The Pawtucket
RED SOX

The Pawtucket
RED SOX

HOW RHODE ISLAND LOST ITS HOME TEAM

James M. Ricci

THE
History
PRESS

Silence, deep, vast, and unbroken save for the sounds of the forest, brooded for centuries over a fall of water that dashed its way into a stream in the midst of a wilderness. Indians broke a trail thither, and tradition says they named the place Pawtucket, meaning the "place of the waterfall." The waters abounded in fish; the redmen built wigwams and speared the salmon which had found the foaming rapids insurmountable and had congregated in the pools at the foot of the falls. And, days of fever and famine being forgotten in the midst of this munificence, the Indians held their revels there.
—Pawtucket Past and Present, Being a Brief Account of the Beginning and Progress of Its Industries and a Résumé of the Early History of the City, *Slater Trust Company, 1917*

At the town line, his headlights flashed on a statue of the Blessed Virgin set up on a knoll between the road and the Edson River. Keeping her back to the town, she greeted each oncoming car with her palms open at her sides, her shoulders hiked in a permanent shrug as if to say, "Welcome to Edson. It's not my fault."
—Bill Morrissey, Edson, *1996*

We're blessed to make our living playing a little kid's game on a field of freshly cut grass.
—Ben Mondor, Owner, Pawtucket Red Sox, *1977–2010*

I hate graveyards and old pawn shops
For they always bring me tears
I can't forget the way they robbed me
Of my childhood souvenirs.
—John Prine, Souvenirs, *1972*

Published by The History Press
Charleston, SC
www.historypress.com

Front cover: On September 26, 2017, former Red Sox and PawSox pitcher Dennis "Oil Can" Boyd rallied proponents at Tolman High School in Pawtucket, Rhode Island, scene of the second Senate Finance Committee hearing on the proposed Ballpark at Slater Mill. *Photo by Ernest A. Brown, from the* Pawtucket Times; David "Big Papi" Ortiz homered in three successive games at McCoy in July 2008. *Courtesy of the Pawtucket Red Sox.*

First published 2022

Manufactured in the United States

ISBN 9781467145633

Library of Congress Control Number: 2021950616

To Alice Mary (Gorman) Ricci
1921–2008

Fox Point, Roberta Plat, Mother

Contents

Preface

On February 23, 2015, news broke that a group of investors had purchased the Pawtucket Red Sox. The group comprised well-known, high-profile, wealthy business leaders and baseball executives from Rhode Island and Massachusetts. The new owners intended to build an $85 million ballpark in Downtown Providence and move the team to the state's capital city. The deal never reached fruition.

The proposal came at an inopportune time. The state was still stinging from the loss of its investment in a computer game development company. It had floated $75 million in bonds to encourage a business called 38 Studios to move its headquarters and associated jobs to the Ocean State. Fourteen months after relocating, 38 Studios was bankrupt. The wreckage from the failed economic development loan colored future public investment in private ventures.

Following the collapse of the Providence Ballpark Plan, PawSox executives and Pawtucket city officials mended broken fences and worked together to keep the team in Rhode Island. The team's lease on McCoy Stadium, its home since 1973, was expiring at the end of 2020. The stadium itself had seen better days. A feasibility study analyzed whether to repair, renovate, or rebuild the stadium. The study suggested exploring a new ballpark in a location that complemented Pawtucket's future development plans. McCoy Stadium needed serious repairs and was missing many features conducive to modern minor-league ballparks; more importantly, it was in the wrong neighborhood.

A better place for the ballpark was closer to Historic Slater Mill, birthplace of the American Industrial Revolution, on a piece of land between Interstate 95 and the Blackstone River. Downtown Pawtucket sat directly on the river's other bank. An interesting building with a distinctive white roof in the form of a ziggurat occupied the site, the home of Apex Companies. On May 16, 2017, PawSox executives, state officials, and city leaders eventually struck a deal to build the Ballpark at Slater Mill on the Apex land, erecting a stunning gateway at the northern entrance to Rhode Island.

Most of the state's leaders said that they did not want to lose the PawSox, as long as it did not have a negative economic impact on taxpayers. The proposal would have kept the team in Pawtucket for another thirty years or more. The Senate Finance Committee vetted the deal during the fall of 2017, revised the bill in December, and passed the enabling legislation in January 2018. With time being of the essence, the Speaker of the House sat on the bill until the last day of the legislative session in June 2018 and then submitted a revised version that eliminated the state's backstop. Without state protection, the cost of the ballpark would rise exponentially.

On August 17, 2018, the PawSox announced that they had accepted a proposal from Worcester, Massachusetts. That city was going to help build a stadium for the team in the up-and-coming Canal District. After fifty years in Pawtucket, the PawSox were leaving for greener pastures. This story explores how Rhode Island lost its home team.

Acknowledgements

Two very special people played significant roles in bringing this story to life. Dr. Susan Turner is an accomplished educator, administrator, and author. Her advice and suggestions significantly improved this manuscript. I think she will be very happy when I finally learn how to make pronouns agree with their antecedents. I can't thank Susan enough for all of her hard work, advice, encouragement, and kind words.

Greg Murphy has strong Pawtucket, baseball, and writing pedigrees. His father, Jim (executive editor), and mother, Jeanne (feature writer), worked for the *Pawtucket Times*. Both are enshrined in the Rhode Island Journalism Hall of Fame. Greg spent many days and nights at McCoy Stadium before becoming a standout first baseman at Tolman High School and Stonehill College. When he learned that I was researching and writing about the PawSox, he immediately offered to help. His incredible memory added background color, and his sharp eye improved the accuracy of the final product.

Two organizations generously provided a number of the photographs used in this book. The Pawtucket Red Sox were particularly helpful with their time and resources, especially Senior Vice President of Communications Bill Wanless and Director of PawSox Productions Joe Jacobs, and I am extremely grateful. The *Pawtucket Times* also provided a number of quality pictures. Special thanks to Group Publisher Jody Boucher and Executive Editor Seth Bromley.

Acknowledgements

While a number of excellent journalists covered the events of this story, Kate Bramson of the *Providence Journal* produced a significant body of work. Her reporting is noteworthy for its quantity and quality and covered almost the entire span of the PawSox stadium drama. At the beginning of my research, Kate spent time sharing her knowledge and insights with me. I am very thankful for that opportunity.

Dr. John Quinn, professor of history at Salve Regina University, provided much-needed encouragement and guidance. Former journalist Brian Gaylord offered sound advice at the outset of this project that proved extremely helpful.

A pair of talented artists captured the essence of important elements of this story. Rhode Island born, bred, and based cartoonist/illustrator Frankie Galasso penned a poignant tribute to Curt Schilling upon his retirement from baseball. Marc Phares produced an image depicting the impact of 38 Studios on Rhode Island. Both illustrations are welcome companion pieces.

Many thanks to Wil Arboleda, Office of the Mayor, City of Pawtucket, for his time and effort. Thank you also to photographer Michael Salerno, who generously contributed photos for this book. Rhode Island Department of State digital archivist Kate Telford and Director of Operations of the I-195 Redevelopment District Amber Ilcisko were both very helpful and accommodating.

I would like to thank Mike Kinsella, acquisitions editor at The History Press, for embarking on a second venture with me. This book took much longer than anticipated, and Mike never lost faith that we would reach the finish line. Thanks also to Ryan Finn, senior editor at The History Press, for putting the final touches on the book.

I am deeply indebted to my wife, Cheryl Kenney, for providing me time, space, and encouragement to explore this story. She will be thrilled that I can now clean up my office. During the early 1990s, one of our first dates was taking in a PawSox game at McCoy Stadium. On Sunday, September 1, 2019, we attended the team's second-to-last game in Pawtucket. We did not go often enough, but we enjoyed every minute when we did.

A State Treasure

On September 2, 2019, an announced crowd of 5,049 sauntered into McCoy Stadium for an early-afternoon Labor Day game, the team's season finale. Donning camouflage-themed jerseys, the PawSox battled the visiting Lehigh Valley Iron Pigs. Nine innings and three hours later, the teams were knotted at three runs apiece. The day belonged to Pawtucket's Cole Sturgeon. In the fifth inning, he belted a two-run homer staking his team to a 2–0 lead. In the eighth inning, he tied the game with his second home run. After the Iron Pigs went ahead with a run in the top of the tenth, Sturgeon blasted a 2-2 pitch for his third homer of the day and a walk-off win for the home team. It was a cracking fine way to end the season.[1]

No one knew it at the time, but that extra-inning win ended up marking the team's last game at McCoy Stadium. The PawSox were supposed to wrap up their fifty-year history on September 7, 2020, but the entire season fell victim to the worldwide coronavirus pandemic. Sturgeon's four-bagger marked the end of professional baseball at McCoy, which dated back to 1946, when the Pawtucket Slaters—the Class B New England League affiliate of the Boston Braves—became the first team to call the stadium home, four years after the $1.5 million ballpark was dedicated. The league folded in 1950, leaving McCoy bereft of pro ball until 1966, when the Pawtucket Indians played at what one reporter described as Pawtucket's "shameful eyesore." The Cleveland Indians' Double-A affiliate left after their second season.[2]

In 1970, the Boston Red Sox moved their Double-A affiliate from Pittsfield, Massachusetts, to McCoy Stadium. After three seasons, the Eastern League team departed to Bristol, Connecticut, clearing the way for the parent club to move its Triple-A entry closer to home. The Louisville Colonels were transported to Pawtucket. In 1973, its first season in Rhode Island, the club won the Governor's Cup, the prize awarded since 1933 to the champion of the International League's annual playoff series. (The Governor's Cup was so named because the original solid silver chalice was sponsored by the governors of Maryland, New Jersey, and New York and the lieutenant governors of Quebec and Ontario provinces.) For that entire season, the team drew a paltry 78,592 patrons to McCoy, an average of 1,077 per game.[3]

The following year, in 1974, despite boasting an outfield anchored by Jim Rice and Fred Lynn, the team struggled on the field, at the turnstile, and in the pocketbook. The team finished with a 57-87 record, hosted an average of 1,115 people per game, and lost close to $400,000. Owner Joe Buzas threw in the towel and sold the team to Philip Anez, an advertising man from Smithfield, Rhode Island. The team fared little better in 1975, finishing last in the International League and drawing only 1,690 fans per game. In the midst of a third straight losing season, owner Anez threatened to move the franchise to Jersey City, New Jersey.[4]

In 1976, Anez renamed the team the Rhode Island Red Sox. Hoping for a boost from the nation's bicentennial, the club adopted a patriotic theme for the cover of its game-day program and embroidered the state's "ri76" logo on its hats. At the end of the season, the team was $2 million in debt and filed for bankruptcy. That December, the International League stepped in and awarded the team to Marvin Adelson, a businessman from Massachusetts. He renamed the club the New England Red Sox and hoped to move it to Worcester. After two months, the league revoked the franchise from Adelson on the grounds that he failed to fulfill contractual terms and conditions.[5]

In January 1977, Ben Mondor, a retired businessman from Lincoln, Rhode Island, was persuaded to step in to reform the bankrupt, disenfranchised baseball team playing its games in an undersized, rickety, hard-to-get-to McCoy Stadium. The former mill owner was a specialist in turning around textile companies. On the heels of the Adelson affair, Red Sox minor-league director Ed Kenney went searching for a new owner and asked Chet Nichols, former Red Sox pitcher and Pawtucket native, if he had any ideas. Nichols recommended the retired fifty-two-year-old Mondor. Upon setting eyes on the ballpark for the first time, the straight-shooting entrepreneur sized up his new asset in three words: "What a dump." At the time, the Pawtucket

Red Sox were one of the worst clubs in the minor leagues and the stadium reflected that lowly status.[6]

Selecting Ben Mondor proved fortuitous and saved professional baseball in the Ocean State. Mondor had the wisdom to follow Kenney's recommendation to hire Mike Tamburro as general manager. Tamburro had just three years of experience—one as an intern in Pawtucket and two as the youngest general manager in baseball with the Elmira Pioneers of the Single-A New York–Penn League. Lou Schwechheimer joined the team full time in 1980, also after learning the ropes during a Pawtucket internship. Tamburro and Schwechheimer became the sons Mondor never had. Together, the trio rescued the team and transformed it into a premier franchise. Longtime PawSox and Boston Red Sox manager Joe Morgan was around when the new ownership arrived. "The field was a wreck, the clubhouse needed work, it wasn't a good situation," he later recalled. "Ben came in and changed everything. As he told me at the time, 'The circus has left town.' He meant it, too."[7]

Reflecting on his purchase, Mondor would later say the situation was so bad "nobody would come near the place." Three weeks before the start of the 1977 season, the players did not have uniforms. The parent club sent down used ones. The home jerseys had "Red Sox" on the front, which was fine, but the road shirts had "Boston" stitched across the chest. Tamburro suggested re-sewing them to read "PawSox." The name stuck. During the first year under their new owner, the PawSox won the league pennant but drew only 70,000 fans. "You couldn't get your mother here," Mondor said. Mondor would later reminisce that fewer than 250 fans showed up for its Governor's Cup playoff game.[8]

But the new owners had a philosophy for success that included hard work, rolling up their sleeves, and doing whatever was necessary to deliver high-quality baseball experiences to working families and their children at a reasonable price. Tamburro said that young fans belonged at McCoy Stadium. Mondor would characterize the ballpark as a "theme park," and baseball was the theme. And like the Disney characters that welcome visitors to the Magic Kingdom, Mondor and Tamburro would greet fans at McCoy's entrance, roam the grandstands during games, and thank them for coming as they left the ballpark. They constantly solicited feedback on how the club could make things better.[9]

The gregarious owner with the hearty laugh would later be tickled when the first generation of children who attended PawSox games with their fathers showed up at McCoy and introduced their children to him. And that the next generation, he hoped, would do the same. The fan-friendly philosophy was tested during the very first game. Tamburro recalled that a busload of the starting pitcher's friends showed up and started having a little too much fun. Tamburro asked them to leave. As the game wore on, the pitcher wondered what happened to his friends.[10]

The owners wanted to make sure that working families could afford to come to McCoy. They offered free parking and kept ticket and concession prices low. In the first quarter century of running the club, the team raised prices twice, and only for a dollar each time. Mondor would frequently say that he had the perfect advertising slogan for the PawSox but that Mike and Lou would not allow it: "You can't go to church as cheap as you can come to McCoy." The team stuck to its knitting and began to prosper.[11]

MAGICAL MOMENTS

Three seminal events contributed to the team's early success and began to cement its special place in the hearts and minds of Rhode Islanders. The first was the longest game in baseball history. The visiting Rochester Red Wings battled the PawSox for thirty-three innings before the home team finally prevailed. The game consumed close to eight and a half hours and extended over three days: April 18, April 19, and June 23, 1981. After a delayed start because two banks of outfield lights blew out, the game started at 8:25 p.m. on Holy Saturday and was mercifully suspended by International League president Harold Cooper on Easter Morning shortly after 4:00 a.m. Lou Schwechheimer later characterized the entire night and early morning as surreal.[12]

At the start of the game, temperatures were chilled by steady northwest winds gusting up to twenty-five miles per hour. At best, it was, as locals say, "raw." By 4:00 a.m., temperatures had reportedly dipped below freezing. By then, it was downright cold for football, never mind a baseball game. The wind made it difficult to hit and knocked at least one potential home run, a towering shot by Sam Bowen that appeared to end the game, back into the playing field. Attempting to stay warm, the players eventually burned broken baseball bats and wooden benches in fifty-five-gallon drums. Nevertheless, of the original 1,740 patrons, 19 die-hards remained until the end, each of whom received a season pass from the PawSox.[13]

Despite the inclement weather, neither team relented. The game was scoreless until Rochester pushed across a run in the top half of the seventh inning. The PawSox evened it up in the bottom of the ninth when fan favorite Chico Walker scored on Russ Laribee's sacrifice fly. Twelve innings later, in the top of the twenty-first inning, the Red Wings scored again, making it 2–1. But the PawSox tied it up when Wade Boggs doubled with two outs in the bottom of the frame. "I didn't know if the guys on the team wanted to hug me or slug me," Boggs later recalled.

The teams rattled on without scoring for eleven more innings. Rochester hurler Jim Umbarger pitched the final ten innings, giving up only four hits while striking out nine. In the top of the thirty-second inning, right fielder Bowen scooped up Tom Eaton's single and threw out John Hale at the plate—and it wasn't even close. Hale was trying to score the go-ahead run from second base. After thirty-two innings, the exhausted players left to rest for their 2:00 p.m. game on Sunday. The sun was breaking through the horizon beyond the first base line. On the way home, PawSox players saw families headed to Easter sunrise services.[14]

A makeshift section accommodated the overflow press corps on hand for the conclusion of the longest game on June 23, 1981. *Courtesy of the Pawtucket Red Sox.*

When the game resumed on June 23, it became the center of the baseball universe. On June 12, major-league baseball players went on strike and would not return until August 9 with the annual All-Star Game. A sellout crowd of 5,746 came through the gates. More than 140 reporters from around the globe jammed into a makeshift press section in the stands. The game lasted just eighteen minutes. In the bottom of the thirty-third inning, Dave Koza drove in Marty Barrett from third with the winning run. The team celebrated as though they had just won the World Series before retreating to a media spectacle in the cramped locker room. The teams still had another game that day. Cal Ripken Jr. played for the Red Wings, joining Boggs as the other future Hall of Famer who played in the longest game in baseball history.[15]

The second event occurred on Thursday evening July 1, 1982, when Mark "The Bird" Fidrych tangled with Dave Righetti. Fidrych, from nearby Northborough, Massachusetts, had been a rookie sensation with the Detroit Tigers in 1976, collecting nine wins before the All-Star Game, to which he was named the American League's starting pitcher. He went on to win nineteen games that season, earning Rookie of the Year honors. Besides being a phenom, Fidrych was one of those colorful characters that comes around every so often in baseball and a genuine fan favorite. He would manicure the mound with his hands, talk to the ball, and shake hands with players in the field after they made good plays. He earned his nickname because his lanky frame and unkempt hair resembled *Sesame Street*'s Big Bird. He injured his shoulder the following year and struggled to regain full effectiveness. The Tigers released him in 1981, and in 1982 he signed with the Boston Red Sox, who assigned him to Pawtucket. The Bird filled stadiums at home and away. Tamburro later recalled that even Toledo, which usually drew six hundred people to its games in that era, sold out whenever Fidrych pitched.[16]

The Columbus Clippers' starting pitcher, Dave Righetti, was also a former American League Rookie of the Year (1981) with the New York Yankees. During the first half of the 1982 season, Righetti suffered control problems and landed in owner George Steinbrenner's doghouse. The Yankees sent the southpaw down to Columbus, the team's Triple-A affiliate, to find his command. His reassignment coincided with an early July series at McCoy. Anticipating the allure of a matchup of former major-league stars, PawSox manager Joe Morgan held back Fidrych's scheduled start one day. The savvy PawSox front office jumped on the opportunity and promoted the heck out of the contest.[17]

It worked, and 9,349 fans jammed into six-thousand-seat McCoy Stadium. People were standing in the aisles four deep and shoulder to shoulder. Tamburro later reflected that they could not squeeze one more body into McCoy. Rejected fans pulled their cars behind the center field fence and watched from there. Righetti left with a 5–3 lead after six innings, giving up just four hits while striking out twelve. But a pumped-up Fidrych got stronger as the game wore on. With the huge crowd encouraging Fidrych's every move, Morgan decided to let him go the distance. It paid off. The PawSox came from behind for a 7–5 decision. The Bird was never the same again—his injured shoulder possibly further damaged by the one-hundred-plus-pitch performance. One year later, on July 4, 1983, Righetti exacted revenge by tossing a no-hitter against the parent Boston Red Sox at Yankee Stadium.[18]

The final event in the troika was a series of games played between September 5 and September 13, 1984. The PawSox earned the final spot in the Governor's Cup playoffs with a late-season surge. They bested top-seeded Columbus in the semifinals, three games to one, winning the first two on the road. The PawSox and the Maine Guides met in the finals. Playing in their first season after moving from Charleston, South Carolina, the second-seeded Guides swept the Toledo Mud Hens in the semifinals. In the best-of-five championship series, Maine won the first two games on the road at McCoy, 8–1 and 8–6. All the Guides needed was one more win on their home turf in Old Orchard Beach. With Maine fans calling for a

On July 1, 1982, former American League Rookies of the Year Mark Fidrych and Dave Righetti squared off in a marquee matchup at McCoy Stadium. *Courtesy of the Pawtucket Red Sox.*

Mike Tamburro and Ben Mondor showing off the Governor's Cup, the prize for winning the 1984 International League championship in stunning come-from-behind fashion. *Courtesy of the Pawtucket Red Sox.*

sweep, the PawSox won the third game, 5–2, and then evened the series with a 4–2 win in Game 4. On September 13, in the final game, George Mecerod shut out the Guides for seven and two-thirds innings as the PawSox won the Governor's Cup with a 3–0 victory. The PawSox ruined the victory party that Guides owner Jordan Kobritz had prematurely arranged for his Maine club.[19]

PAWSOX NATION

The longest game, Fidrych versus Righetti, and the come-from-behind Governor's Cup championship catapulted the PawSox's reputation throughout the minor leagues and, more importantly, elevated the team's stature in southeastern New England. Tamburro claimed that those games "solidified the franchise" and "began the process of turning the PawSox into one of the most respected teams in the industry." Slowly but surely, the team was becoming a Rhode Island institution. McCoy Stadium's fading charm added to the experience. It was simple but quaint. The stands perched above the field, extending in an arc from first base to third base. Team dugouts sat at field level, entombed into the structure supporting the grandstands. It became a McCoy tradition for young fans to fish for autographs before each game by dropping lines from the grandstands, dangling pens and pails in front of the players.

Between 1985 and 1999, the PawSox and its stadium evolved into an attraction. Buoyed by Mondor's fan-friendly approach and accentuated by the opportunity to see future major-league stars on their way up and existing stars on rehabilitation assignments, more and more people went to PawSox games. The team's steady rise in attendance illustrated this success. During the 1970s, the PawSox averaged 1,385 fans per game. The average jumped to 2,903 during the 1980s and to 6,091 in the 1990s. The 1990s had its share of special moments, including a record-breaking 30–7 start to the 1994 season, welcoming its 4 millionth fan in 1994, and announcing the 25th Anniversary Team in 1997, which included Rice, Lynn, Boggs, Roger Clemens, Mo Vaughn, John Valentin, Nomar Garciaparra, and manager "Walpole Joe" Morgan.[20]

By the late 1990s, McCoy Stadium was in pretty rough shape. At the time, Tamburro was a member of the Minor League Baseball Board of Trustees and was aware of forthcoming changes to Triple-A ballpark standards. He knew that McCoy could not comply with the new rules and feared the team might have to move. After the 1998 season, PawSox ownership renovated and expanded McCoy, pouring $16 million of public and private money into the stadium. Team executive Lou Schwechheimer would later recall that a number of visionary legislative leaders at the time "also happened to hail from the northern part of the state…Blackstone Valley guys, Pawtucket guys, East Providence guys." They "understood what McCoy meant to the quality of life in the community" and "what it meant in terms of civic pride." Those leaders forged a partnership with the team to fund the project.[21]

Construction began immediately following the final game of 1998, continued through the winter, and wasn't completed until hours before the home opener on April 14, 1999. The transformation was so complete it marked the birth of "the New McCoy." In a span of eight months, the team added four thousand seats, a six-story entrance tower, luxury boxes, an expanded press box, seating spaces for fans with disabilities, picnic areas, updated clubhouses, indoor batting cages, a concourse, parking lots, new sod, and the signature outfield berm. The team introduced its new

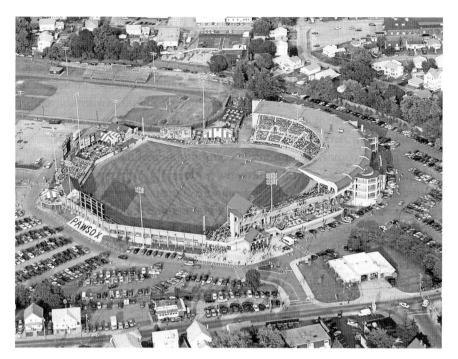

The "New McCoy" opened on April 14, 1999, to much fanfare and acclaim. *Courtesy of the Pawtucket Red Sox.*

polar bear mascot, Paws, and the city renamed the roadway leading into the ballpark "Ben Mondor Way." The New McCoy opened with requisite ceremony, including marching bands, balloons, and a cannonade. TV color commentator Mike Stenhouse, enthusiastic about the transformation, proclaimed, "If you thought McCoy was a great place to watch a game you haven't seen anything yet." Schwechheimer would later proclaim the improved stadium was "the will of one man, Mike Tamburro."[22]

The team's success at the box office continued through the 2000s, as the team drew 9,038 patrons per game. Between 1999 and 2010, average attendance equated to 89 percent of McCoy's seating capacity (excluding the berm). Throughout New England, from Bangor to Block Island, baseball was at a fever pitch, mainly a result of the Boston Red Sox's sustained success and popularity. Between May 15, 2003, and April 10, 2013, the parent club sold out 820 consecutive games at Fenway Park, a professional sports record. In Rhode Island, the PawSox continued to expand their lore on the playing field and in the community. On June 1, 2000, Tomo Ohka spun a perfect game, and on August 10, 2003, Bronson Arroyo matched the feat. These were just the third and fourth perfect games in 125 years of International League history. In 2003, McCoy hosted its 10 millionth fan. The team went on to reach the Governor's Cup playoffs, losing to the Durham Bulls in the finals. In 2004, McCoy was the scene of the annual Triple-A All-Star Game, complete with a three-day festival that engaged the local community.[23]

In 2005, 11,629 fans packed the ballpark to see Curt Schilling's rehab assignment in Pawtucket. That season, the PawSox averaged 9,561 fans per game, establishing an attendance record of 688,421. In one electric three-game stretch in July 2008, David Ortiz imprinted his personal stamp on McCoy Stadium. Big Papi hit home runs in each game as McCoy welcomed crowds of 11,460, 11,140 and 10,675. That year, the PawSox set a club-best eighty-five wins, and Mike Tamburro received his record-setting fifth International League Executive of the Year Award. In 2009, the PawSox completed a string of six consecutive seasons entertaining more than 600,000 fans, bringing the total attendance since Ben Mondor purchased the team in 1977 to almost 13 million.[24]

During the 2010 season, fifteen Boston Red Sox stars rehabbed at McCoy, including Jacoby Ellsbury, Josh Beckett, Mike Lowell, Dustin

Pedroia, and Jason Varitek. A disconcerting trend, however, showed early signs. Despite the cavalcade of stars, the team failed to break the 600,000 fans mark and posted a decline in average attendance per game of 7 percent from the previous year. The Great Recession and bridge repair work on I-95 were contributing factors.[25]

During the off season, a cloud descended over PawSox nation. On Sunday, October 3, Ben Mondor died at his home on Warwick Neck. He was eighty-five and had owned the team for thirty-four of those years. Mike Tamburro reflected on the sad news. "We have lost a true Rhode Island treasure. Ben was a man who brought people together— whether it be at the business table or the ballpark. His love for the fans and the community were unsurpassed." Tamburro was optimistic about a future without his

David "Big Papi" Ortiz captured the spotlight and captivated the crowds at McCoy Stadium. Attendance during his three-game visit in July 2008 averaged 11,092. Ortiz homered in each game. *Courtesy of the Pawtucket Red Sox.*

mentor. "It's not going to end now," he promised. "This operation will continue to grow and flourish because of him and in his memory."[26]

During the 2012 season, the PawSox dedicated a life-size statue of Mondor outside the ticket gate at McCoy Stadium. Why the statue? *Boston Globe* columnist Bob Ryan rhetorically asked then answered: because he took "a bankrupt and untrustworthy franchise…and turned it into as an important social, cultural, and philanthropic institution as there is in all of Rhode Island." Upon that occasion, Ryan reminisced how over time he began to think, "Why couldn't Ben be 20 years younger?" Tamburro said that he and Ben were "attached at the hip." When Mondor died, Tamburro felt as though he had "lost a limb." Ryan was content that the team's future was secure. He observed, "The PawSox are the PawSox, and always will be with Ben looking over his flock. The team was in good hands." Now Ryan wondered, "Why can't Mike and Lou be 20 years younger?" He implored the people of Pawtucket, "I hope you realize how good you have it."

Statue of revered owner Ben Mondor near where he enjoyed greeting fans arriving for games. *Photo by James Ricci.*

In 2011, the slide at the gate continued, though at a slower pace, despite the PawSox fielding one of their most accomplished teams. That edition won the International League North title, set records for defensive and pitching prowess, and reached the Governor's Cup finals, all while sending twenty-one different players to Boston. The PawSox won their third Governor's Cup in 2012, beating the Charlotte Knights in the finals three games to one. They made it back to Governor's Cup in 2013, losing to the Durham Bulls three games to one in the championship series. In 2014, the PawSox clinched their fourth Governor's Cup and second in three seasons, capturing the title series three games to two over Durham, following an epic Game 3 extra-inning thriller in North Carolina.

Nevertheless, in 2014, the fewest number of fans ventured to McCoy since the stadium expanded in 1999. The team averaged 7,367 per game. Attendance dropped 6 percent from the previous year. During the winter, majority owner Madeleine Mondor, Mike Tamburro, and Lou Schwechheimer decided to sell the team. The future of the franchise transferred to a new ownership group comprising powerful and wealthy Rhode Islanders and Boston baseball executives who touted keeping the PawSox in Rhode Island as one of their primary objectives. The drama surrounding the PawSox over the subsequent three years bared the soul of Rhode Island and reinforced that not all stories have happy endings.

CHAPTER 1

The Bloody Sock

A FOREBODING SENSE OF DOOM

The specter of a bond deal gone bad hovers over the state of Rhode Island. It even has its own name: 38 Studios. And beware the unfortunate public servant who fails to fear its presence. Any project requiring public funding must genuflect at the altar of the apparition, and the ghost has spooked more than one well-meaning expenditure into oblivion. There's one thing you can say about Rhode Islanders: they have long memories.

It began innocently enough and from an unlikely source. In 2004, the Boston Red Sox were on their way to extinguishing their own curse, one wrought eighty-five years earlier when the team lost its star player, Babe Ruth, to its bitter rival, the New York Yankees. In the early twentieth century, the Red Sox won five World Series, including the modern-day inaugural in 1903. Its last championship came in 1918. The following year, after a lackluster sixth-place finish in an eight-team American League, owner Harry Frazee sold Ruth to the Yankees, supposedly to help finance a Broadway play he was producing. During the remainder of the twentieth century and into the new millennium, the Red Sox failed to win another World Series, giving rise to what became known as the "Curse of the Bambino."[27]

The club came close to breaking the curse a number of times. In the 1946 World Series between the Red Sox and St. Louis Cardinals, Game 7 was knotted with two outs in the bottom of the eighth inning when the Cardinals' Enos Slaughter tried to score from first on a hit to left field.

Red Sox shortstop Johnny Pesky seemingly froze for one critical moment before throwing the relay to home. He was shocked to see Slaughter's "mad dash" attempt to score. Then, in 1967, the Red Sox came from behind in Game 6 of the World Series to force a showdown of pitching aces. St. Louis fireballer Bob Gibson ended the Impossible Dream by besting Red Sox star Jim Lonborg, 7–2. Lonborg had pitched brilliantly in Games 2 and 5, giving up just one run on four hits total, but was gassed when he took the mound in Game 7 on only two days' rest.

The 1975 World Series included an epic Game 6 that included Bernie Carbo's dramatic game-tying, three-run, pinch-hit home run in the bottom of the eighth inning. The game remained knotted until Carlton Fisk launched his iconic twelfth-inning game-ending home run off the top of the left field foul pole. The next night, the Cincinnati Reds squeaked out a one-run win in the series finale. In 1978, the Yankees and Red Sox swapped regular season collapses before facing off in a one-game playoff for the AL pennant. Light hitting Bucky Dent sunk the Sox with an unlikely late-inning three-run homer. And finally, in 1986, after going up two runs in the top of the tenth inning of a potential World Series–clinching Game 6, the Red Sox bullpen squandered the lead after getting two outs with nobody on base. The New York Mets' rally was punctuated by a two-out ground ball that slithered through Bill Buckner's legs. As was his custom during the closing weeks of the season, Manager John McNamara failed to replace Buckner with Dave Stapleton for late-inning defensive purposes.

Boston fans came to believe that anything that could go wrong would go wrong: no lead was safe, an All-Star player in July would burn out in September, the ace would contract a sore elbow, the closer would lose his ability to paint the corners, the manager would make a boneheaded decision, and the general manager would trade away the wrong phenom or fail to pick one up at the trading deadline. By the turn of the twenty-first century, the curse had become so persistent that many fans and players were tired of hearing about it. In 2001, ace pitcher Pedro Martinez boldly proclaimed, "I don't believe in damn curses. Wake up the damn Bambino and have him face me. Maybe I will drill him in the ass."[28]

In the fall of 2003, the wraith reared its ugly head once more. In the American League Championship Series (ALCS), the Yankees and Red Sox battled to a seventh game. After losing Games 2, 3, and 5, the Sox were on the brink of elimination before outslugging the Bombers, 9–6, in Game 6 at Yankee Stadium. Game 3 had set the tone. Red Sox ace Pedro Martinez faced off against New York's Roger Clemens in perhaps the Big Hoss's last

Pedro Martinez, who debunked the "Curse of the Bambino" by claiming that he would throw at Babe Ruth, was a frequent visitor to McCoy as a special assistant to the Boston Red Sox general manager. *Courtesy of the Pawtucket Red Sox.*

game at Fenway Park. A bench-clearing brawl erupted in the second inning. Don Zimmer, the seventy-two-year-old Yankee bench coach and former Red Sox manager, charged Martinez, who deftly sidestepped the charging senior and forced him to the ground.

In Game 7 at Yankee Stadium, the Red Sox swiftly quieted the hometown fans with three runs in the second inning and held a 5–2 lead going into the bottom of the eighth. Sox skipper Grady Little chose to leave a tiring Pedro Martinez in the game after he had thrown more than one hundred pitches. The results were predictable. The Yankees tied it up. Then, in the eleventh inning, third baseman Aaron Boone, playing the role of Bucky Dent, homered off knuckleballer Tim Wakefield. Another year, another devastating, heartbreaking loss.[29]

DIRT DOGS

The rivals met again in the 2004 ALCS. The series could not have started worse for the Red Sox. The Yankees swept the first two games in New York. In Game 1, a hobbled Curt Schilling served up six runs in just three innings, while a late-game rally fizzled, yielding a 10–7 final. Jon Lieber outdueled Pedro Martinez for a 3–1 win in Game 2. Spirits remained high as the series moved to Boston, but a 19–8 thrashing by the Yankees all but extinguished any hope for this solid Red Sox team that had won 98 regular season games, 3 behind New York's 101. There was good reason for despair. No team had ever come back from a 3-game deficit to a win a 7-game series in baseball history.

On Sunday, October 17, 2004, with 35,828 fans packed into Fenway Park, the Boston franchise took a small but significant step in exorcising its demons. The Yankees secured a 2–0 lead in the third inning when Alex Rodriquez took Derek Lowe deep. The Red Sox manufactured three runs in the bottom of the fifth with nothing more than a couple of singles and a few walks off Yankee starter Orlando Hernandez, posting a 3–2 edge. The Yankees took it back in the top of sixth, touching Lowe and reliever Mike Timlin for two more tallies, and held that lead through the eighth frame. Here we go again, thought Red Sox Nation.

This team of "dirt dogs" was not giving up. Kevin Millar drew a walk on five pitches from future unanimous Hall of Fame closer Mariano Rivera. First-year skipper Terry Francona immediately sent in late-season acquisition Dave Roberts to pinch-run for Millar. Boston had acquired Roberts on July 31, the trade deadline, for just this reason. Everyone in the stadium knew Roberts was going to try to steal second. Rivera threw over to first base three times trying to pick off the speedster, which he nearly did. At the least, he tried to keep Roberts from getting a big jump. Roberts took off on Rivera's first pitch to Bill Mueller. When the dust settled, Roberts was standing on second and umpire Joe West was signaling safe. Mueller drove Rivera's next pitch through the box into center field, scoring Roberts from second. The game stayed tied until the bottom of the twelfth inning. At 1:22 a.m., Monday morning, David Ortiz, the Big Papi, arguably the greatest clutch hitter in team history, launched a Paul Quantrill offering deep into the Boston night, halfway between the bullpen and the right field corner. Miraculously, the Red Sox lived to fight another day.

Just sixteen hours after one of the most emotionally draining games in the storied Red Sox/Yankee rivalry, the teams returned to Fenway Park for

Game 5 and a rare 5:11 p.m. starting time. This one featured Mike Mussina, who in Game 1 had carried a perfect game into the seventh inning, staking the Bombers to an 8–0 lead before he was chased after two outs when the Red Sox mounted a five-run, two-out rally. This time he would face off against Pedro Martinez. A pitching duel of aces was anticipated. The Red Sox broke the ice with two runs in the bottom of the first, but Bernie Williams parked Pedro's first pitch in the top of the second, after which both teams were silenced until the sixth inning. The Yankees loaded the bases off Martinez with a pair of singles and a hit batsman as prelude to Derek Jeter's bases-clearing double. New York held a 4–2 lead going into the bottom of the eighth. David Ortiz started that frame with a solo home run off former Red Sox closer Tom Gordon. After Jason Varitek sacrificed Dave Roberts in from third, the game was knotted at four runs apiece.

The teams remained deadlocked for six more nail-biting innings. In the bottom of the fourteenth inning, as the clocks on the Eastern Seaboard struck 11:00 p.m., Yankee reliever Esteban Loaiza walked Johnny Damon and Manny Ramirez, bringing up Big Papi with two outs. On the tenth pitch of the at bat, with a 2-2 count, after spoiling off five two-strike pitches, David Ortiz fisted a Texas League blooper into center field, scoring Johnny Damon from second base. In almost eleven hours, within a span of two days, the rivals had played twenty-six innings of heart-stopping baseball. The Yankees still held a one-game lead and the home field advantage. With little rest, the teams headed for a Tuesday matchup at Yankee Stadium.[30]

The starting pitchers were set. Jon Lieber, who had silenced the Red Sox in Game 2, faced Curt Schilling, who was tattooed in Game 1, the result of an injured right ankle. Schilling was questionable. A painful torn tendon hampered his ability to push off the rubber. Boston team doctor Bill Morgan performed an unusual surgery on Schilling the previous day, suturing the torn tendon sheath back onto Big Schill's skin. Morgan had practiced the procedure on a cadaver to gauge its efficacy. Thoughts that Schilling might wear high-top shoes to help support the ankle were dismissed when he took the mound after a scoreless top half of the first. The TV cameras zoomed to a close-up of Schilling's foot. Blood was seeping through his sock. Boston fans held their collective breath as Schilling wound and fired a high fastball, enticing Derek Jeter to pop softly to right. Schilling was going to be all right.

Schilling mowed down the first eight batters before Miguel Cairo hit a shot to left-center field that hopped into the stands for a ground-rule double. Jeter could not capitalize, flying out to center. Rolling into the fourth inning, the game was scoreless. Lieber, who had sported a 12-3 record at home

In October 2004, Curt Schilling had a tendon sheath in his right ankle sutured into place before becoming the hero of Boston's pivotal Game 6 victory over the New York Yankees. Schilling, who rehabbed with the PawSox at McCoy, was captured here walking in from the left field bullpen. *Courtesy of the Pawtucket Red Sox.*

during the regular season, lured ground outs from Big Papi and Trot Nixon. Kevin Millar drilled a double down the left field line and moved to third on Lieber's wild pitch to Varitek. The Sox catcher singled up the middle, scoring Millar for a Red Sox lead. Shortstop Orlando Cabrera, a fortuitous late-season acquisition, singled to left, bringing Mark Bellhorn to the plate with runners on first and second.

The switch-hitting second baseman lofted an opposite field fly that drifted to the wall over Hideki Matsui's head in left field. At first it appeared to ricochet off the fence, scoring Varitek and Cabrera. In actuality, the ball bounced off a fan wearing a dark jacket. Spurred on by the pleadings of manager Terry Francona, the umpires convened and made the correct call: home run. Red Sox 4, Yankees 0.

Big Schill pitched a scoreless sixth inning, which was critical given the weary state of Boston's bullpen, depleted from the previous two thrilling victories. He took the mound for the seventh inning. This was exactly the kind of outing the Red Sox brass anticipated when they flew to Arizona the previous Thanksgiving and convinced Schilling to join the team. After Matsui grounded to first, Bernie Williams roped one down the right field line into the second deck, making it 4–1. Schilling retired the next two batters and trudged to the Boston dugout. It was a brilliant performance. Throughout the game, the TV coverage highlighted the bloody sock. Schilling later said in a postgame interview he "was touched by God." Francona said that Schilling pitched with heart, especially after the fifth inning, when he appeared exhausted.

But Game 6 wasn't over. Bronson Arroyo relieved Schilling in the eighth. After striking out Tony Clark, Miguel Cairo doubled to right. Derek Jeter promptly singled home Cairo, and the Yankees cut into Boston's lead, making it a 4–2 game. Alex Rodriguez followed with a chopper down the first base line. Arroyo picked the ball up and tagged Rodriguez. The ball squirted out of Arroyo's glove and bounded into right field. Jeter scored from first and A-Rod landed on second. The Yankee faithful rejoiced. But wait. Rodriguez swatted the ball out of Arroyo's glove. Rodriguez was called out and Jeter returned to first. Yankee fans voiced their displeasure by throwing baseballs onto the field. The umpires cleared the field until order was restored. Police SWAT teams lined the periphery during the top of the ninth inning and then retreated into the stands in the bottom of the frame—a surreal scene, even by Red Sox/Yankee standards. The Red Sox held on for a 4–2 victory. The series was all square at three wins each. This Red Sox team just might "reverse the curse." If it did, the "bloody sock" would no doubt go down in history as a symbol of the improbable.

With 56,129 fans packed into the old Yankee Stadium, Game 7 decided it all. Yankee starter Kevin Brown squared off against resurgent postseason star Derek Lowe, whom manager Terry Francona had earlier left out of the postseason rotation. In the top of the first, Damon singled to left and then immediately stole second base. After Mark Bellhorn struck out swinging, Manny Ramirez singled to left under a diving Derek Jeter, but Damon was gunned down at the plate, Matsui to Jeter to Posada. Just when it looked like Brown might escape unscathed, Big Papi roped a two-run homer into the left field stands, shushing Yankee fanatics.

But the game belonged to Johnny Damon. After loading the bases in the top of second with just one out, Brown gave way to Javier Vazquez. Damon pulled a first-pitch inside fastball down the right field line for a grand slam. The Red Sox lead jumped to 6–0. The Yankees pushed one across in the bottom of the third, cutting the gap to five runs. In the top of the fourth, Vazquez walked Orlando Cabrera to start the inning. Once again, Vazquez offered a first-pitch inside fast ball to Damon. Just as before, Damon hammered it down the right field line, depositing the ball in the upper deck. Boston held an 8–1 lead en route to a 10–5 American League Championship Series–clinching win.

Over a span of four straight October nights, the Red Sox accomplished what no other baseball team had ever done: come back to win a postseason series after losing the first three games. The team had grit and resolve. Its clubhouse leader was Kevin Millar, a former Florida Marlin, who joined the team during Spring Training in 2003. Before the Red Sox rescued him, Millar was on his way to the Chunichi Dragons of the Japanese Central League. He is credited with christening the team the "dirt dogs" and the "idiots"—two apt monikers. It was Millar who proclaimed after the Game 3 pounding that the Yankees better not let the Red Sox win one because they would take them all after that. An unlikely prediction, but not out of character for the lead dog, the head idiot. He knew that the Red Sox had Schilling, Martinez, and Lowe.

The World Series turned out to be anticlimactic. The Red Sox swept the St. Louis Cardinals. The first game was the closest contest. The teams battled back and forth in the brisk October New England night. The Cardinals finally tied things up in the sixth inning at 7–7, but Boston went out in front again by two in the bottom of the seventh. The Cardinals tied it again at 9–9 in the top of the eighth. After Varitek reached first on an error by sure-handed shortstop Edgar Renteria, Mark Bellhorn drove one into the right field grandstand. The Red Sox made the 11–9 lead hold up to the conclusion of another four-hour game.

In Game 2, Schilling throttled the Cardinals for six innings. The "bloody sock" made an encore performance. He left the game in the capable hands of Boston's relievers at 6–1. The Cardinals mustered just three hits and a walk off Schilling. The run was unearned. The Cardinals tacked on a run off Mike Timlin in the eighth for a 6–2 final. In Game 3, Pedro Martinez tossed a seven-inning gem, yielding just three hits and two walks en route to a 4–1 victory. Derek Lowe spun a masterpiece in Game 7, twirling seven innings of three-hit ball, as Boston shut out St. Louis, 3–0. Joe Castiglione's call of the last out echoed throughout the region: "The Red Sox have won the World Series. Can you believe it?"

Red Sox Nation breathed a collective sigh of relief. Children visited their fathers' graves to pass along the news. Generations of Red Sox fans who thought they would never see this day wept tears of joy. The city hosted a Duck Boat parade to celebrate the team that put an end to the specter of Babe Ruth.

Curt Schilling was already a "big time" pitcher before the 2004 World Series. He was known to rise to the occasion when the postseason rolled around. He had played major roles in two previous World Series—one with

By the time he retired in 2009, Curt Schilling and the "Bloody Sock" had reached mythic proportions in New England baseball folklore. *Courtesy of Frankie Galasso.*

the Philadelphia Phillies and the other with the Arizona Diamondbacks. He already had two World Series rings and was co-MVP with teammate Randy Johnson of the 2001 Fall Classic. He was also known for his candor. Schilling spoke his mind. He also amassed a portfolio that one day might open the door to Cooperstown. His statistics bolster his credentials as one of the dominant pitches of his era. The *Sporting News* ranked Schilling as one of the eight best pitchers that never won a Cy Young Award. Yet it is the "bloody sock" that has become a symbol of his strength, determination, and perseverance. He could have easily opted out of Game 6 in 2004. He did not have to endure doctors stitching his slack tendon to the skin on his foot. He later released photos of the gruesome scar to dissuade haters who fashioned it a hoax. It looked like a body part that Dr. Frankenstein might have applied to his monster.[31]

But the "bloody sock" also has a strong link to how the PawSox came to leave Pawtucket, Rhode Island, its home since 1973. It is a long, winding story with its roots firmly planted in that memorable fall of 2004 when the

Red Sox finally broke through and exorcized their demons. Enamored of Schilling's athletic prowess, Rhode Island leaders hoped that he possessed the capabilities and business acumen to help boost the state's sagging economy, so much so that Rhode Island offered Schilling $75 million to relocate his video game production company to Providence from Maynard, Massachusetts. The state guaranteed the economic development bonds floated to fund the move—60 percent of the entire $125 million earmarked for all such projects. When it was done, the 38 Studios shingle would have a Rhode Island address.

CHAPTER 2

38 Studios

Courtship

38 Studios burst into the collective consciousness of Rhode Islanders between its heralded announcement to move to the state in the spring of 2010 and its public shuttering two years later. In a mere twenty-four months, the promise of hundreds of computer game entrepreneurs, designers, programmers, artists, and writers transforming Providence's Jewelry District into a miniature Silicon Valley collapsed amid an acrimonious feud between the company's founder and the state's governor. What started as a venture full of hope and optimism was shattered by finger-pointing about mismanagement from one side and claims of pulling-out-the-carpet from the other. When the dust settled, both parties were irreparably damaged.

The one-time benefactor of the venture's economic development promise—the State of Rhode Island—remains as scarred by the 38 Studios deal as was Hawthorne's Hester Prynne by her scarlet letter. Curt Schilling's reputation as an entrepreneur, businessman, and creator of massively multiplayer online roll-playing computer games (MMORPG) lay crippled under the weight of accusations and personal attacks. A shadow still follows many of the supporting characters associated with the deal—from its inception as a panacea for the state's anemic economy to the special jobs creation bill passed by the general assembly to the state agency that brokered the loan arrangement to the lack of oversight into the company's progress and fiscal condition to the final curtain of bankruptcy to the comprehensive lawsuit, and ultimately to the investigation into what really happened and who was responsible. All were tarnished by the same brush. The miasma settled into the state's heart and soul, ultimately coloring any government-supported scheme, including the opportunity to keep the Triple-A Pawtucket Red Sox in Rhode Island.

The popular version of Rhode Island's courtship of 38 Studios marks its starting point as March 6, 2010, when then-governor Donald L. Carcieri attended a fundraiser for the World War II Foundation hosted by Curt and Shonda Schilling at their estate in the tony Boston suburb of Medfield, Massachusetts. In December 2009, World War II Foundation founder and documentary director Tim Gray included the governor's name on a list of suggested invitees. Gray's list included a who's-who of influential Rhode Islanders, such as the current or former CEOs of CVS, Hasbro, Gilbane Construction, FM Global, Textron, GTECH, Nortek Industries, Amica Insurance Company, VIBCO, Paolino Properties, and Fleet Financial Group. Many of these folks had ties to the Rhode Island Economic Development Corporation (RIEDC), which would eventually assume the lead role in enticing Schilling's 38 Studios to Providence.[32]

During the new millennium, Rhode Island was a perennially poor economic performer. It was one of the first states to feel the impact of an economic downturn and one of the last to rebound. *Sluggish* and *stubborn* were two popular words used to describe the state's economy as it clawed its way out of the Great Recession of 2008. In February 2010, for example, the state's unemployment rate lingered around 12.7 percent, three points higher than the national average. Many leaders, including Governor Carcieri, feared that it would get worse in the upcoming months.[33]

Carcieri followed the road less traveled to the Rhode Island State House. He was not a politician. Carcieri grew up in the West Bay coastal community of East Greenwich, population then around 3,800. His father coached football and basketball at the local high school and bull-raked quahogs off the bottom of Narragansett Bay during the summer. Don subsequently played the traditional big-three sports—baseball, basketball, and football—at East Greenwich High School. He was awarded an academic scholarship to Brown University, where he earned a degree in international relations while playing varsity football and baseball.[34]

Two weeks after graduating from college, Carcieri married his high school sweetheart, Suzanne Owren, the first-ever Miss East Greenwich. He followed his father's footsteps into education, teaching math at Newport's Rogers High School and then at Concord-Carlisle Regional High School in Concord, Massachusetts. After a few years, he joined Old Stone Bank, eventually becoming an executive vice-president during his ten-year stint in finance. In 1981, the Carcieri family moved to Kingston, Jamaica, where Don ran the Catholic Relief Services, West Indies, and Sue taught science in the local high school. After two years, the family returned to Rhode Island, where Carcieri assumed leadership of a start-up subsidiary of Cookson America Inc., eventually becoming chief executive officer of Cookson America and joint managing director of Cookson Group Worldwide. He retired from the company at age fifty-five, primarily because he did not want to move his family to London, along with a growing skepticism of the company's direction.[35]

Harboring a deep love for his home state, and based on his record of continual success, Carcieri believed that he could make a significant difference in government. He was an action-taker and a problem-solver. In 2002, that seemed exactly what the state needed. He jumped into the race for governor with a solid plan. First, control government spending. Between 1996 and 2002, the state's budget had ballooned 55 percent. Second, hold government accountable. Too many of the state's elected officials often forgot the constituents they represented. Third, draw the line on new taxes. The state's property tax ranked fifth highest in the country. Fourth, achieve excellence in education. Rhode Islanders needed to stop rewarding failure and start demanding results.[36]

Carcieri won the Republican Party primary, defeating endorsed candidate James Bennett. He then routed progressive liberal Myrth York 55 percent to 45 percent to capture the governorship. It was State Senator York's third consecutive bid to become the first female governor of Rhode Island. Her run faltered when she tried to shame Carcieri for the deaths of Brazilian miners whose company was doing business with Cookson America. She then failed to fulfill Carcieri's request to disclose the companies in her personal portfolio—the implication being that her investments weren't exactly squeaky clean.

Carcieri's political platform rested on his sense of community, fair play, cooperation and pragmatism, all built on a foundation of Roman Catholic virtues. His background mirrored much of his constituents' heritage. At the turn of the twenty-first century, about 20 percent of Rhode Island's population claimed Italian American heritage—the highest of any state. He became Rhode Island's sixth Italian American governor since John O. Pastore ascended to the post in 1945 when President Harry S Truman appointed then-governor J. Howard McGrath to be the U.S. solicitor general. Likewise, more than half of the state's population was Roman Catholic. Furthermore, despite being long beholden to the Democratic Party, Rhode Islanders had a penchant for electing Republican governors, especially between 1985 and 2002. Carcieri became the thirty-second Republican governor in the state's history (out of seventy-three); three of his previous four predecessors emanated from the GOP.

Carcieri's stint as governor got off to a rocky start. He was vacationing in Florida when a President's Day weekend blizzard dumped two feet of snow on the state. Then, four days later, on Thursday, February 20, one of the biggest tragedies in the state's modern history happened. That evening, an inferno engulfed The Station nightclub in West Warwick, ultimately claiming the lives of 100 and injuring an additional 230 of the 362 people gathered for the Great White concert. Carcieri was still in Florida but rushed back early Friday morning. He earned high praise for his leadership during the fire's aftermath. His down-to-earth humanity and deep empathy for the victims and their families were evident to anyone paying attention. Throughout the remainder of his two terms, though, he was embroiled in constant battles with the Democratic plurality of the General Assembly.[37]

On January 26, 2010, entering his final year in office, the term-limited Carcieri delivered his last State of the State Address. He reminded leaders that Rhode Island was experiencing its "most severe economic turmoil of the last 30 years, maybe longer." Of the state's 1 million people, 73,000 Rhode Islanders were out of work, the governor said, "with little sign that employment will improve anytime soon." He suggested that the thirty-five thousand small businesses in the state could fuel an economic engine. The state needed "more tax payers, not taxes," he said. Carcieri deputized the RIEDC, under the leadership of Newport resident Keith Stokes and its new board of directors, to focus on the problem.[38]

Carcieri was a Republican governor in a deep-blue state. He preached bedrock fiscal and entrepreneurial values as the engine for moving the state's economic needle. Carcieri extolled efficiency, ingenuity, innovation, resourcefulness, improved education, less government spending, municipal consolidation, and lower taxes. And he pleaded for the legislature to put aside party differences and

Donald L. Carcieri, seventy-third governor of Rhode Island, believed the state's economic revival would come from jobs generated by small businesses. *Courtesy of the Rhode Island State Archives.*

work together. He urged the gathered legislators to search their "hearts and souls" and "summon the courage and determination to do right" to honor the sacrifices of their forbears and for the legacy of future generations.[39]

Hope

As Carcieri headed to the fundraiser at Schilling's home that Saturday in March 2010, the state's economy remained stalled. Schilling, meanwhile, was struggling with growing 38 Studios, his Maynard, Massachusetts–based gaming software development company. He was having difficulty raising capital through private equity firms. Schilling was unwilling to surrender control of his company in order to realize his dream. He had also become disenchanted with the lack of support from the Commonwealth of Massachusetts, which offered little help. Governor Deval Patrick's administration turned Schilling down because it determined that 38 Studios was not a good investment.[40]

The stars were aligned. Carcieri's state needed an economic catalyst that the governor hoped would come from jobs through small businesses. Schilling needed money to complete his quixotic quest of producing an alternate-universe role-playing computer game code named "Copernicus." Carcieri told Schilling he should consider moving his company to Rhode Island. Schilling thought that would be a solution to his inability to raise funding from other sources. It is unlikely that either man foresaw how this introductory meeting would shape their fates, let alone the subsequent reputational and financial carnage that would follow.

Within four days, the governor connected Stokes with Schilling to get the ball rolling. From that moment on, the RIEDC and 38 Studios sped their way to achieving the single objective of negotiating a satisfactory arrangement. It would be a chaotic, fast-paced effort with many moving parts and a number of characters filtering in, around, and about the scene. The critical work was accomplished in just five short months, between March and July 2010. And, as might be expected in such a rapid courtship, the result was far from perfect.

On Tuesday, March 16, Stokes and Schilling met to set the process in motion. The meeting must have been constructive. In a follow-up thank-you note, Schilling said he sincerely appreciated "the time and effort already provided by the State of Rhode Island, from the speaker on down." Already provided? From the Speaker of the House? So, as early as mid-March, the hand was tipped that somebody associated with the state was already engaged with Schilling, well before the World War II fundraiser. In reality, House Speaker Bill Murphy and/or House Majority Leader Gordon Fox had been working behind the scenes with 38 Studios and its man in Providence, Michael Corso, attorney-at-law and tax credit aficionado.[41]

Stokes and Schilling agreed to meet again the following Monday. Stokes invited his agency's legal counsel and board secretary, Rob Stolzman, and its deputy director for capital and finance, J. Michael Saul, both of whom, Stokes said, had firsthand experience in business development, investment projects, public finance, and legislation. Schilling forwarded the note to 38 Studios board member Tom Zaccagnino, who in turn looped in Corso. Stolzman, Saul, Zaccagnino, and Corso would become principal players in the drama.[42]

By March 26, 2010, just ten days following the aforementioned Stokes-Schilling powwow, the parties were negotiating a letter of intent. RIEDC and 38 Studios exchanged marked-up drafts over the weekend of March 27. RIEDC would lend 38 Studios $75 million. In return, the company would relocate its headquarters to Rhode Island, along with 125 full-time jobs paying annual salaries of approximately $75,000 by December 31, 2010; an additional 175 jobs in 2012; and 150 more in 2013. All told, 38 Studios would add 450 jobs to the state over three years, with salaries totaling close to $34 million. Stolzman took the opportunity to locate a potential landing place for 38 Studios. He mentioned in an e-mail to Corso his desire to show company representatives a building owned by his in-laws, writing, "If I can be helpful with this it would be great to help a company and my in-laws."[43]

The drafts passed over the weekend stated that RIEDC understood that 38 Studios needed $75 million to complete Project Copernicus and begin its relocation to Rhode Island and that the proceeds of the loan would provide such necessary financing. As negotiations wore on, however, this would become a major point of contention. 38 Studios needed the full $75 million. RIEDC planned on deducting reserves and expenses, thereby providing much less than the "necessary" $75 million. Other conditions included an analysis by a qualified expert on the economic impact of the company's move to the state and a review of the company's financial projections. At least someone had the good sense to strike RIEDC's trite baseball reference: "While some might call moving 38 Studios to Rhode Island a home run, since pitching wins ball games, we are more inclined to compare it to the more subtle but equally thrilling complete game."[44]

As the negotiations between RIEDC and 38 Studios steamed forward, leaders in the state legislature cleared the decks for a deal. Whether the governor knew about it or not, operatives in or with ties to Rhode Island government had been plotting to lure 38 Studios to the Ocean State months prior to the Medfield fundraiser. There is strong indication that as early as July 21, 2009, Fox had dinner with 38 Studio representatives Corso and Zaccagnino; whether the friends discussed the opportunity is unknown. Zaccagnino had befriended Schilling and offered to help establish a board of directors for 38 Studios and fill it with businessmen. Such a board was intended to add gravitas to the enterprise and help lure investors. Also, Schilling and Zaccagnino had apparently targeted states receptive to providing incentives, perhaps in the way of tax credits, in return for moving the business within their borders. Rhode Island was on that list.[45]

Later that fall, House Speaker William Murphy toured 38 Studios in Maynard. A lifelong Red Sox fan, Murphy jumped at the opportunity to meet World Series hero Schilling. Murphy said that Schilling recruited him to gain an introduction to the Massachusetts Speaker of the House. Schilling would later disabuse that notion, wondering aloud why one of the more recognizable sports figures in the Bay State would need an introduction to one of its politicians. Schilling had actively campaigned for then Massachusetts senator Scott Brown. Murphy would later say the visit afforded him a firsthand look at a repurposed mill that was put back on the tax rolls—even though there were plenty of such examples dotting the landscape of his own state. On or around October 8, Murphy, Fox, and Corso signed nondisclosure agreements with 38 Studios, the reason for which remains undisclosed. Then there was the December 2009 meeting that Murphy stumbled upon in Fox's office between Corso and Zaccagnino.[46]

In early 2010, Governor Carcieri was planning to pump $50 million into a loan guarantee fund to jumpstart economic development in the state. He included the item in his annual budget. The state-backed loans would be added to RIEDC's toolbox to encourage expansion of Rhode Island companies and perhaps bring to fruition the long-planned "knowledge district," where technical innovation could flourish in and around Providence's Jewelry District. Once state leaders learned that 38 Studios needed $75 million, they pivoted to a new plan. Fox, in his role as House majority leader, and Steven Costantino, then chair of the House Finance Committee, promoted the idea of boosting the loan guarantee program to $125 million. The increase equaled the exact amount 38 Studios said it needed. The revision was fast-tracked. Costantino outlined the plan to Stokes in mid-March 2010. Fox and Costantino wanted to include the program in the 2010 fiscal year supplemental budget.

On April 6, the House Finance Committee commenced hearings on the bill. It would permit the state to issue loans to companies. The loans would be funded by issuing "moral obligation" bonds, meaning they would not be secured by the state's full faith and credit. Moral obligation bonds differ from appropriation bonds, in that the latter require the General Assembly to "appropriate" funds in the state's annual fiscal budget to pay the interest expense. Because they are riskier, they pay a higher yield. Republican representative Laurence Ehrhardt, of North Kingston, saw the potential danger of giving a large portion of the pot to a single company. He sought to limit funds for any single company to $10 million and wanted to submit an amendment as such. The governor asked Stokes to talk with Ehrhardt. Stokes urged Ehrhardt to trust RIEDC to do the right thing. The amendment never surfaced.[47]

Keith Stokes pondered a dilemma. On one hand, he questioned whether the legislation was moving too quickly. On the other, he wondered if 38 Studios' desire might dissipate in the midst of a month's delay. He chose to move forward and ended up testifying in favor of the job creation financing program. The funding found its way into the state's supplemental budget. Prior to his testimony, Stokes sent an e-mail to RIEDC's board members informing them about the Job Creation Guaranty Program legislation. Even though efforts to entice the company to Rhode Island were well underway, Stokes supposedly avoided any mention of the 38 Studios opportunity when delivering the information to the RIEDC Board.

On May 19, 2010, Costantino redirected the loan guarantee program to a separate bill, which the House passed six days later. The legislation sailed through with only one nay vote. Robert Watson, Republican leader in the Rhode Island House of Representatives, objected. He issued a prophetic warning: "Scandal finds money." Watson warned, "Scandal finds a pool of $125 million with sketchy, sketchy strings attached. Scandal will find this bill some day and your vote will aid and abet it." On June 11, Carcieri signed the bill authorizing the state to issue up to $125 million of economic development bonds into law, clearing the path for the 38 Studios deal.[48]

The Briefing

When 38 Studios saw the $75 million figure in the early term sheets, it immediately notified RIEDC staff that it would need all of that, plus more, to move to Rhode Island and complete "Copernicus." Anything less would be unsatisfactory. Without the entire amount, 38 Studios would need to raise additional capital from other sources, which, based on past experience, would not be easy. The company had already tried and failed to attract infusions from venture capitalists. Such inability to raise funds from the private sector should have made RIEDC extremely cautious. Throughout April, May, and early June, the teams tried to reach a mutually agreeable term sheet.

RIEDC staff engaged consultants to assist with its due diligence. Wells Fargo Securities, which would ultimately become the placement agent for the RIEDC bonds, provided an analysis of the current state and future prospects of the gaming industry. Wells also provided detailed six-year financial projections for 38 Studios. Strategy Analytics, a Boston-based technology research consultancy, was asked for insight into the video gaming industry. RIEDC staff also wanted to learn about critical success factors in attracting, retaining, and growing a gaming cluster in Rhode Island. The economic development agency sought knowledge into the gaming industry's structure and whether 38 Studios could serve as an effective anchor in the state. Strategy Analytics would in turn consult with gaming expert Perimeter Partners.

Despite the lingering discrepancy on how much 38 Studios would receive at closing, the RIEDC staff was ready to present the opportunity to its board of directors, which, up to this point, had not been formally introduced to the deal. On June 9, 2010, in executive session, RIEDC's Deputy Director Saul delivered the opportunity to the board. He said the staff had "completed normal due diligence" that showed the gaming company would be able to meet its repayment obligations. Saul told the board the due diligence process also relied on input from gaming industry experts Wells Fargo Securities and Strategy Analytics.

The formal presentation occurred five days later, on Thursday, June 14, when the RIEDC Board of Directors met at its offices at 315 Iron Horse Way in Providence. Governor Carcieri called the meeting to order at 4:00 p.m. Item no. 4 on the agenda was "Consideration of New Business or Industry to be Located in Rhode Island." Saul served as moderator.[49]

Strategy Analytics presented first. The company's president, Harvey Cohen, described video game clusters and where they existed in North

America. He told the board that jobs in the gaming development field pay above average wages. Rhode Island, Cohen said, was well suited to support a video game cluster. Its colleges—especially RISD, Brown, and URI—offered excellent programs to educate future game developers. The state already had companies in place that could participate in the gaming industry, such as GTECH and Hasbro. 38 Studios would bring 458 jobs to the state with an average salary of $72,500. The direct benefit to Rhode Island would be $33.2 million. In addition, Rhode Island would see an increase of 1,113 indirect jobs at an average salary of $54,500, adding $60.7 million more in payroll. All totaled, bringing in 38 Studios as the anchor tenant for a gaming development cluster would add 1,571 jobs reaping salaries of $93.9 million.[50]

Strategy Analytics pointed out the risks associated with the gaming industry in general and in particular with 38 Studios. Clusters need more than an "anchor" tenant and "collaboration between industry, academia, and government." The consultants acknowledged the risk that 38 Studios was pre-revenue and lacked brand recognition. However, although industry cycles exist, 38 Studios was targeting a market with the potential to sustain "double-digit growth over the next five years plus." Regarding cluster development, Rhode Island had the advantage of learning from other states. Plus, Rhode Island could compete with other states because it could "offer an attractive package to entice additional game studios to the region given its strong academic culture and pro-business posture." (Strategy Analytics must not have been privy to the state's notoriously unfavorable business climate or the well-publicized failures of the very same Economic Development Corporation to which it was presenting.) As to 38 Studios being pre-revenue, Strategy Analytics determined such a risk would be mitigated by the company's "strong management, first rate technical and creative talent, and a strong distribution partner."[51]

Wells Fargo's Mark Lamarre was up next and delivered an optimistic picture of the interactive entertainment market. The bank estimated that industry revenues worldwide would grow from $81.9 billion in 2009 to $124.1 billion in 2013, a compound annual growth rate of 11 percent. In the United States alone, projected revenues rose from $32.8 billion in 2009 to $43.2 billion in 2013, a growth rate of 7.1 percent. Over the previous six years, the interactive entertainment sector had grown substantially, while other entertainment sectors such as movies, books, and music were flat to slightly down.[52]

Wells Fargo listed a number of current industry trends and drivers. The positive side of the ledger included increased penetration of broadband in homes, more powerful PCs/laptops at lower prices, improvement in the quality of games, longer console lifecycles, growth of cellphones and handheld devices that support gaming applications, and changing demographics. As inhibitors, the firm identified microeconomic weakness and uncertainty, piracy, free content available on the internet, platform incompatibility, and the high bar to produce sophisticated titles—they were costly and time-consuming to develop.[53]

Curt Schilling introduced 38 Studios to the RIEDC Board. He started by thanking the RIEDC for its interest in his company over the last six months, reaffirming that he was in communication with state leadership before he first met Carcieri. He told the directors he had been "into gaming" for more than thirty years. He used video games to stay in touch with his sons when he was on the road throughout his major-league baseball career. He also realized the games were educational for his boys.[54]

38 Studios was the result of Schilling's twenty-year vision to create the best video game development company in the business. He cited people, accountability, and philanthropy as the most important attributes of his company. The studio's board of directors possessed strong leadership skills. Most of them were present. Some had traveled from Europe. Schilling read letters of support from Todd McFarlane, 38 Studios' executive art director, who was unable to attend in person, and from a representative of Electronic Arts (EA), a leading video game distributor that was already working with 38 Studios on its first production, *Kingdoms of Amalur: Reckoning*.[55]

The company's president, Jennifer MacLean, introduced the management team and board members. The managers of 38 Studios all had significant experience in designing and developing video games. Her presentation provided information about "Copernicus," the downloadable remote-player offering that would be available by subscription. The release date had not been determined. One-third of the company's artists, MacLean told the RIEDC board, were either RISD students or alumni. And, she added, the company had a philanthropy manager who oversaw the company's charitable activities.[56]

The RIEDC Board voted unanimously to grant preliminary approval to pursue funding for 38 Studios to relocate its corporate headquarters to Rhode Island and complete development of "Copernicus." The "inducement resolution" adopted by the board that evening endorsed the Jobs Creation Guaranty Program as an RIEDC program and granted preliminary approval to issue bonds not to exceed $75 million to finance a loan to 38 Studios. RIEDC's staff disclosed 38 Studios would receive net proceeds from the loan but did not say the gaming company had long required the entire amount plus more later. The approval was subject to "receipt and satisfactory review of Project budget, specifications, plans, and essential contract." Stolzman noted the staff would need to come back to the board at a later date for final approval.[57]

The very next day, June 15, Governor Carcieri announced that Curt Schilling would be moving 38 Studios to Rhode Island. Carcieri's public statement may have been a bit premature based on the number of gaps that needed to be closed.

Don't Do It

Leading up to the presentation to RIEDC's board, Saul asked the agency's financial portfolio manager, Sean Esten, to prepare an internal credit memo. As early as May 28, Esten was alarmed. "Have you read the Wells Document?" he questioned Saul. It did a "nice job summarizing the company, the industry, and the talent," Esten wrote, "but nothing about the opportunity itself." There was no financial information. There was no analysis about the company's ability to perform. "To be honest," Esten told Saul, he "had more information on the typical $10k micro loan" than he had on a $75 million request. "This is a problem."[58]

Three days later, Esten wrote to Saul with a request for additional information. He took the opportunity to convey further concerns. 38 Studios said the worst-case scenario was that it would produce "a new, commercially successful RPG (role playing game)" every two years. 38 Studios' subsidiary, Big Huge Games, was nearing completion of *Reckoning*, which was due out in early 2011. The business plan called for each successive game to eclipse its predecessor's marketability. "Is this realistic?" Esten queried. "No one bats 1,000." His assessment was far from rosy. The more he looked at the deal, the less comfortable he became. Further, the financial analyst proclaimed, "I don't think I can support a $75 million guarantee to any single company in this industry due to the wide volatility in commercial success in game releases." Saul told Esten to forget the internal credit memo. Allegedly, none was ever produced.[59]

By June 1, 2010, Perimeter Partners' gaming expert, Jason Della Rocca, provided input to Strategy Analytics' inquiry concerning the 38 Studios deal as a building block to establishing a gaming cluster in Providence. It asked Della Rocca to provide a thorough list of risks associated with public investment in that industry. His opinion was frank and perhaps not quite what Strategy Analytics or RIEDC's staff wanted to hear. Della Rocca pointed out that while the gaming business had massive potential, it was not conducive to a "field of dreams" model, referring to the if-you-build-it-they-will-come formula espoused in the movie of the same name. The success of growing a gaming cluster, Della Rocca wrote, "requires ongoing, aggressive and strategic deliberate cultivation and support." He was clear on this point: "The biggest risk is making one move and assuming the job is done." Della Rocca warned that "the government should not get into the VC [venture capital] business." They should not try to pick individual winners. Rather, they should focus on setting up "the systems, programs, infrastructure and atmosphere that enable entrepreneurs and innovators to flourish."[60]

Strategy Analytics asked Della Rocca whether follow-on businesses would relocate or if new businesses would be prone to sprout up because an anchor was in place, which would be essential for a successful gaming cluster to develop and flourish in Providence. Della Rocca opined that "it comes down to two triggers: 1) access to talent, and 2) low/cost risk of doing business." He elaborated, "A successful anchor tenant is a 'symptom' of a region that is providing both #1 and #2." The anchor tenant is rarely the driver. Della Rocca did not see 38 Studios "having much impact" in the short term, as they "have yet to succeed, and there is no 'proof' that #1 and #2 are sufficient in RI to produce success on a consistent basis." Further, Della Rocca told Strategy Analytics, he did not see 38 Studios as a model for drawing additional gaming activity to the state. "RI will not be competitive without ongoing aggressive activity to build the cluster."[61]

Della Rocca advocated for a government approach focusing on a "meta/macro model." "The best model for cluster development is nurturing a complex ecosystem," he wrote. Additionally, while he granted that informed strategic decisions could be made, "ultimately, everything is unpredictable." It would be wise to "make as many bets as possible," Della Rocca advised. "We don't know which seeds will grow and flourish in the RI environment, so you want to plant as many seeds as possible." He was calling for a "system/approach that allows for and can tolerate some failure as part of the learning process." Della Rocca was describing a completely opposite methodology for success than what was unfolding in Providence. Rather, the state was putting most of its eggs in one basket, 38 Studios. When asked on a June 2 conference call with Strategy Analytics and RIEDC staff if he would do the deal, Della Rocca answered, "No."[62]

Jason Della Rocca influenced at least one person. Sean Esten listened intently to Della Rocca's concerns. Esten later characterized "the substance of that conference call as extraordinarily negative." He believed that it was unlikely the deal would go forward. After the meeting, he "was reassigned to other matters and no longer worked on the 38 Studios deal."[63]

Meanwhile, on July 14, the day before the presentation of the term sheet to the RIEDC Board, another concerned voice surfaced. It came from Rosemary Booth Gallogly, the State of Rhode Island's director of administration. Gallogly addressed a memo to Governor Carcieri under the subject line "38 Studios." After ceding a lack of expertise in venture capital and video gaming, Gallogly trumpeted her "experience in looking out for the taxpayers' best interests." She wanted to share her concerns with the governor, which, she believed, "should be weighed at the Board meeting."

Gallogly did not mince words. First, the Jobs Creation Guaranty Program had just been approved. It was so new RIEDC had not even developed rules, regulations, or general policies on which decisions for granting loans would be made. Second, 38 Studios was "pre-revenue." The viability of the company was dependent on the success of its first release, the console game *Kingdoms of Amalur: Reckoning*. If it failed, she warned, "the business plan for the subsequent chapters is unlikely to be realized." Third, the risk/reward might not be appropriate for such a hit-driven business venture. The state was putting up $75 million for a potential $40 million equity score. Fourth, the loan lacked "key person" provisions, despite the importance given to the value of the knowledge and experience of the development team. Fifth, the term sheet required disbursing $25 million to 38 Studios before it moved to Rhode Island. And sixth, the borrowing would not be favorably priced "due to the nature of the 'project' and the debt will be considered state tax-support debt for rating agencies purposes."[64]

Carcieri later acknowledged he received Gallogly's memo but did not act on her observations. While Carcieri valued Gallogly's opinion on a number of matters, he did not believe she possessed any special knowledge or expertise related to the 38 Studio deal. "I felt most all of the issues she was raising were issues that had already been raised or would have been raised in the course of the board meeting," Carcieri said. He added that Gallogly "did not have the benefit of any presentations, any of the information that went to the full board."[65]

On July 16, 2010, one day after the board reviewed the term sheet but ten days before it granted final approval of the authorizing resolution, Gina Raimondo sent a note to Stokes outlining her concerns. At the time,

Before being elected Rhode Island's general treasurer, Gina Raimondo penned a letter to RIEDC director Keith Stokes citing concerns about the fledgling 38 Studios deal. *Courtesy of Michael Salerno.*

Raimondo was a partner in a Rhode Island–based capital firm, Point Judith Capital. She was on a path to become the State of Rhode Island's general treasurer and subsequently its governor. She relayed to Stokes a number of concerns she and her partners had about the 38 Studios loan. Her company knew a number of investment firms that had evaluated 38 Studios and passed on the opportunity. One in particular did not believe 38 Studios' platform was "compelling" and had a number of issues "with their approach." Raimondo urged caution. There were more than two hundred venture capitalists in Boston, she told Stokes. It was telling that the company could not find funding in its own backyard, which was a "very hot area for gaming." Raimondo informed the RIEDC director it was "well known that most gaming companies don't succeed" and those that do "consume tremendous amounts of capital (hundreds of millions of dollars)."[66]

Raimondo added that 38 Studios was "pre revenue, pre profit, and the company has not launched a successful game." Like Della Rocca, Raimondo advised if the state was going to pursue companies in the gaming industry, it would be better to fund a portfolio of them, rather than a single venture, "given that companies of this nature have a high failure rate." Raimondo proved particularly prescient. She was worried about the company going "out of business in the next couple of years, the state losing its money, people losing jobs and going forward there is much less appetite to fund companies of this nature." She warned if the 38 Studio deal failed, it would be hard to bring in start-up or innovation companies in the future. Later in the year, embroiled in a campaign for general treasurer, Raimondo characterized the deal "as high risk a venture as you can find."[67]

THE AYES HAVE IT

38 Studios was not happy about what transpired at the June 14 RIEDC Meeting of Directors. Zaccagnino delivered an e-mail to Saul the following

evening, saying it was imperative that he and Saul meet as soon as possible. 38 Studios' board was concerned that if the initial funding was insufficient to cover relocation expenses and distribution costs, and the remaining funds were tied to basic non-discretionary milestones, the risks to 38 Studios were too high. There was "simply too much at stake for the Company, our employees, and their families," Zaccagnino wrote to Saul. 38 Studios had been "an open book" concerning its "risks and requirements" from the get-go, especially the need to be "fully capitalized with the $75 million at closing." The company's enthusiasm was also tempered by only receiving a preliminary approval by the RIEDC Board. Zaccagnino feared the two parties were "headed in the complete opposite direction."[68]

By Friday, June 18, four major points remained unresolved: how much money 38 Studios would receive at closing; the timing of lease milestones relative to closing; the ability of 38 Studios to leverage tax credits; and a date for executing a final resolution. The parties remained at odds about the amount of funds available to 38 Studios following the loan closing. RIEDC staff was internally aligned on the conditions and were certain they had made them clear to 38 Studios. The loan would be for a maximum of $75 million. Reserves and fees would be required, so the company would receive less than the loan amount. Also, the company needed to have a lease for office space in Providence before RIEDC would close on the deal. Saul wrote internally that the optics on the deal would be "very bad without a signed lease." And RIEDC was at least willing to discuss tax credits as a way to fill the gap between net and gross loan proceeds.[69]

Four days later, RIEDC staff and 38 Studios met in Providence to address the financing issue. Representatives from Wells Fargo Securities also attended. The gaming company once again reiterated that its business plan to relocate to Rhode Island and complete "Copernicus" would not work without sufficient capital above and beyond the gross proceeds of the $75 million loan. They had always said they needed more than the initial $75 million. Now the $75 million would be trimmed by reserves, fees, and disbursement based on milestones. By 2012, the company would need money from additional sources, approximately $20 million, but as of late June it had not secured such funding. Without it, 38 Studios knew it would have a cash flow shortfall of $23.8 million in 2012.[70]

On July 1, 2010, Saul delivered a term sheet to 38 Studios president Jennifer MacLean that reflected the RIEDC staff's position concerning loan proceeds. It stated that 38 Studios would receive net proceeds from the loan. This would be the term sheet presented to the RIEDC Board during an executive session scheduled for July 15. The purpose of that special meeting was for the board "to review, discuss and hopefully approve the final negotiated term sheet."[71]

Director Stokes, Deputy Director Saul, and First Southwest, the RIEDC's financial advisor in the transaction—whose duties included helping develop the term sheet—presented the information to the board. The proposition was straightforward. RIEDC would loan 38 Studios $75 million. 38 Studios would relocate to and subsequently expand in Rhode Island. The company would hire 450 direct employees and generate an additional 1,113 indirect jobs. These employees would average $67,500 per year. 38 Studios was in the process of completing Project Mercury, code name for the *Kingdoms of Amalur: Reckoning* game being published and distributed by EA. Upon moving to Providence, the company would complete its MMO game, code named "Copernicus."[72]

The loan agreement required 38 Studios to locate within Rhode Island's "Knowledge Economy." The term of the loan would be for ten years but amortized over twenty years. RIEDC would require a debt service reserve based on the first year's interest owed on the loan. The interest rate was not to exceed 7 percent. It would also establish a Balloon Payment Fund of 25 percent of the remaining loan proceeds that would be released upon specific milestones of relocation, job creation, and game development. 38 Studios would incur a penalty of $7,500 for each job short of 450. RIEDC needed to approve the bond underwriter.

The RIEDC staff told its board that companies like 38 Studios lacked access to conventional capital markets. Investors looked at moral obligation bonds on non-essential government projects to avoid putting underlying revenue streams at high risk. 38 Studios would likely be rated A, with bond pricing between 5.25 percent and 7.0 percent. Someone will buy them, even though investors would mostly pass on the offering.[73]

There were risks, the RIEDC staff told its board. 38 Studios was pre-revenue. The company was basing its success on a hit-driven product, which was far from a sure thing. The amount of the loan to 38 Studios would consume 60 percent of the Job Creation Guaranty Program's $125 million. And there was equity risk "given no debt market exits without 100 percent credit enhancement." After obtaining the board's approval, an item to obtain final board approval of an "authorizing resolution" was included on the board's July 26 meeting agenda.[74]

But the staff may not have told the board everything. They allegedly failed to mention that their own portfolio analyst, Sean Esten, could not make financial sense of the deal. Or that gaming industry experts, such as Jason Della Rocca, advised against the deal. Or that a venture capitalist and general treasurer candidate, Gina Raimondo, called to their attention how other private investors and public agencies steered clear of the company. Or that a trusted state employee and taxpayer watchdog, Rosemary Booth Gallogly, had stuck her neck out to warn the governor. But more importantly, the RIEDC staff portrayed the net proceeds of the loan as providing sufficient funding for the company to move to Rhode Island and complete "Copernicus," even though they knew it was not the case. All of this would later form the basis of a comprehensive lawsuit brought by RIEDC against advisers and financial institutions (Wells Fargo Securities, Barclays Capital, First Southwest Company, and Starr Indemnity and Liability Company), 38 Studios' former executives (Curt Schilling, Thomas Zaccagnino, Richard Wester, and Jennifer MacLean), lawyers and law firms (Robert Stolzman, Adler Pollock & Sheehan P.C., Mosses Alfonso Ryan Ltd., and Antonio Alfonso Jr.), and RIEDC executives (Keith Stokes and J. Michael Saul).[75]

The staff figured the pros outweighed the cons. 38 Studios possessed an experienced management team with a successful game development track record. *Reckoning* had a publishing agreement with highly regarded EA and was on schedule. Equity investment in the company to date was $51 million, although most of that was Schilling's own money. They claimed the gaming industry had a favorable future and aligned with "high potential" Rhode Island assets, meaning RISD, Brown, Hasbro, and GTECH. There was a potential for adding 1,500 jobs in the state over the upcoming five to seven years. 38 Studios and its gaming industry affiliates create "compelling opportunities" for the state's graduates, and their "presence and spawning fosters increased entrepreneurialism." Not to mention, if successful, the investment in 38 Studios would yield a return on investment of 47 percent.[76]

The RIEDC Board approved the proposition. Only one of its thirteen members dissented. That was Karl Wadensten, owner of VIBCO, one of the country's leading manufacturers of industrial vibrating equipment. He knew it almost always takes twice as long as expected to bring a product to market. And, he thought, if the economy continues to stall, some number of parents would probably curtail purchasing video games.[77]

A New Sheriff in Town

And so it came to pass that 38 Studios loaded up its vans and moved to renovated office space at One Empire Plaza in Downtown Providence. The office occupied a prominent spot atop a gradual rise extending from Memorial Boulevard up Westminster Street, through the financial district, and overlooking the theater district nestled below. The six-story, 104,000-square-foot brick building was the former headquarters of Rhode Island Blue Cross and Blue Shield until it relocated its main office to the new Waterplace Towers. The health insurance company wanted to consolidate its 1,100 employees who were scattered about the city.

Schilling entrusted Tom Zaccagnino with the transition. On September 1, 2010, 38 Studios announced its decision to move into the Blue Cross

38 Studios moved into the former Blue Cross and Blue Shield building at One Empire Plaza in Providence. *Photo by James Ricci.*

building. The space required extensive renovations. The infrastructure had to be upgraded to support the high-tech company. It also needed a face-lift. Zaccagnino relied on Michael Corso to oversee the renovation. Zaccagnino told people to copy Corso on all work orders and invoices related to the build-out. By the time the company moved in on April 8, 2011, the improvements had rung up a bill of $12.5 million, far more than anticipated. Knowing that it faced a certain financial shortfall, 38 Studios tasked Corso to secure bridge financing for the company.[78]

The year 2010 was a gubernatorial election year in Rhode Island. The incumbent, Don Carcieri, was term limited. Lincoln Chafee was looking for work. He had previously served as the popular mayor of Warwick throughout the 1990s. In 1992, he became the city's first Republican mayor in thirty-two years and was reelected for three additional terms. His father, John H. Chafee, was one of, if not the, highest regarded local leaders during the second half of the twentieth century, first as governor from 1962 to 1968 and then as senator from 1972 until his unexpected death in October 1999. Governor Lincoln Almond appointed Linc Chafee to serve out the few months remaining of his father's term.

In the 2000 race for U.S. senator, the Republican Chafee retained his seat by handily defeating Democrat U.S. Representative Robert Weygand, 57 percent to 41 percent. Chafee subsequently lost in 2006 to Sheldon Whitehouse, who painted Chafee as tied to conservative Congressional leaders whose positions were unpopular with the state's overwhelming majority of liberal voters.[79]

It was a broad leap to believe that Chafee was tied to the right wing of the Republican Party. During his term, he strongly opposed a number of President George W. Bush's policies, particularly on issues concerning the environment, tax cuts, women's choice, and the war in Iraq. He was the only Republican to vote against that war, which he carried as a badge of honor. As a U.S. senator, liberal groups ranked him high and conservative groups ranked him low, lower than even some Democratic senators. Chafee ended up bolting from the Republican Party shortly after losing his senate seat to his solid blue opponent, 54 percent to 46 percent.[80]

Linc Chafee is a different kind of politician. Upon graduating from Brown University with a degree in classics, Chafee headed west. He enrolled in Montana State University's Farrier School and then traveled the United States and Canada, shoeing horses at harness racing tracks. He claims to have once shoed the fastest trotter on the circuit. "When you're around horses, you tend to be a quieter person," Chafee once said. "Horses don't talk. That's one of their advantages." He made up his own mind on issues, finding it difficult to feel comfortable in either major political party.[81]

On January 4, 2010, Chafee announced his candidacy for governor of Rhode Island. Around July, he learned that RIEDC had approved the 38 Studios loan commitment. Something about the deal did not feel right. Leading up to and immediately following the RIEDC Board's final approval of the loan on July 26, Chafee voiced his disapproval. He criticized the process as well as the deal. It was "fundamentally flawed," Chafee said, and "every step possible should be taken to right this wrong." Chafee also called out RIEDC's meeting irregularities. He even tried to get on the RIEDC meeting agenda to speak against the proposal but was denied. Chafee was skeptical about the state going all-in on the computer gaming industry. The odds were long. "I don't see why we need a video game," he chided, "when so many of our politicians are already living in an alternate reality."[82]

Chafee made 38 Studios a plank in his campaign. His position was clear: he was against it. Chafee believed the state should not be putting such a large percentage of the funds approved for the Jobs Creation Guaranty Program into one company. The RIEDC staff, he reasoned, should have issued a request for proposals and selected the best applicants from a pool of respondents. "I have said again and again that this deal is too much of a gamble for Rhode Island taxpayers to bear the burden of responsibility," he said. "We're talking about $75 million of taxpayer money—60 percent of our loan guarantee fund—to one unproven company in a risky industry segment, without seeking out any other firms or taking any other bids."[83]

Chafee released his comments from the Warren, Rhode Island home of TPI Composites, which had retooled its Rhode Island–based operations from yacht building (Pearson Yachts) to wind turbine blade manufacturing. TPI had just announced that it was opening a wind blade innovation center in nearby Fall River, Massachusetts, where it anticipated creating between thirty and fifty new jobs. To Chafee, the state should be as focused on helping existing Rhode Island companies as it was on bringing in new unproven ventures.[84]

Chafee didn't just dislike the 38 Studios deal—he also didn't like Curt Schilling. He claimed that Schilling's teammates didn't like him either. Chafee thought Big Schill was a bit of a salesman. On the day of his inauguration, the governor went so far as to relate a story he heard about one of Schilling's teammates saying the bloody sock was fake—that Schilling painted the sock red. Chafee learned later the story was false but reportedly never apologized. The new governor's distrust for Schilling presaged a rocky future. There was

Elected governor of Rhode Island in 2010, Lincoln Chafee was a vocal critic of the process that incentivized 38 Studios to relocate to the Ocean State. *Courtesy of the Rhode Island State Archives.*

a new sheriff in town. Chafee stared down Schilling like a western lawman studying a desperado's triggerfinger during a high noon gunfight. The first wrong move might be the last. It would not take long.[85]

Chafee retained Stokes as director of RIEDC, mainly because he recognized that Stokes was a longtime friend of then Senate president and fellow Newport resident M. Teresa Paiva Weed. He did jettison one key figure, dismissing Rob Stolzman in favor of David Gilden as the agency's lawyer. Remarkably, despite being the largest investment it had ever made and despite the agency holding a number of various meetings between September 2010 and May 2012, the RIEDC Board had not monitored the financial health of 38 Studios. Rather, it believed it had hired a consulting division of IBM to provide oversight of the gaming company. In reality, IBM was contracted to 38 Studios and did not deliver a single report to the RIEDC Board of Directors.[86]

38 Studios had a lot on its plate. The company's viability rested on a significant financial infusion from the sales of its console game, *Kingdoms of Amalur: Reckoning*, which was being completed by its Maryland-based subsidiary. In Rhode Island, 38 Studios focused on developing its very complicated MMORPG, Project Copernicus. Schilling paid his employees well, on average $86,000 per year, and provided them with "as good a health care plan as anyone in the world." For a significant number of employees relocating to Rhode Island, 38 Studios assumed responsibility for their home mortgages until the houses sold. At the same time, the company had to hire hundreds of new employees to meet the quotas established in the loan agreement. It also engaged best-selling fantasy author R.A. Salvatore as executive creator of games "to create a fantasy world with 10,000 years of back story." The company rang up a $2 million payable to the writer.[87]

Within the first few months of his administration, Chafee and Patrick Rogers, his chief of staff, visited the Maynard facility and met with 38 Studios' executives and employees. Chafee was encouraged by the meeting, being favorably impressed by the company's experience, talent, and professionalism. The 38 Studios team was striking, from Salvatore to artistic visionary Todd McFarlane to Executive Designer Ken Rolston. They had a "chief people person," Peggy Freeman, who had been with the company since its inception in 2006. And there were more, each with a number of years in the industry and with much experience in their jobs.

This was not Chafee's deal, though. After vigorously opposing it during the campaign of 2010, he tread cautiously. He was mindful of his actions being perceived as bringing 38 Studios down, especially just a few short months into his administration. He knew others were watching his every move with the company, just waiting for a misstep. And according to the milestone-based funds distribution schedule, approximately 75 percent of the allocated money was going to be disbursed to the company during his watch. Chafee claimed that he was committed to making the deal work. The state made a major investment in the company, and he was going to do everything he could to help it succeed. It was in the state's best interest to do so.[88]

In 2011 and early 2012, 38 Studios was burning through several million dollars of cash each month. On February 7, 2012, the company released *Amalur*. Schilling welcomed around 150 people to a Bellingham, Massachusetts video game store where it went on sale at midnight. Priced at $59.95, the game received positive initial reviews and within a month was listed among the top five selling video games for that month. Unfortunately, it was less of a success than the company was planning. *Amalur* would sell 1.2 million units within ninety days, which was a promising debut for a start-up company in the challenging video game business but not enough to help the company secure the additional financing it knew it needed from the very start. Chafee labeled the game a failure, saying it had to sell 3 million copies to break even. 38 Studios was still banking on the tax credits it believed would be eventually forthcoming from the state. The company knew it needed an immediate lifeline.[89]

38 Studios was in deeper financial trouble than anyone at RIEDC really understood. The release date for "Copernicus" had slipped from September 2012 to June 2013. Because of the slippage, the company needed more money to finish the product than originally planned. Schilling had been desperately trying to raise cash since January 2012. During that month, tax credit broker Michael Corso arranged an $8.5 million loan from Bank RI. The collateral included 3,200 gold coins from Schilling and $14.3 million in tax credits Corso secured from the Film Tax Office. 38 Studios believed the state had committed the tax credits long ago.[90]

In April, Schilling invited Chafee and House Speaker Fox to 38 Studios' Empire Plaza offices. Schilling told Chafee and Fox the gaming company was going to need more money. "They were tapped out," Chafee said. "We were stunned." 38 Studios failed to make payroll for three straight weeks. Nevertheless, its 379 employees continued to show up for work, even though their pay failed to materialize. One pregnant employee reportedly found out from her doctor that her healthcare benefits had been canceled.[91]

On May 1, 38 Studios missed its $1.1 million loan payment to RIEDC, possibly even intentionally. 38 Studios was hoping to raise a level of concern that would require Chafee to help obtain the tax credits. The governor refused to take the bait. Two weeks later, on May 14, 38 Studios executives meet with Chafee and RIEDC staff to review the company's financials. "What is at stake," the governor said, is "keeping 38 Studios solvent." Chafee summoned the RIEDC Board to meet on May 16 to discuss the situation. Curt Schilling also attended and asked the board to forgive the then-overdue loan payment and to help deliver the tax credits. Without such help, the company would have to close up shop.[92]

Marc Phares's graphic represents the devastating impact of the failure of 38 Studios on the State of Rhode Island. *Illustration by Marc Phares © Phares Studios, LLC.*

The next day, May 17, RIEDC director Keith Stokes publicly announced that he was resigning. That same day, 38 Studios sent over a $1.1 million check to RIEDC. It later called to say that the bank account did not have sufficient funds to cover the check. The company funded the rubber check the very next day, thereby avoiding a technical default of the loan. Once the state had good funds, Chafee announced that 38 Studios had been unable to obtain outside financing or tax credits. In addition, he doubled-down on his assessment of *Reckoning*, claiming that video game insiders considered it "an abject failure."[93]

On May 24, 38 Studios laid off its entire workforce, including three hundred Rhode Island–based employees. Schilling blamed the company's financial woes on the state for failing to fulfill its promises and on Chafee for making "devastating" comments about the company's financial health. It filed for bankruptcy on June 7 in Delaware. The state immediately initiated liquidation proceedings to soften the blow of future losses.

Denouement

And just like that, the company that was intended to help lift Rhode Island out of economic stagnation by promising jobs and establishing the foundation for "Knowledge District RI" flamed out in spectacular fashion, just over one year after laying down roots in the Ocean State. As Chafee feared, some people blamed him for the company's demise. Others fingered Schilling. Many blamed both. They were the two best-known personalities holding the bag when the music stopped. It was not unusual to hear that it was Chafee's naïveté and stubbornness that brought 38 Studios down or that it was Schilling's arrogance and extravagance that nailed the company's coffin shut.

Schilling himself said the two people most responsible for the company's failure were he and Chafee. He believed that 38 Studio was on the brink of accomplishing what no other company in the gaming business ever had. "The company went bankrupt," Schilling wrote in an opinion-editorial article published in the *Providence Journal* after the dust settled, "and that was on me." He continued, "My failure to raise the final tranche to complete Copernicus was, in the end, our death blow, and I will take that to the grave." Schilling recounted Chafee's first visit to the company and how, at the end of the tour, the governor vowed to do everything in his power to help 38 Studios succeed. Schilling claimed making that statement was the last thing

Chafee did to help his company. The governor rang the company's death knell when he refused to release the tax credits Schilling desperately needed to stay afloat.[94]

Schilling claimed that the company had done everything the state asked, including providing monthly financial statements and meeting with the agency quarterly, more frequently when requested. According to Schilling, 38 Studios met the letter of the loan agreement without exception. No state official was "ever in the dark" about where they stood developmentally or financially, "unless they chose to be," he said. Schilling claimed that Chafee did not desire to know the details. He did not want to micromanage the company. To Schilling, Chafee's behavior at meetings was extremely odd. Schilling characterized the governor as inept. The opinionated, outspoken Schilling was known to say whatever was on his mind. It would get him in trouble on more than one occasion.[95]

Chafee agreed with Schilling on one point: he did not view micromanaging 38 Studios as part of his duties as governor or as chairman of the RIEDC. That role belonged to the agency's professional staff. Keith Stokes was the architect of the deal, the governor said, and as such, Chafee believed that Stokes should have done everything in his power to protect the state's investment, including providing oversight and ensuring that 38 Studios complied with the provisions of the loan agreement and bond issuance. He believed RIEDC's staff should have established appropriate monitoring and raised issues or concerns to the board. Others might argue it was incumbent on Chafee and the RIEDC Board to ensure the staff did just that. So, the lack of oversight was an institutional failure on many levels: the governor and chairman (Chafee), the director (Stokes), the RIEDC staff, and the RIEDC Board.

In reality, the failure of 38 Studios was baked into the deal. Schilling and 38 Studios continually made it clear the company needed $75 million to move to Rhode Island and finish "Copernicus." The company knew and informed RIEDC negotiators that even with the full $75 million, it would need to raise additional capital, at least $25 million more. On the other side of the ledger, RIEDC informed the company over and over that the gross amount of the loan was $75 million and that it would actually receive much less. That condition was delivered in verbal conversations, e-mail communications, and term sheet drafts.

The only people who allegedly did not know the $75 million loan was insufficient were the members of the RIEDC Board. Nobody told the board—just the opposite, actually. The RIEDC staff informed the board that the agency's staff had conducted detailed due diligence and determined that a loan of $75 million gross was sufficient funding to ensure the company's success. That narrative was reinforced by consultancies and legal representatives. The RIEDC Board was led to believe that the deal was "a calculated risk well worth taking." The lawsuit eventually brought by RIEDC against Wells Fargo et al. was built on the premise that the defendants "knew or should have known" that precisely the adverse was true and allegedly failed to disclose those particular facts to the RIEDC Board.[96]

Upon closing the loan, 38 Studios received less than $50 million. Most of the remainder was secured away in a capital reserve fund, a capitalized interest account, loan guarantee fees, and bond fees. Reserve funds were released according to a schedule of milestones the company was required to meet. Eventually, before filing bankruptcy, 38 Studios received about $57 million—nowhere near what the company always said it needed. Meanwhile, Rhode Island taxpayers were "morally obligated" to make good on the entire $75 million bond.[97]

The State of Rhode Island eventually recovered $61 million in damages from defendants named in the lawsuit. Of that, attorneys were awarded $11.3 million, leaving the state $49.7 million. Nevertheless, it could take years for the state to fully mend from the 38 Studios episode. The scars inflicted on the fragile psyche of the state could last generations. Skeptics will no doubt look askance at public funding proposals that benefit specific limited enterprises. After all, no one yearns to be the author of "another 38 Studios." One victim hit the radar screen in early 2015 when the new owners of the Pawtucket Red Sox began their quest to relocate the team to Providence. They hoped for public funding to help make it happen. Unfortunately, by that point, the wound that was 38 Studios had hardly begun to heal.

CHAPTER 3

The Providence Ballpark Plan

A Once in a Generation Opportunity

Interstate 95 (I-95) cuts a diagonal swath through Rhode Island. Drivers heading north from Connecticut enter the smallest state at the town of Westerly and exit forty-three miles later after Pawtucket. Visitors are welcomed to Providence by the Roger Williams Park Zoo, slammed fast against the eastern embankment of the highway. The city border is marked by a brown rectangular sign welcoming you to "Historic Providence." From this vantage point, there does not appear to be anything truly "historic" about the place. But as you exit at number "22A Memorial Boulevard—Downtown Providence" and meander through the city's streets, you begin to see its charm. Colonial-era buildings are mixed with remnants of mid-nineteenth-century mercantile warehouses, early twentieth-century offices, and contemporary mixed-use buildings, with samples of architecture from five centuries, the seventeenth through the twenty-first, cohabitating each with the other—the result of a strong historic preservation ethic and the city's inability to recover quickly from economic downturns that protected the city's structures from destruction, contributing to an attractive built environment, desirable to captains of industry and struggling artists alike, along with a smattering of everyone in between.

These are the bones of Providence's resurgence, that time in the late twentieth century when the moribund capital city was resuscitated by a fusion of culture, commerce, higher education, sports, and a vibrant nightlife buoyed by restaurants and clubs. This is the place that city planners and public leaders, led by charismatic mayor Vincent A. "Buddy" Cianci Jr., helped transform into America's Renaissance City by moving rivers, uncovering others, importing gondoliers, and promoting an event called Water Fire, where thousands still gather on summer evenings to promenade along the river alight with crackling wood-fired braziers and awash in Venetian opera.

It is also the beginning of Interstate 195 (I-195), the highway that runs from Providence dead east to Cape Cod. The confluence of the two highways once formed the most dangerous intersection in the region. The east–west highway bisected the city, cutting off the Jewelry District and Fox Point from Downtown, Providence's central business district. The highways, built in segments between 1955 and 1965, contributed to the malaise that afflicted Providence at the time. In four decades, the city's population had dropped 30 percent, from 253,500 in 1940 to 179,000 by 1970. Many settled in the surrounding suburbs; others were displaced to make room for the postwar interstate system. By 1974, as one scholar later described the scene, "Providence was too old, too overbuilt, and too little valued to meet the challenges of the post-war years. The city was emptying out, and the Downtown, once a built expression of industry-driven wealth, was becoming a stony preserve of orphaned symbols."[98]

The newly elected mayor painted a more colorful picture of the city circa January 1975. "On the night of my inauguration," Cianci said, "the police got an emergency phone call that several monkeys were escaping from our zoo. You know you're in trouble when your monkeys are trying to get out of town."[99]

It became clear to planners and visionaries that Providence needed significant improvement. The idea surfaced in a 1974 master plan called Interface:Providence. It was the fruit of Rhode Island School of Design students enrolled in a course called "High Speed Rail, Any Effect on Providence?" under the tutelage of architecture professor Gerald Howes. Its publication was buoyed by a National Endowment for the Arts grant. The plan provided a way to remedy the decentralizing impact of the automobile on late twentieth-century American metropolises while diminishing the impact of the then-raging "gas crisis" brought on by the Arab oil embargo of 1973. Their answer revolved around reinvigorating the modern city by reestablishing its importance as a local and regional mass transportation hub.[100]

Interface:Providence established a blueprint for the city that Cianci and other civic leaders eventually parlayed to rejuvenate Providence. It kick-started a series of initiatives designed to accentuate the city's inherent attractiveness. In 1978–79, the Providence Foundation, an organization dedicated to creating an environment conducive to growth and sustained investment, developed a plan to upgrade existing railroad facilities and convinced the Federal Railroad Administration to relocate tracks, thereby speeding construction of the planned I-95 Civic Center interchange. It also called for preserving the existing train station by turning it into offices and retail space.[101]

In 1984, Rhode Island DEM director Bob Bendick and visionary William Warner formulated the Providence Waterfront Study, which detailed plans for relocating rivers, uncovering others, and extending Memorial Boulevard. In 1987, the city took down its famed War Memorial statue, whose rotary over the covered river below was so confusing it was affectionately called "Suicide Circle." Construction started in 1988 on Citizens Plaza and other Gateway Center buildings. By 1991, work on extending Memorial Boulevard and reconfiguring the Woonasquatucket River and Waterplace Park was underway. Memorial Boulevard opened in 1993, followed by the Convention Center, the Westin Hotel, and Waterplace Park. In 1999, the Providence Place Mall opened its doors with Filene's, Nordstrom, and Lord & Taylor as anchor tenants. The Providence Renaissance was in full bloom.[102]

That same year, the Rhode Island Department of Transportation (RIDOT) initiated tangible steps to relocate the bottleneck that was I-195. The Providence Foundation had floated a plan to realign the highway a half mile south over the iconic Fox Point Hurricane Barrier. That structure was built to thwart the devastating effects of storms like the September 1938 hurricane, whose surge flooded the city with fourteen feet of water and left more than $300 million of damage (the equivalent of $5 billion today) and Hurricane Carol, which raged in late August 1954, pushing a twelve-foot storm surge up Narragansett Bay into Providence. In 1993, RIDOT and the Federal Highway Administration (FHA) reached consensus on the highway's new path and announced reasons for selecting it, including improving safety, reducing impacts on historic districts, facilitating implementation of the Old Harbor Plan, enhancing India Point Park, improving access to Rhode Island Hospital, and causing the least disruption to traffic during construction, which would ultimately begin in 1997.[103]

The plan would free up valuable property along the Providence River; relink long-separated local neighborhoods; create a mixed-use educational, medical, and high-tech enterprise center; and establish an urban linear park with a pedestrian bridge to add to the city's civility. At its inception,

During the relocation of I-195 through Providence, the highway and its new signature I-Way Bridge over the Providence River were placed half a mile south to cross with the city's Hurricane Barrier. *Photo by James Ricci.*

the estimated cost of the project was $450 million. In the end, it would run closer to $625 million. The project took decades to complete but was well worth the wait. When the original I-195 was built, the viaduct was intended to carry 75,000 vehicles a day. By the turn of the twenty-first century, it was handling 180,000 each day—and not well. During morning and afternoon rush hours, traffic jams routinely backed up five miles to the Massachusetts state line. Destruction of the old highway began in 2000. In August 2006, the bridge builders floated the attractive new four-hundred-foot center span from Quonset Point in North Kingstown, Rhode Island, and placed it on the substructure stretching over the river. The I-Way Bridge opened in October 2007, preceded by a public walk attended by ten thousand people.[104]

Providence soon experienced a once-in-a-generation opportunity. The highway relocation opened up nineteen acres of prime real estate for redevelopment. In October 2011, Governor Lincoln Chafee signed a bill creating the I-195 Redevelopment District Commission to plan and guide redevelopment activities. The commission's first job was to acquire the land from RIDOT, which needed approval from the FHA. Then an infrastructure of roads, utilities, sewers, and drainage was built before soliciting bids from real estate developers. All of this work was not moving fast enough for some prominent Providence leaders. In 2014, former mayor and real estate developer Joseph Paolino raised the issue when he questioned rhetorically, "They are taking forever, aren't they?"[105]

The I-195 Redevelopment District Commission would oversee twenty-two lots totaling twenty-six acres. As a condition of the FHA for the land transfer, three of these parcels comprising seven acres were reserved for open space. From a bird's-eye view, the corridor resembles an elongated letter *A*. Beginning in Fox Point, it angles north up the east side of the Providence River along Water Street to James Street, crosses over the river, reaches a peak where Dyer Street meets Peck Avenue, and from there drops south and west to Imperial Place in the Jewelry District.[106]

At its apex sits P4, a trapezoid shape of five acres. On almost every map, it stands out as a keystone of open space—virtually always distinctive in its green coloring. From the early stages, P4 was sacrosanct. It was to be an urban park, the centerpiece of the redeveloped corridor. It even had its own plan, developed by Boston landscape architects Brown, Richardson

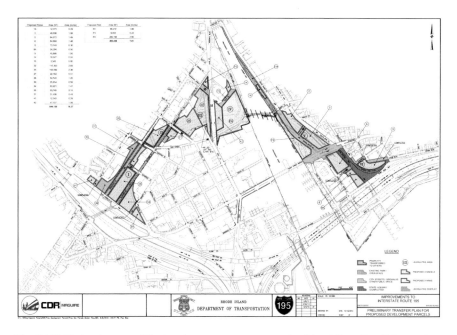

The I-195 Redevelopment District plan encompasses parcels of land from Fox Point on the east side of the Providence River to the Jewelry District on the west. Parcel P4 is located at the base of the Providence Pedestrian Bridge. *Courtesy of the I-195 Redevelopment District.*

and Rowe. A pedestrian bridge would traverse from P2 on the east side of the river to P4 on the west, forming the seven-acre linear open space that would later become known as Providence River Park. The green section caught the attention of a group of investors who would reveal that they had purchased the Pawtucket Red Sox and wanted to move the team to Providence…particularly to the newly freed land that once lay beneath the I-195 viaduct—specifically to P4 and Parcel 42, as well as an adjoining parcel owned by Brown University. It would not take long for the vitriol to rain down.[107]

WE ARE ALL RHODE ISLANDERS

The news broke on Monday, February 23, 2015. A group of investors had purchased the Pawtucket Red Sox the previous Friday from Madeleine Mondor, widow of beloved Ben Mondor, and minority owners Mike Tamburro and Lou Schwechheimer. The sale was no surprise. Rumors were rife that something was afoot. The buyers—a group of Boston and Rhode Island business leaders led by Providence lawyer James Skeffington and Boston Red Sox president/CEO Larry Lucchino—included Fenway Sports Management, which held an interest in the parent Boston Red Sox; Bernard Cammarata, chairman of the board of TJX Companies; William P. Egan, founder and general partner of Alta Communications and Marion Equity Partners; Habib Y. Gorgi, managing director of Nautic Partners LLC; and Arthur E. Nicholas and Frank M. Resnek, both partners in the Boston Red Sox. Rhode Island was well represented, especially by prominent local business leaders J. Terrence Murray (former CEO of Fleet Financial Group) and Thomas M. Ryan (former CEO of CVS). Each of the ten partners would own 10 percent of the team. Skeffington was named president.[108]

The Boston Red Sox were training in Fort Myers, Florida, where temperatures that Monday reached eighty-one degrees by noon. Outside McCoy Stadium, the totem pole of Paws, the PawSox mascot—his arms forever stretched out in welcome embrace to families who would eventually visit later that spring—stood in frozen solitude, surrounded by a snow-encrusted landscape. It was a biting twenty-eight degrees in Providence. By midnight, it would plunge to minus two degrees. For Pawtucket residents, the news release did little to warm their hearths. The new owners, it said, planned to move the team to Providence. Not far away, but still, out of Pawtucket—despite the lease with the State of Rhode Island the team signed the previous year, signaling its intention to keep the PawSox put at least through 2020, with a five-year extension available on top of that. Worse yet, the press release said, the team was going to drop its PawSox name.[109]

In a conference call, Skeffington said the owners planned to build a new ballpark near Downtown Providence. They had identified a site in the redeveloping I-195 corridor, evoking a scene of home run balls splashing into the Providence River, reminiscent of San Francisco's new ball yard where dingers end up in McCovey Cove. The Providence stadium would be built with private funds, Skeffington said, but the owners would be looking for state and local assistance. Ballparks for Triple-A franchises, he noted, generally cost between $60 and $70 million. "We are trying to keep the team in Rhode Island," Skeffington emphasized. "That's my desire. That's my wish."[110]

The new ownership group was impressive, especially for a team that would be looking to build a new stadium. Larry Lucchino was renowned for doing just that. He specialized in building or renovating urban ballparks with unique architectural features that accentuated artifacts of the local landscape, like in Baltimore and San Diego. At Fenway Park in Boston, he helped retrofit the ancient shrine with modern features. He seemingly had a Midas touch for such ballparks. These urban stadiums were highly acclaimed for contributing to the rejuvenation of, and the quality of life in, their surrounding neighborhoods.

No doubt the inclusion of Skeffington, Murray, and Ryan as part of the ownership group gave some people in the Ocean State a sense of permanence and the assurance that any new stadium would remain true to its Rhode Island roots. After all, Jim Skeffington was a Providence-based lawyer who had counseled some of the largest public developments in the state, including the Rhode Island Convention Center and Providence Place Mall. Terry Murray steered the Fleet Financial Group to become one of the largest and most successful financial firms in the country. It maintained headquarters in Providence until it merged with Bank Boston and then Bank of America. Tom Ryan grew a regional drugstore chain once known as Consumer Value Stores into the largest pharmacy/health chain in the country, CVS Caremark, while retaining its main office in Woonsocket, Rhode Island. The people of Rhode Island would have been hard-pressed to find stronger representation. Even though Pawtucket was getting the bum's rush from the new owners, the team was trying to stay in Rhode Island. As Skeffington said, "Our sense is that if the state wants us here, it should be the Rhode Island Red Sox. We're all Rhode Islanders."[111]

New owners Jim Skeffington and Larry Lucchino celebrate their group's acquisition of the Pawtucket Red Sox. *Courtesy of the Pawtucket Red Sox.*

In Pawtucket, Mayor Don Grebien did not share the owners' exuberance. Devastated by the news, he had only learned about it the day before. The new owners briefed Pawtucket officials on Sunday. They were clear with Grebien about their intention to leave McCoy Stadium, offering little chance the team would stay in Pawtucket. "This will rip the heart right out of us," Grebien said. "It's really the psychological impact this will have."[112]

TOM McCOY'S FOLLY

McCoy Stadium was named after the man most responsible for its existence, Thomas P. McCoy, the son of Irish immigrants who ascended through labor union leadership to become the boss of the city. Born in 1883, two years before Pawtucket was incorporated as a city, McCoy eventually scratched his way onto the political scene. He was one of seven children born to first-generation Irish parents, and his early childhood paralleled those of other urban, working-class newcomers to America during the late nineteenth and early twentieth centuries. His primary school education was truncated in the eighth grade when, as he said, "a turn in the fortunes of my family compelled me to go to work." He hustled his way from a milk wagon delivery boy to the Union Wadding Company, a firm that made stuffing for bedding and furniture. While employed there, McCoy took classes in English and shorthand at Brown.[113]

In 1904, McCoy became a conductor on the Providence–North Attleborough leg of what eventually evolved into the Union Electric Railway Company. He joined the Carman's Union, where he polished his debating and persuasive skills fighting for his fellow employees. The loquacious conductor entered politics after befriending passenger John J. Fitzgerald, the former progressive mayor of Pawtucket who, at the time, was making a run for governor. In 1920, Democrat McCoy won the House seat from the city's Tenth Representative district in the face of local and national Republican Party landslides. In the General Assembly, McCoy pursued progressive policies under the notion that the government should play a positive and active role in uplifting its citizens. In 1932, as the Great Depression lingered, McCoy worked on the successful Pawtucket mayoral campaign of John F. Quinn and assumed a leadership position in the new administration as city auditor. McCoy built a powerful political machine, but by 1935, Quinn and McCoy were embroiled in disagreements. Quinn chose not to seek reelection to his mayor's seat, opening the path for McCoy to win the post.[114]

As mayor, Thomas McCoy established firm control of the city and maintained a strong voice in state policy. He controlled the city council, its aldermen, ten House representatives, and one senator. In adherence with his paternal view of government, McCoy pushed building a sports complex for the benefit of his constituents. By initiating a construction project, he could provide employment to hundreds of families in need of paychecks. By building a sports stadium, the mayor could grant the gift of baseball to city residents as a diversion to their daily routines and a tool to help Americanize them. He selected Hammond's Pond as the site for the stadium, which required reclaiming the land from mud and silt.[115]

The project began in 1938, during the lingering years of the Great Depression. It was funded by the Works Progress Administration. The mayor deployed hundreds of workers to shore up the structure's swampy foundation, spawning stories of support piers and construction equipment sinking into oblivion. The pond consumed cement at prodigious rates. The stadium opened in 1942 at a cost of $1.5 million, two and a half times its original budget, the equivalent of $25 million today. It was called Pawtucket Stadium before being renamed in 1945, after the colorful mayor's early death at age sixty-two.[116]

Pawtucket's McCoy Stadium and its surrounding neighborhood as it looked from the air in the 1960s. *Courtesy of the Pawtucket Red Sox.*

The Triple-A PawSox had called McCoy Stadium home since 1973. Now the team's future relationship with the city was in jeopardy. Grebien was well aware that the PawSox had become an institution in the hardscrabble Blackstone Valley city. On this bleak late-February day, the future prospects of the city and its stadium looked far from bright.

Before the announcement, the new ownership group had already talked to Providence officials about a new ballpark. To gain leverage for future negotiations, the team raised the possibility of moving to Massachusetts if they couldn't do business in Providence. The message was unambiguous: we would like to stay, but we need cooperation. The owners' desire for a new ballpark seemed to mesh with the city's imminent need to redevelop the I-195 corridor. It soon became evident that they were targeting the site reserved for the proposed urban park, along with an adjacent acre parcel controlled in part by Brown University. The owners did not specify how they were going to wrestle P4 away from its current owner, the I-195 Redevelopment District Commission, but Skeffington was promoting the idea that a ballpark would speed additional development along the corridor.

THE BIG ASK

On April 15, 2015, the owners released plans for a new stadium. The conceptual designs had all the elements expected of a modern, signature, transformative, urban ballpark: brick exterior walls, exposed structural steel, and high arched openings—all architectural features that blended with the surrounding neighborhoods. The new ten-thousand-seat stadium would have a wraparound concourse, covered seating, picnic areas, Wiffle ball fields, and a requisite grassy berm. Beyond the center field wall would sit a lighthouse, intended to remind fans that this was, after all, the Ocean State. The proposal incorporated the previously approved pedestrian bridge that would connect the city's east and west sides.[117]

The owners estimated the new ballpark would cost $85 million. The stadium itself would run $70 million. Participation in an adjacent parking garage was pegged at $10 million. It was projected to cost $5 million to move storm water, wastewater, and gas utilities from beneath the land. The owners needed help from the state, though, as they could not build the stadium alone. Skeffington noted twenty-seven of the thirty Triple-A stadiums around the country were owned by governments.

In return for their investment, the owners proposed a scheme whereby they would lease the ballpark to the state for $5 million. The team would in turn sublease the stadium back from the state at $1 million each year. Rhode Island taxpayers, therefore, would be asked to pony up $4 million per annum for thirty years, totaling $120 million over the term of the arrangement. They were hoping to secure 9.5 acres of land as a gift or lease it for $1 per year. The owners had their eyes on P4, Parcel 42, and Parcel 14 of the I-195 Redevelopment Plan. In addition, the owners were

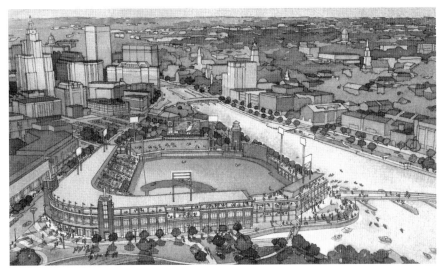

Providence Ballpark rendition at P4 in the I-195 Redevelopment District, with Downtown Providence as a backdrop in left field and the Providence River and East Side framing center and right fields. The lighthouse holds down a prominent position in straightaway center field. *Courtesy of the I-195 Redevelopment District.*

asking for an exemption from real estate taxes for thirty years. And they also needed a zoning change from the city to build a ballpark on the site. The owners wanted an option to purchase the land at fair market value after thirty years.[118]

The cost to the state would be cut in half from revenues the new owners said would flow in from sales taxes, income taxes, and hotel taxes at a rate of $2 million per year. They projected Providence would receive $170,000 a year in additional tax revenues. During construction, the project would create $20.4 million worth of jobs for 405 workers. Once completed, the team would employ between 30 and 40 full-time employees, along with another 300 to 350 seasonal workers. The annual payroll would run around $6.8 million. When asked about the details, the owners did not attempt to itemize those numbers, saying only that their consultants, Brailsford & Dunlavey, provided the estimates.[119]

Governor Gina Raimondo immediately praised the idea as "exciting," while reiterating that her top priority was "getting Rhode Islanders back to work." She said the state had "very limited resources to invest in economic growth—especially in the face of a large structural deficit." She was committed, she said, to working with the mayor of Providence and the state legislature to evaluate whether the project "was in the best interest of Rhode Island and whether we can afford it."[120]

The original plans for the Providence ballpark envisioned a cove in right field where home runs would go to rest. *Courtesy of the I-195 Redevelopment District.*

House Speaker Nicholas A. Mattiello said he was interested in keeping the team in Rhode Island. He intended to consult with his House colleagues and its Finance Committee and promised to review the proposal in an open and transparent hearing process before drawing any conclusions. Senate President M. Teresa Paiva Weed also promised that the proposal would be thoroughly vetted by the full Senate. These seem like cautious statements from the three political leaders in a state badly in need of economic stimulation. If they did not play their cards right, the future of Triple-A baseball in Rhode Island could be jeopardized. No one mentioned the ghost of 38 Studios that day, but judging by their guardedness, they most certainly felt its presence.[121]

The Opposition

Opposition had been brewing before the owners released their plans. Two lawmakers had read the tea leaves correctly. Three weeks earlier, state senators Patricia Morgan and Blake Filippi co-sponsored a bill calling for a referendum allowing Rhode Island voters to have their say on a land-lease deal for the Providence ballpark. A few weeks before that, red flags started flying when Skeffington hinted the team might need a lease from the state. Morgan and Filippi did not want a repeat of the Convention Center approval process, which, Morgan claimed, was "going to cost the taxpayers three-quarters of a billion dollars," and the people of Rhode Island "never had a chance to vote on it." Interestingly, Skeffington played a major role in that project, committing Rhode Island taxpayers to pay expenses related to the Convention Center, including debt service, operating expense, and maintenance costs.

The advocates for a referendum invoked the ghost of 38 Studios. "The history of 38 Studios has shown the weakness in giving a small group of internal policy makers sole authority," Morgan pointed out. "That proposal, which is costing the state over $100 million, was never adequately researched, examined or understood," with disastrous results for the taxpayers. After referral to the House Finance Committee, the stadium bill that would have put the question to the public was held for further study. In other words, it was dead on arrival.[122]

On April 2, Rhode Islanders got another whiff that the owners would be asking for something. Skeffington drew a crowd of reporters and other interested parties as he ventured down to P4 to "walk" the potential site. He liked what he saw—so did the consultants, who had already completed

PawSox CEO Jim Skeffington meets with reporters in 2015 following the acquisition of the team by the new owners and their announced desire to move the team to Providence. *Courtesy of the Pawtucket Red Sox.*

engineering, environmental, and transportation studies. Skeffington announced the Narragansett Bay Commission would have to move storm water utilities currently buried beneath what would become left field. He also said the new owners were eyeing more land than they originally envisioned, including the 1.08-acre Parcel 42 between the ballpark and Dyer Street and a relatively newly built Brown University continuing education facility on 2.19 acres at 198–200 Dyer Street. The building would have to go. The I-195 land was not just acceptable, Skeffington said—it was "perfect for a ball field."[123]

Grass-roots opposition to the Providence Ballpark Plan did not take long to formulate. And for a number of reasons. First, the plan was complicated. On one hand, the owners said they were building the ballpark with their own money. On the other, they were looking for Rhode Island taxpayers to provide financial support for the stadium in a lease/sublease arrangement. Second, the owners were all highly successful individuals, with a reported combined net worth between $8 and $10 billion. At the time, that would make them the tenth-wealthiest owner of any sports team in the United States. Subsidizing a stadium for them would not sit well with the average Rhode Islander, whose median household income in 2015 was a smidge over

$58,000. Third, the 38 Studio bankruptcy weighed heavily on the minds of Rhode Island politicians, opinion makers, and citizens. Any decision to provide taxpayer funds to bolster a private enterprise would be hard-pressed to garner necessary political and public support.[124]

Fourth, the new plan had designs on P4. The I-195 relocation plan was required to set aside open space for public use as a condition of the approval for the project. In its 1997 impact statement, the FHA stipulated that 14.7 acres of the redevelopment zone be dedicated to parks, "including 4.5 acres in the 'waterfront district west shore,'" seemingly specifically reserving P4. Fourteen years later, the Rhode Island state legislature passed the "I-195 Redevelopment Act of 2011," which codified that P2 and P4 "shall be developed and continued to be used as parks or park supported activity." When RIDOT asked the FHA in June 2015 if it could modify the configuration of open space as long as it retained the 14.7-acre commitment, the FHA replied that it saw no need for any alteration to the original plan. In fact, it declared, "any change to the use of these parcels would require the return of these properties" from the I-195 Redevelopment District Commission to RIDOT, which, in turn, could resell the land and apply the proceeds according to Title 23, the provision that regulates the use of money from highway land sales. Based on previous sales, P4 would be worth at least $10.8 million. The owners' attempt to grab P4 was a bold move.[125]

Finally, Ben Mondor was beloved for the family-friendly environment he nurtured at McCoy. Low ticket prices, free parking, affordable concessions, and generous exhibitions of fireworks, just to name a few aspects, were staples of Triple-A baseball in Pawtucket. Rhode Islanders expected no less from the new ownership team.

The more nuanced *bête noire*, however, reared up the day after the owners released the Providence Ballpark Plan. It accompanies most requests for public expenditures for stadiums nationwide. New ballpark proposals often proclaim that the new stadium will breathe life into the surrounding area. Then they typically place a value on that contribution, which is exactly what the new PawSox owners did in their April 15 press release.

Such estimates are difficult, if not impossible, to verify. They are typically boasted as reliable by proponents because they are the product of expert consultants who spend months analyzing the economics. Unfortunately, the optimistic consultants are usually hired guns by the folks trying to build the ballpark. The opponents find their own experts to dispute the projections spouted by the proponents' consultants. When not serving as paid consults, many of these economists, planners, and public policy professionals hold the pessimistic opinion that baseball stadiums rarely, if ever, pay off for the community.[126]

One ballpark expert, Holy Cross professor Victor A. Matheson, provided perspective on the Providence Ballpark Plan. Matheson, along with Lake Forrest College professor Robert A. Baade, had previously published a white paper titled "Financing Professional Sports Facilities." Shortly following the unveiling of the Providence Ballpark Plan, Matheson opined, "Take what stadium boosters are telling you and move that decimal point one place to the left." The Providence Proposal, Matheson assessed, was "absolutely a silly economic idea." Moving the team five miles from Pawtucket to Providence made no sense, he said.[127]

The professors' study found that minor-league baseball teams do not attract visitors from beyond the area, nor do they spur meaningful incremental spending. A new ballpark, Matheson said, "simply shifts where people spend money." If people choose a ballgame for entertainment, it might actually have a negative impact on other local business such as movies and restaurants. Besides, Matheson observed, "owners of ballparks want fans to spend money on food, beverages and souvenirs inside the park, not outside." Taxpayer-supported stadiums, he said, are not sound investments for taxpayers. "A small number of people stand to make profits from a large number of people who support the stadium." Matheson's opinion was not what the new owners hoped to hear.[128]

Gary Sasse—the director of the Hassenfeld Institute for Public Leadership at Bryant University and the former director of the Rhode Island Public Expenditure Council, the Rhode Island Department of Administration, and the Rhode Island Department of Revenue—agreed with Matheson's assessment of the Providence Ballpark Plan. "A reasonable effort should be made to keep the PawSox in Rhode Island," he declared. "However, on first read this proposal appears to heavily favor the owners not the taxpayers."[129]

Johnson & Wales University professor of management Lee Esckilsen provided a different view. Professional baseball teams add "to the quality of life" and provide "a social stimulus" that would be missing if the team left Rhode Island. A study by the Federal Bank of Kansas City uncovered similar findings. There are benefits associated with major-league baseball parks that transcend economics. "A strong case can be made," the report says, "that the quality-of-life benefits from hosting a major league team can sometimes justify the large public outlays associated with doing so." The benefits are similar to those stemming from "parks, zoos, museums, and theaters."[130]

Within three days of the Providence Ballpark Plan's unveiling, it was evident the stadium was going to be a hotly debated issue. For his part, Skeffington said the team's proposal was intended to start a conversation, including counterproposals. It is hard to say if they anticipated such an initial response. Some critics even suggested that if the state were going to spend $120 million for an $85 million stadium, why not just purchase the team outright? The new owners reportedly paid $20 million for the PawSox, which some pessimists believed was too much. The tsunami of negative reaction had an immediate impact. Before the end of April, the new owners were prepared to make an offer to purchase the land.

During the first week of May, Speaker Mattiello hired a renowned critic of publicly supported ballparks to help sort it out for the state legislature. Andrew Zimbalist earned a doctorate in economics from Harvard University and was a professor at Smith College. His views were well known to sports economists through papers and books, including *Baseball and Billions: An Intriguing Look Inside the Big Business of Our National Pastime* (1992) and *May the Best Team Win: Baseball Economics and Public Policy* (2003). Zimbalist had been a member of the editorial board of the *Journal of Sports Economics* since 1999 and had guided cities and states concerning ballparks in San Francisco, Anaheim, Wisconsin, Missouri, and Tennessee. Mattiello engaged Zimbalist to analyze proposed deals and provide advice as negotiations progressed. He wanted to know if the deal offered by the PawSox owners was "competitive and consistent" with others. From his vantage point, Zimbalist said that a deal can look attractive, but "it's got to have the right price." Zimbalist was brought on to help the state figure that out.[131]

Later in the week, after a series of closed-door meetings with the team, it appeared that Governor Raimondo was warming up to the idea of consummating a deal during the current legislative session. The PawSox owners were hoping for a similar outcome. Raimondo characterized the meetings as constructive, saying the team had been "open-minded" and willing to listen to the state's suggestions. "If there's a good deal here for the people of Rhode Island," the governor said, "then I am going to find that deal and do it." If not, she said, "We will kill it."[132]

Three days later, Zimbalist provided some initial advice to Mattiello. He characterized the PawSox offer as "aggressive" but "not completely outlandish." He pointed out that during the past twenty years most ballparks received larger public subsidies than the proposed Providence plan, but he warned, "That doesn't mean it's a deal you want to take." The team's proposal was a starting point from which to negotiate. Zimbalist pointed out a number of variables the state could negotiate to make the deal more attractive—for example, percentages of ticket or advertising revenue. Zimbalist needed more time to review the specific economics of moving the team from Pawtucket to Providence, but he said, "Basically the idea is to cut a better deal, or cut a good deal and how you can do that."[133]

A TRAGIC LOSS

The conversation had barely got started when tragedy struck. On Sunday, May 17, one month and two days after unveiling the Providence Ballpark Plan, James Skeffington died from a heart attack while jogging near his home in Barrington, Rhode Island. He was seventy-three years old. Even had he not been in the news recently as the new leader of the Pawtucket Red Sox, his death would have been noteworthy in Rhode Island.

Skeffington had been a well-known, longtime business and civic leader in the state. He was an accomplished counsel to quasi-public agencies in Rhode Island such as the Port Authority and Economic Development Corporation, the Housing and Mortgage Finance Corporation, and the Convention Center, among many others. Skeffington played major roles in economic development projects such as bringing General Dynamics and Fidelity Investments to the state, relocating and expanding Women and Infants Hospital, moving Roger Williams University and Bryant University to new campuses, developing the Convention Center, and building the Westin Hotel and the Providence Place Mall.

A philanthropist, Skeffington helped start the Coalition for Community Development and the Ocean State Charity Trust. He served as chairman emeritus of the John E. Fogarty Foundation for the Mentally Retarded, was a former member of the Georgetown University Law Center Board of Visitors, and generously supported the American Heart Association, for which he was awarded the Rhode Island American Heart Association Gold Heart Award in 2009. Skeffington served on the Greater Providence Chamber

Jim Skeffington, seen here with mascots Paws and Sox, died in May 2015 before plans for a ballpark in Providence could reach fruition. *Courtesy of the Pawtucket Red Sox.*

of Commerce Board of Directors and as a trustee of Bryant University, Providence College, the Providence Performing Arts Center, Women and Infants Hospital, and Butler Hospital.

By all accounts, Jim Skeffington loved Providence and the state of Rhode Island. He was born in the shadow of the State House on Smith Hill and educated at St Augustine's School, LaSalle Academy, Boston College, and Georgetown University Law Center. He worked as an attorney for the Locke Lord firm. His partner, Charles F. Rogers, said that Skeffington was "larger than life. A force of energy, a whirlwind, and it's kind of like Superman died. He seemed invincible in a lot of ways." Rogers lamented Skeffington's passing by noting, "The state's lost a great advocate, and the state's a lesser place today than it was yesterday."

That sentiment was echoed throughout Rhode Island. Jim Skeffington was a legend. He made an indelible mark on the community. His death left a void that would be hard to fill. House Speaker Mattiello called Skeffington "a gentleman in every sense of the word and a real champion for all that is good about Rhode Island." Mattiello called it "tragic that he did not live long enough to see his vision for the Pawtucket Red Sox come to fruition." In the months leading up to his death, that meant building a new stadium on P4. That proposal had not been well received even with Skeffington at the helm. Now, without his leadership, drive, savvy, and influence, the new owners had to revise their approach.[134]

LARRY

The void left by Skeffington's death was filled by another highly regarded figure, Larry Lucchino, who remained committed to realizing Skeffington's dream of "a beautiful, state-of-the-art, multi-purpose, well-located ballpark near the heart of downtown Providence." If there was one man who could make that happen, it was Lucchino.

Lucchino was born on September 6, 1945, in Pittsburgh, Pennsylvania. After starring in basketball and baseball at Allderdice High School in the city's Squirrel Hill neighborhood, he enrolled at Princeton and joined its basketball team. In his sophomore year, the Tigers reached the NCAA Final Four in Portland, Oregon, where they lost in the semifinals to the University of Michigan, which in turn succumbed to John Wooden's UCLA Bruins. Princeton was powered by future New York Knicks sharpshooter, Basketball Hall of Famer, and U.S. senator Bill Bradley.

Larry Lucchino assumed the PawSox CEO responsibilities upon Jim Skeffington's death and continued to push for a Providence ballpark. *From the* Pawtucket Times.

Of local interest, Princeton drubbed Providence College in the East Region Finals by 40 points, 109–69, to advance to the Final Four. That 1965 Friar edition was ranked number three in the nation. It was led by Jimmy Walker but also featured Dexter Westbrook, James Benedict, William Blair, and Mike Riordan, who later joined Bradley on the Knicks. The Friars, who were favored to beat Princeton, angered the Tigers by cutting down the nets after PC's semifinal victory over St. Joseph's College. Also, prior to the regional final, Westbrook personally annoyed Bradley by saying that he was overrated. Bradley poured in 41 against PC, while Friar star Jimmy Walker scored 27 points before fouling out. Bradley later said that Lucchino "was a good basketball guard." Larry "wasn't as quick as our other guards—but he always worked hard at his game," Bradley remembered. "I never saw him slack off."[135]

Upon Lucchino's graduation from Yale Law School, the prestigious Washington, D.C., law firm of Williams & Connolly recruited him to join its fold, where his mentor was famed trial attorney Edward Bennett Williams. Williams had ownership interests in the Washington Redskins and the Baltimore Orioles. Much of Lucchino's legal work centered on those two franchises and led to a seat on the Redskins Board of Directors from 1975 to 1985. When Williams purchased the Orioles, Larry became vice-president and general counsel. Williams appointed Lucchino president in 1988, where he stayed until 1993. He led the San Diego Padres as president and CEO from 1995 to 2001. In December 2001, Larry joined the Boston Red Sox ownership team and assumed a similar role. Lucchino is chairman of the Jimmy Fund, a philanthropy that supports the Dana-Farber Cancer Institute and has been long associated with the Boston Red Sox. Lucchino has an additional relationship with the charity, though, as it helped him win his battle against non-Hodgkin's lymphoma.[136]

Lucchino is the only known person to have five World Series rings, a Super Bowl ring, and a Final Four watch. Along with his many accomplishments, Lucchino has been the guiding light of the urban ballpark reformation that began in the last quarter of the twentieth century. The movement was a reaction against the cavernous, symmetrical, multi-purpose stadiums surrounded by acres of readily available parking that sprouted up in the 1970s. A major premise of the retro urban model is that baseball parks can breathe new life into the city neighborhoods in which they reside. They also add to the character and desirability of their surrounding areas by embracing the charm of old-time ballparks, incorporating modern amenities, adapting conforming architectural features, and repurposing nearby landmarks. Lucchino's major disciples in the movement are longtime associates Janet Marie Smith, ballpark architect extraordinaire, and Charles Steinberg, public relations maestro.

Lucchino was the driving force behind Baltimore's Oriole Park at Camden Yards, which contributed to the resuscitation of that city's Inner Harbor district. Built between 1989 and 1992 at a cost of around $110 million ($231 million today), it was the first application of the retro urban ballpark motif. As a Pirate fan growing up, Lucchino witnessed the impact on the community when "charmless" Three Rivers Stadium replaced the "charming" Forbes Field. That transformation informed his idea of what ballparks should and should not be. He replicated the methodology in San Diego, situating Petco Park in the city's Gaslamp Quarter, which helped jump-start redevelopment in surrounding downtown neighborhoods. Since then, major-league cities across America have embraced the fashion: from New York to Atlanta on the East Coast to Pittsburgh and Philadelphia in the Keystone State; Detroit, Cleveland, Cincinnati, and Milwaukee in the Midwest; Arlington and Houston in Texas; and Phoenix, Seattle, San Francisco, and Anaheim out west.[137]

In 1999, Boston Red Sox CEO John Harrington advocated abandoning Fenway Park as obsolete. He famously proclaimed that it would be easier to straighten the Leaning Tower of Pisa than save Fenway Park. Harrington was not the only one who felt that way. Fenway was out of date and in need of significant repairs. Though structurally sound, paint was peeling, asphalt was cracking, and wooden chairs were breaking. There was movement afoot to build a new stadium in the Seaport District. The baseball park could be located near the new convention center and become part of a sports complex along with a modern football stadium for the New England Patriots. Preservationists rallied to "Save Fenway," and eventually proposals surfaced to build a replica of the bandbox across the street. That option carried a price tag of $545 million ($865 million today) and required taking land from existing owners by eminent domain.

The new owners had other plans. Henry-Warner-Lucchino considered their options and decided to refurbish Fenway. The bones were still good.

It helped that the original engineers used steel and concrete when they built the stadium, but the place needed modern amenities. Between 2002 and 2012, the owners put more than $270 million ($350 million today) into renovating the ballpark. The improvements eventually included improved player facilities, two new rows of "dugout seats" parallel with the first base and third base foul lines, a roof deck atop the right field bleachers, luxury boxes ringing the field from foul line to foul line, pavilion seating behind home plate, expanded concourses, and seats above the Green Monster—all of which look as though they might have been there when the stadium opened in 1912. The new owners added a digital Jumbotron above the center field bleachers but wisely retained the manually operated scoreboard on the face of the Green Monster. Fenway Park was added to the National Register of Historic Places in 2012, the same year it celebrated its 100th anniversary.[138]

A GIFT FOR FUTURE GENERATIONS

After taking over for Skeffington, Larry got right to work. In an opinion piece published in the May 27 op-ed page of the *Providence Journal*, Lucchino summarized the team's case. It was as well constructed as it was written. He emphasized the major points of the Providence Ballpark Plan. "Affordability," Lucchino penned, "a key to Ben Mondor's success, is a value we commit to honor." The games would be affordable to families by keeping 25 percent of tickets for each game at $8 or less for the first five seasons. The new ballpark would spur redevelopment in the I-195 corridor, inspiring "private investment in biotech, retail, hotel, restaurants and residences." It would stimulate the economy to the tune of $14.9 million annually in direct spending, not to mention indirect spending, and generate $2.5 million in new taxes, more than double taxes created by McCoy Stadium. There would be new jobs designing, building, and operating the ballpark.

The new ball yard, Lucchino said, would become an urban asset situated at the mouth of the Providence River, "a beacon of welcome, a new 'front door.'" It would be an asset to a vibrant downtown, and "vibrant downtowns that attract businesses and residents are desirable." The ballpark would be a public gathering space, "a draw that supports small business year-round." And it would help preserve professional baseball in Rhode Island, protecting the state's "great baseball traditions that date back over 136 years to the National League's Providence Grays of 1878."

"It is a commitment," Lucchino wrote, "that outlasts all of us—a gift for future generations."[139]

Curiously, Lucchino's sentiments were published less than a week after Pawtucket mayor Donald R. Grebien wrote him an open letter. The new owners had dismissed the option of keeping the team in Pawtucket mainly because they wanted to build a new ballpark, but they also cited that renovating McCoy Stadium would cost $65 million. In his letter, which was publicized through numerous local media outlets, Grebien asked Lucchino to release the feasibility study—not to dispute it, but to understand the "true need and costs" of the stadium. Grebien invoked the spirit of Ben Mondor, whom he said "helped foster that bond with the City and State which is a big reason why he was so revered." The implication was that the new owners seemed to have overlooked the importance of the team to Pawtucket—and, for that matter, Pawtucket to the team. Grebien was trying to keep the city relevant and its hopes alive. His letter was public affirmation that Pawtucket was not going to lose its franchise without a fight.[140]

And Pawtucket wasn't the only city signaling interest in the team. By the middle of May 2015, at least three Massachusetts communities—Worcester, Springfield, and New Bedford—were prepared to make a pitch if Rhode Island bobbled away the opportunity. After all, one journalist following the drama observed, "These teams don't hit the market too often."[141]

The PawSox owners hoped that the Rhode Island legislature would consider the proposed ballpark before it adjourned, which would be between the middle to the end of June. Since it was clear that the original scheme was not going to pass muster, the PawSox and Rhode Island leaders were trying to craft a new deal for a Providence ballpark. Everyone involved was keeping the details under wraps. The new owners were optimistic that an agreement was within reach, as was Speaker of the House Nicholas Mattiello. Governor Raimondo, on the other hand, was less certain. She continued to stress that negotiations were complicated and that many pieces needed to fall into place. Whatever the case, the new approach was not likely to be a carbon copy of the original plan. Both the Speaker and governor repeatedly emphasized that any ballpark plan involving Providence had to make financial sense for the state and its capital city.

As the sun set on the month of May 2015, Larry Lucchino ratcheted up his plea. He took the opportunity to accentuate the Providence Ballpark Plan's roots by once again calling to mind its late leader, Jim Skeffington. "Jim was the chief cook and bottle washer…the passionate advocate for this downtown ballpark project," Lucchino told the *Providence Journal*.

He then laid out what he felt were three good reasons for continuing to push for a deal. First, it was "a very good idea with demonstrable public benefits." Second, it worked "well for the baseball team." And third, it was "Jim's dream and goal and we're motivated by trying to honor that legacy." Lucchino added that he was interested in speaking with Pawtucket's Grebien, although he was uncertain whether he would be able to release the feasibility study the mayor requested.[142]

Lucchino kept the pressure on during the first week of June. Comments coming into Governor Raimondo's office were tracking at 98 percent opposed to the plan. Lucchino flew in the head of Minor League Baseball, Pat O'Connor, from his office in St. Petersburg, Florida, to address local politicians, business leaders, union officials, and the media. It must have seemed like a good idea at the time. Instead, the homespun O'Connor lectured Rhode Islanders on the benefits of a new ballpark for one of Minor League Baseball's prize possessions. Without equivocating, O'Connor said that the economic impact of the downtown stadium would be "really significant." He stressed that it was "an opportunity to elevate the state of Rhode Island." And Minor League Baseball was here to help, just like it had helped other cities facing "the same problems as you have and have turned around things." O'Connor continued to rankle: "I think y'all got some problems outside of this…and this is an easy target for some stray bullets." As for McCoy, O'Connor said, "That pig ain't going to sing anymore." It is unlikely that O'Connor's visit tipped any scales in the PawSox's favor, singing pig or not.[143]

Lucchino immediately tried to minimize any damage inflicted by O'Connor. Within the week, he dispatched Dr. Charles Steinberg to a forum sponsored by WNRI-FM and Brown University's Taubman Center. Steinberg, one of Lucchino's top lieutenants since the Baltimore days, was a mastermind of special events. He helped elevate Fenway Park's reputation from legendary to magical through such hallmark events as Opening Day celebrations for previous years' World Series champions and the 100th anniversary of Fenway Park. Lucchino called Steinberg the "best in the business" on ballpark presentation and community relations. Sports economist Victor Matheson and urban planner Jack Robbins joined Steinberg on a panel moderated by WRNI political reporter Ian Donnis. More than 250 people attended the presentation. The owners were hoping to forge a fresh start on the proposal, saying, "Let this be the beginning of a discussion statewide." Matheson reiterated there was no doubt that Downtown Providence would be a great location for a ballpark, but the

Charles Steinberg preparing for a special occasion at McCoy Stadium. *Courtesy of the Pawtucket Red Sox.*

real question was whether taxpayers should subsidize it. Robbins called the ballpark a very complex issue. He stressed, "You have to make decisions on such big things on something other than sentiment."[144]

Meanwhile, emotions were rising on another element of the I-195 Redevelopment District. The signature pedestrian bridge had long been a major element of reinvigorating the corridor. Now its future was in jeopardy. RIDOT director Peter Alviti signaled that his agency was reevaluating the pedestrian bridge in light of the many other bridges that needed repair. He had been advocating for a comprehensive plan to address the state's many deteriorating bridges and roads. Alviti and Raimondo had a plan afoot for funding the repairs. It was called RhodeWorks, and it would eventually involve tolling trucks to help defray costs—the idea being that those putting the most stress on the state's infrastructure should contribute to its maintenance. One could interpret Alviti's pessimism about the pedestrian bridge as a pawn to help gain support for the larger RhodeWorks plan. RIDOT spokesman Charles St. Martin explained the dilemma, "We need to make the highest and best use of the limited funding we've got, and the highest and best use is to maintain the roads and bridges that are active and structurally deficient."[145]

RIDOT's statement upset some neighbors and students who valued the future City Walk footpath and bridge. Transportation officials had told the I-195 Redevelopment District Commission that it would begin building the bridge in the spring of 2015. Design changes to the bridge pushed that date out a year. Now, Alviti's comments tossed the bridge's future up in the air. That did not sit well with Arthur Salisbury, president of the Jewelry District Association. Salisbury was adamant about the bridge getting built. "Let's face it," he said. "We're going to make sure of that." The success of the bridge became correlated with defeating the PawSox's Providence Ballpark Plan. "We're going to protest," Salisbury said. "When we're protesting against the ballpark, we're going to protest for the bridge." The 450-foot pedestrian bridge would take three years and $22 million to build, ultimately opening on August 2, 2019.[146]

THE LISTENING TOUR

As June became July, very little substance escaped from the backroom negotiations between the PawSox and state and local officials. The regular legislative session concluded without a ballpark bill. The team now hoped the general assembly would hold a special session in the fall to consider and approve legislation for the plan. Speaker of the House Mattiello was amenable to such a session to contemplate the ballpark and Raimondo's RhodeWorks scheme. Senate President M. Teresa Paiva Weed, however, was refusing to reconvene that body, and both sides of the legislature were required to pass bills.

Then, on July 3, Lucchino announced that the PawSox owners were going to conduct a Listening Tour. They intended to meet and speak with people in each of the thirty-nine cities and towns in the state. Steinberg was enlisted to carry out the sessions. The first was scheduled for Smithfield on July 7, followed by Portsmouth, Richmond, and Johnston. The PawSox also announced they would hold tours on the proposed ballpark site each Monday at 5:00 p.m.[147]

Steinberg and the new PawSox owners received an earful during their first Listening Tour in the upstate town of Smithfield, where nearly forty people convened at the Smithfield Senior Center. Steinberg began with a parable. He had worked with Lucchino on major-league ballparks in Baltimore and San Diego. When the story took place, Lucchino was recruiting Steinberg to help in Boston. "To build?" Steinberg asked. "Have you learned nothing?"

Lucchino replied. "You don't destroy the Mona Lisa." Steinberg asked the audience if McCoy was the Mona Lisa. He must have been a little taken aback when more than a handful of people said, "Yes." Don Murphy of Warwick chimed in, "No debate here. It's the Mona Lisa, pal."[148]

After a contentious exchange between Steinberg and Murphy, cooler heads prevailed. They wanted to hear what Steinberg had to say. But there was little news, only that the original funding proposal was no longer an option. The locals told Steinberg it was unfair to compare a proposed minor-league ballpark with major-league stadiums. Some feared going to Downtown Providence with its urban problems of crime and murder. Others said that the family-friendly pricing of McCoy would be difficult to replicate in Providence, where parking and traffic would become issues. Steinberg said there was no deal yet, but PawSox owners and state leaders were working hard toward one. That, said Lauren Gresh of the nearby town Glocester, is the crux of the matter. "The vision doesn't mean anything unless we know what we're paying for."[149]

Steinberg and the new owners received another dose of criticism the following Monday when they held the first open house on the proposed future site of the Providence ballpark. Most of the fifty visitors were protestors against the plan. The sentiment among them was the city already had a plan for property's best use. "It's not right to put a stadium where there's supposed to be a park," one proclaimed. Another favored saving McCoy Stadium and keeping the PawSox in Pawtucket. "Pawtucket is a much more depressed area," added another protestor, "so why take away something from them?" Steinberg observed there remained a passion for keeping the team in Pawtucket but added that the Providence proposal showed "what could be better somewhere else."[150]

On July 22, the Providence City Council passed an ordinance granting fifteen-year tax breaks to developers whose projects ranged between $10 million and $50 million and additional incentives for projects over $50 million. The tax breaks were intended to accelerate development in the I-195 Redevelopment District. For all the objections and protestations about granting public subsidies to the PawSox, the city would now reward other private developers with tax incentives.[151]

By late July, the Listening Tour was losing steam. Steinberg did not attend the Barrington session on Monday, July 27. He was with former Boston Red Sox pitcher Pedro Martinez, who was being inducted in Baseball's Hall of Fame that coming Sunday. Instead, the team sent Cyd McKenna, a Durham, North Carolina resident who summered in Rhode Island and worked with Steinberg; Daniel Rea, another special assistant to Lucchino; and Jeff White, financial advisor to the Red Sox. In a possible attempt to quell open dissent, participants were asked to write their questions on pieces of paper.[152]

As the evening wore on, one resident cut to the chase. How, he wanted to know, could the owners learn anything when they had not asked any questions yet? Wasn't that the point of a "Listening Tour" to solicit ideas from the people of the state? It seemed as though the Listening Tour was really a Telling Tour. One resident said they wanted more parking. Another said taxpayers did not want to be left holding the bag. "Ask Curt Schilling about that," someone said. White explained that 38 Studios was a new business, whereas professional baseball had been around a long time and was a proven good corporate citizen.[153]

The PawSox owners must have felt they had received enough feedback. After the Barrington meeting, no future sessions were scheduled. The team's ownership made it through only seven of the state's thirty-nine cities and towns. Meanwhile, an opposition group calling itself the Providence Campaign Against the Stadium attracted about 125 people to an organizational meeting at Providence's Rochambeau Public Library.[154]

DURHAM, NORTH CAROLINA

Rather than additional Listening Tour events, the owners announced a new approach. They were going to host a trip to Durham, North Carolina, to show thirty to forty Rhode Islanders the kind of stadium they envisioned and what it could mean to Downtown Providence. Invitations were delivered to representatives from business, government, labor, real estate, and media to see firsthand "the transforming effect a Triple-A ballpark can have on a community." The trip was scheduled for August 5. Governor Raimondo, Commerce Secretary Stefan Pryor, House Speaker Mattiello, and Senate President Paiva Weed all said that they would not be making the trip. So did stadium opponent Sharon Steele, who characterized the trip as a "quid pro quo," saying the PawSox were trying to "buy the support" of those who accepted Lucchino's all-expenses-paid junket.[155]

Despite the objections, Lucchino rustled up thirty-nine guests, enough to make the trip worthwhile. Eight others on their way to North Carolina returned to Providence because a storm disrupted travel and connecting flights could not deliver them in time. The tour was delayed as stragglers arrived later than expected, including two who rented a car in Washington, D.C., and drove the remaining four hours to Durham, as well as others who pressed a shuttle bus into service.[156]

Those who made it to North Carolina received a full dose of southern hospitality. Durham had supported a team since 1902. They were first called the Bulls in 1913. In 1988, the team co-starred with Kevin Costner, Susan Sarandon, and Tim Robbins in the popular movie *Bull Durham*, about a new owner who wants to relocate the team to Miami. James F. Goodmon, president and CEO of Capitol Broadcasting Company, told the visitors that his company purchased the team from owner Miles Wolff in 1991. The new owners wanted to move the Bulls to a more central location outside Durham, but local opposition foiled those plans. Instead, the city built the new Durham Athletic Park, which opened on April 6, 1995, with 10,886 fans in attendance. Goodmon told the Rhode Islanders that they should move beyond their differences and get a ballpark built in Downtown Providence— if, that is, it is a good and fair financial deal for all sides.[157]

Other Durham leaders spoke of the stadium being a catalyst for development and of the beneficial synergies being shared among the ballpark, a nearby theater, and local businesses, some of which were spreading out across the railroad tracks where new commercial space was being built or renovated as the immediate area approached capacity.[158]

Lucchino took the opportunity to release some guarded news. The PawSox had "dramatically renegotiated" a deal with the General Assembly and Governor Raimondo's office. He did not want to release any details before elected officials were ready, but he was hoping to do so within the next few weeks. Speaker Mattiello's office confirmed Lucchino's assessment that the state and the team were getting "very close" to agreeing on a new proposal, characterizing it as "a good deal and in the best interest of the state." The governor's office, however, reiterated its consistent realistic refrain: there was still much that needed to happen, like "various approvals from regulatory agencies and other stakeholders."[159]

The Straw that Broke the Camel's Back

Two weeks after the Durham trip, on August 19, Mattiello began signaling that the House might not take up the PawSox proposal during a special fall session after all. It now looked like the issue would be pushed to the regular session convening in January 2016. Mattiello pointed out two thorny issues remained unresolved: one with Brown University concerning a parcel of land that reared up a few days previously and the other a long-discussed storm water runoff problem during stadium construction.[160]

Public opinion against the ballpark continued to swell. The overwhelming majority of letters, calls, and e-mails to public officials (including Governor Raimondo, Senate President Paiva Weed, Providence mayor Jorge Elorza, and the I-195 Redevelopment District Commission) were against the Providence Ballpark Plan—800 of the 828 records, or 96.7 percent, were opposed. One e-mail petition sent to Paiva Weed contained 3,528 opposition signatures, and two boxes delivered to her office reportedly contained 13,000 opposition letters. (Speaker of the House Mattiello's office said it did not keep such records.) The data clearly indicated there was significant sentiment against the proposal.[161]

The situation did not improve during the evening of August 25, 2015, when Leadership Rhode Island and the Harvard Business School Association of Southeastern New England sponsored a forum on the Providence Ballpark Plan at Point Street Dueling Pianos in Providence's Davol Square. About 240 people showed up, close to 210 of them opposed the plan. The debate centered on the best use for the land west of the Providence River: a public park or a baseball stadium. PawSox spokeswoman Patti Doyle and team community outreach director Cyd McKenna presented the argument for the ballpark. It would be a park within a park with three acres of open space surrounding the stadium. Doyle said the team wanted to build a multipurpose ballpark because "a well-located, well-designed and well-built [stadium] can be transformative for a city."[162]

Jewelry District Association past chairwoman Sharon Steele and Ethan Kent of New York City's Project for Public Spaces spoke against the project. Steele reinforced that the long-planned destiny of P4 was as a park, the centerpiece of the I-195 redevelopment corridor. Kent confirmed that a ballpark was not the highest and best use of the land, saying that "a ballpark is a private, exclusive space. You have to pay a lot of money to come into these spaces, and it's closed a lot of the time. We can do better." Scott Wolf, a former pollster and political strategist then serving as director of Grow Smart Rhode Island, which had not taken a formal stance on the plan, wondered aloud if, given the prevailing sentiment for fiscal conservatism, the "owners have the public feel or are they too obtuse and arrogant to be public stewards of a project of such scope?"[163]

The next day, Lucchino was spotted examining Victory Place, an eight-acre vacant lot on Eddy Street. PawSox owners had previously dismissed the site as being too far from downtown. Victory Place was the former site of a jewelry factory and recent benefactor of an environmental cleanup. It would be accompanied by a tax stabilization plan capping city taxes at $20.6 million over thirteen years. No taxes would be owed on a development there during the first three years. Lucchino said the lot was not under serious consideration for the new ballpark.[164]

During the first week of September, Mattiello announced what sounded like the end of the road for the Providence Ballpark Plan: it would not be considered by a special legislative session. The Speaker said, "The PawSox is an issue that's just not ready." More ominously for future prospects of a ballpark in the heart of the I-195 Redevelopment District, Mattiello added, "And it may never be ready to be addressed. I don't know if the ballpark is going to happen or not."[165]

Brown University and the new owners could not reach a deal on a piece of real estate needed by the PawSox to stitch together the 9.5 contiguous acres necessary to fulfill their vision. For its part, Brown University released a statement saying it was supportive. "If the City, State and people of Rhode Island determine that a stadium is desirable," said Cass Cliatt, Brown's vice-president for communications, then the university would be willing to sell any of its land needed for the project "at a fair price that fully compensates Brown for its significant investment in the real estate and associated programmatic requirements for our School of Professional Studies and Office of Admission at 200 Dyer Street." The statement elaborated, "It is our responsibility to our community to ensure an equitable outcome for any transfer of the land."[166]

The City of Providence wanted a piece of the action for "hosting" the stadium. Mayor Elorza made it clear that "the city cannot be out of pocket for a dime of the cost of building or operating a stadium on that site." Secondly, the proposed ballpark did not fit in with Elorza's vision for the I-195 land, which, he said, had "always been an opportunity to build the economy of the future" and that "any proposal must leave a clear path for surrounding development to achieve that goal." The other fly in the ointment was the Federal Highway Administration wanting fair market remuneration for the land once designated as parkland "if a commercial enterprise were built there."[167]

All of this led Mattiello to conclude that the parties might not reach a deal. "No matter how you look at it, the deal's only so big: There's only so much money the ballpark's going to generate," Mattiello said. "Every time you have someone looking for a piece of the revenue…it makes it more difficult to go forward." The Speaker did acknowledge that he believed a stadium along the riverfront would be "a nice attraction" and a "catalyst" for Providence, but he would not support it if they "could not get it to a point where it is in the public's best interest." "If the cost is too great," Mattiello said, "then it is not a project that is ever going to materialize."[168]

The death knell came two weeks later. The news was splashed on the front page of Sunday's *Providence Journal*. Mattiello said Lucchino told him that the PawSox had ended their pursuit of moving the PawSox to Downtown Providence. There would be no ballpark built on P4. Lucchino said Governor Raimondo had made it clear that the location was not possible. "We were told it was not going to be a suitable site and there were too many obstacles that remained," the team chairman said. "And we…heard loud and clear what we were being told." Lucchino said, "The formal decision was largely made for us." Spokeswoman Patti Doyle released a statement saying the team still believed the site would have been "exceptional." Going forward, the team was going to be open to all options and proposals. As for the immediate future, they would now focus on preparing for the 2016 baseball season.[169]

Speaker Mattiello hinted that the straws that broke the camel's back were Brown's desire to get $15 million for the 0.88-acre Parcel 42 and Elorza's desire for "potentially millions" to cover the City of Providence's costs for supporting a stadium, including police, fire, and street widening. "There's too much capital cost, and if you can't secure the land at a reasonable cost, there's no possibility of working an agreement that serves everybody's interest," Mattiello said. As for McCoy, it needed too much money to renovate, and no one was going to invest in "a model that no longer works," Mattiello added. I-195 Redevelopment District Commission chairman Joseph F. Azrack pushed for the state and city to work with the team to find a suitable site. He continued to advocate for Victory Place, even though Lifespan had purchased the land earlier in the month. His statements elevated the concern that the PawSox might look outside Rhode Island.[170]

At least one group publicly rejoiced the Providence Ballpark Plan's demise. Samuel Bell, chairman of Stop the Stadium, an opposition group formed a month earlier, praised it as an "incredible victory." "They said it couldn't be done," Bell proclaimed. "They said the fix was in. They said we had no chance. But we won!" He thanked all of "the volunteers who braved the summer heat to collect signatures or to go door-to-door in Mattiello's district," trumpeting a belief that such a tactic had a role in the proposal's final death.[171]

As the window closed on the Providence Ballpark Plan, the future of the Pawtucket Red Sox in Rhode Island was sent completely up in the air.

CHAPTER 4

The McCoy Stadium Study

Rapprochement

The City of Pawtucket had good reason to hold a grudge. In February 2015, the new PawSox ownership immediately and publicly dismissed any hope that the team would stay in the city. They said McCoy Stadium lacked the necessary amenities required for Triple-A baseball in the new millennium. It was also far too expensive to renovate the old ballpark to modern standards, they claimed. Besides, the new ownership group wanted to move the team to Providence. Pawtucket's mayor, Don Grebien, was caught unaware. The new owners did not consult with him or other city leaders concerning what was about to go down. It is safe to say that the PawSox paid little respect to the community that had hosted the team for the previous forty-five years. The city had full right to be apoplectic.

The announcement by the new owners to move the PawSox out of McCoy and into a new ballpark in the state's capital left Grebien in an awkward position. If the team moved to Providence, Pawtucket would indeed lose its franchise, but at least the team would remain in Rhode Island. If it could not secure a home in Providence, perhaps the team would reconsider Pawtucket as an option. The mayor tried to keep Pawtucket relevant. When the Providence Ballpark Plan collapsed, Grebien was ready to help pick up the pieces. The new owners wanted to focus on the upcoming 2016 season. Grebien and his city were prepared to do everything they could to keep the PawSox from leaving, even though the new owners' attempted abandonment of Pawtucket for its more populous and glamorous neighbor did little to engender goodwill with its hometown fanbase.

Yet on February 2, 2016, with spring just beyond the horizon, Pawtucket mayor Don Grebien and PawSox honcho Larry Lucchino buried the hatchet. The instrument of choice was a joint letter from the city's mayor and the team's chairman to a mailing list of 100,000 Pawtucket Red Sox fans. It was reprinted on the *Providence Journal*'s opinion-editorial page. The authors acknowledged that 2016 was a critical time for the city, the team, and "the deep-rooted traditions of professional baseball in Rhode Island." Mrs. Mondor transferred "stewardship" of the "historic franchise" to the new owners "one year ago this month." The transition was "not without bumps and bruises," the letter said. It called out team president Jim Skeffington's "unexpected death," along with his dream of "a new, widely-used, state-of-the-art, multipurpose ballpark in the heart of Providence," which "fell short of public and fan support." As the new ownership entered its second year, the club "has heard the people of Rhode Island loud and clear and has refocused itself." The team's primary focus in 2016 was going to be "on our fans and the McCoy Stadium experience."[172]

Ballpark planning was relegated to the back burner, the letter said. The relationship between the team and city had "rebounded" and was now described as "open, candid and collaborative." The ballpark issue would need to be addressed, as there remained "serious challenges to the PawSox given the competitive advantages newer facilities afford many clubs in the International League, and the troublesome decline in attendance at McCoy Stadium over several years." The team was "determined to reverse that trend." The new owners also recognized that the 2015 decline was, in part, because many fans felt slighted "over the unsuccessful roll out of the plan to move to Providence."[173]

Grebien and Lucchino called on the PawSox community to join them "in making this a fresh start in the next great era of Rhode Island, PawSox and Red Sox baseball." The mayor and chairman hoped to revive and strengthen the baseball traditions and roots that "run deeply in this part of the country, and probably nowhere more deeply than right here in Pawtucket." The pair concluded by urging "every member of the PawSox community, from whatever zip code, to provide comments to us directly regarding your PawSox opinions and experiences" and thanking fans for continuing to support the team.[174]

For Grebien, the future looked significantly brighter at the beginning of 2016 than it had at any time in 2015. Pawtucket now possessed a real chance of keeping its Red Sox. On February 9, Lucchino reinforced the joint letter's sentiments to nearly five hundred business and civic leaders gathered at Twin River Casino for the Northern Rhode Island Chamber of Commerce's twenty-fifth annual dinner. Lucchino was the keynote speaker. He said the team, the city, and the state were considering commissioning a joint study on McCoy Stadium. When the new owners were pushing the Providence plan, Skeffington revealed that consultants conducted an analysis of McCoy and concluded the old ballpark needed $65 million of improvements in order to compete with other International League teams' state-of-the-art facilities. Grebien repeatedly asked to see the report, but the team never shared it with the city, or anyone else for that matter. Lucchino claimed the enhancements were more accurately stated as between $50 million and $65 million, ramping down the previously stated findings.[175]

Lucchino told the audience that the PawSox were focusing on baseball, which included reversing the recent woes at the turnstile. The chairman acknowledged that PawSox home game attendance had "been on a downward trend for a decade." In 2015 season, the team drew 466,600 patrons. That was the lowest since 1999, the year McCoy was renovated and its capacity expanded to accommodate 10,000 fans per game. Lucchino said he could not promise the team would remain in Pawtucket. The PawSox owners had heard from a number of other communities, but they were not pursuing any of them. Lucchino said the team was slowing things down on that front. He drew enthusiastic applause from the crowd, however, when he mentioned the team would take a "good, comprehensive look at McCoy Stadium."[176]

The lease agreement between the team and the city called for a joint study of McCoy. The new owners had skirted the provision when they were attempting to move the team to Providence. The lease was set to expire in January 2021. The team was planning to celebrate the seventy-fifth birthday of McCoy Stadium during the 2017 season. Going forward, Lucchino laid out the team's four guiding principles: first, create a comfortable, hospitable, high-quality ballpark without peer in Triple-A baseball; second, construct baseball teams worthy of its fans' support while providing affordable family entertainment; third, be fully engaged in the charitable and civic life of the surrounding community; and fourth, create a top-notch player development machine for the Boston Red Sox.[177]

THE MAYOR

By the time Lucchino and Steinberg arrived in Pawtucket, they had turned ballpark pageantry into an art form. The new owners had become particularly adept at installing memorable rituals and staging grand productions at their previous addresses, most recently Fenway Park. The seminal event occurred on Opening Day, Monday, April 11, 2005, when Lucchino and Dr. Charles produced a celebration for the reigning World Champions, the team that ended the eighty-six-year drought between titles. The planning began in earnest in March. The organizers staged numerous walk-throughs until they were certain their ideas could be executed.

The spring extravaganza was worthy of the team's fall accomplishment. To start, each contributor publicly received a championship ring. Then, banners from previous Red Sox World Championship seasons (1903, 1912, 1915, 1916, and 1918) were unfurled in sequence, beginning at the left field

Steinberg and Lucchino checking out the script for a carefully planned ceremony. *Courtesy of the Pawtucket Red Sox.*

foul pole and skirting the Green Monster to the center field triangle. The 2004 banner followed, covering the other five, in a sense eclipsing all of the franchise's previous accomplishments. Finally, a giant U.S. flag dropped to span the entire expanse of the left field wall. As if by magic, legendary representatives from Boston's other major sports teams emerged from the Green Monster: the Celtics' Bill Russell, the Bruins' Bobby Orr, and the newly minted Super Bowl champion Patriots' Richard Seymour and Tedy Bruschi. Each walked in from left field to the vicinity of the pitcher's mound and simultaneously threw out an opening pitch. The Red Sox punctuated the ceremonies by handily beating the rival New York Yankees, 8–1.

The Pawtucket Red Sox's 2016 season opened at McCoy Stadium in grand fashion. It wasn't surprising that Lucchino and Steinberg reserved a key role on Opening Day for Don Grebien. The mayor stood out in his bright-red PawSox jersey. The new owners had presented it to him on "truck day" just a few months earlier. On that occasion, the team's equipment truck had just barely started on its perennial journey from Fenway Park to Jet Blue Park in Fort Myers when it detoured off Interstate 95 South and stopped at McCoy Stadium. The visit was a symbolic nod connecting the major-league team to its Triple-A affiliate, an olive branch arranged by the PawSox's new owners and, perhaps, a precursor to what many Rhode Islanders hoped would continue the long-standing team/city relationship.

Grebien grew up in Pawtucket's Fairlawn section. After graduating from Davies Career and Technical High School in 1985, he attended the Community College of Rhode Island, earning an ABA degree in business administration. After college, he joined American Insulated Wire Corporation, where as an operations manager he prepared budgets, supervised team members, and negotiated labor contracts. He also supervised logistic, freight, and warehouse processes for two of the company's major facilities.

In 1997, Grebien was elected an at-large member of the Pawtucket City Council. He ran for mayor in 2008, but incumbent James E. Doyle prevailed by a margin of 54 percent to 46 percent. Doyle did not seek reelection in 2010. Running on a platform of "A New Direction," Grebien handily defeated Henry S. Kinch Jr. in the Democratic primary and then waltzed to victory unopposed in the general election. On the morning of November 3, 2010, at the age of forty-three, Donald R. Grebien found himself mayor-elect of Rhode Island's fourth-largest city.

To the rest of Rhode Island, the city of Pawtucket is best known for two things: being the birthplace of the American Industrial Revolution and

Historic Slater Mill on the falls in Pawtucket. At right is the Pawtucket City Hall, which is also in the National Register of Historic Places. *Photo by James Ricci.*

being the home of the Pawtucket Red Sox. By the time children in the state finish high school, many have visited Slater Mill. In 1793, at the request of industrialist Moses Brown, Samuel Slater built a mill to spin cotton at the falls along of the Blackstone River. It was the first enterprise in North America to use a water-powered spinning frame to mechanize textile manufacturing consistent with the principles espoused by English industrialist Richard Arkwright. Slater employed families to work in the factory, establishing a child labor scheme that became known as the "Rhode Island System." It is highly likely that those same students who visited Slater Mill had also been to McCoy Stadium for a PawSox game.

The start of the PawSox's 2016 home season was delayed one day because the field was saturated. Earlier in the week, a rare April storm dropped seven inches of snow on Pawtucket. Subsequent rain compounded the problem. So, the 2016 campaign at McCoy commenced on Friday, April 9, at the relatively early start time of 6:15 p.m. Opening Day ceremonies kicked off at 5:45 p.m., replete with the flair the new owners had sharpened to perfection during their days in Boston. A blue tarp covered a structure in center field that, when dropped, revealed an oversized sign in red and blue lettering embracing fans with the words "Welcome to Pawtucket." Kaya Rose Giroux, a sixteen-year-old local high school student and opera singer, unleashed an inspiring rendition of the national anthem. And an ebullient Don Grebien threw out the first pitch.

No one was more deserving than Grebien to be so honored. It was he who protested the loudest when the new owners snubbed his city in favor of Providence. It was he who challenged the new owners when they said it would cost $65 million to renovate McCoy. It was he who maintained a cordial working relationship with the new owners despite their public shunning of his city. It was he who continued to keep alive the hope that if the Providence Ballpark Plan fell through, which it did, the new owners would consider remaining in Pawtucket. It was he who "never made it personal" despite being "emotionally attached." It was he who understood that this was business, not personal, and that his administration was going to "fight passionately" for the community, but "not to the point of shooting arrows." With the Rhode Island winter of 2015–16 in the rearview mirror, the signs were clear: the new owners yearned for detente with the city the team had called home since 1973.[178]

A Window of Exclusivity

The strong bond between the PawSox and the city of Pawtucket seemed like a birthright to the generations of Rhode Islanders coming of age in the final quarter of the twentieth century. In 2016, the Triple-A Red Sox affiliate wanted nothing more than to restore that privilege. Following the debacle that unfolded in 2015, the PawSox named Dr. Charles Steinberg team president and Dan Rea general manger. In February, Steinberg identified the first step in mending the relationship: "engage in personal connections" with the fans. Over the winter, the team conducted as much direct face-to-face contact with the team's fans as possible, "so that people could feel our love and could sense our sincerity in wanting them to love their PawSox the way they have over the years." Team representatives met with fans of all ages, from elementary school students to senior citizens, and planned to do so throughout the spring. One idea Steinberg said the PawSox planned on implementing was "My Hero Mondays." Fans would nominate local people and causes for recognition during Monday home games at McCoy Stadium. Such promotions would help salve open wounds and, perhaps, increase attendance while doing so.[179]

Just one month earlier, the team organized a two-day open house it called "Moonlight Madness" and "Daylight Savings." The event replaced the traditional "Hot Stove" rally at which fans and media could meet and speak with PawSox players. The updated version allowed fans to play catch with Boston Red Sox center fielder Jackie Bradley Jr., chat with PawSox pitching coach Bob Kipper, call games with PawSox announcer Will Flemming, and take pictures with the Boston Red Sox World Series trophies or Carl Yastrzemski's silver bat, a memorial to his Triple Crown season in 1967. The event was well attended—about four hundred people showing up each day. Ticket sales were so brisk they surpassed the previous season's entire opening weekend.[180]

The PawSox front office considered the event a sign of progress in recovering from the previous year's public relations missteps. General Manager Rea saw "a lot of positive sentiments and feelings" during the weekend. He wanted the fans to judge the organization by its actions. The team was focusing "on the 2016 season at McCoy Stadium," Rea said, "and we will be here for the foreseeable future." The owners wanted "to make this a great place that does great things." Rea claimed that the fans he spoke with at the two-day open house were of the same mind. The proof would come in September when the team tallied its season-long receipts.[181]

After the 2015 season, Lucchino said that the PawSox would listen to all offers. When discussing ballpark options, he noted, "We've taken a position that we're open to everything, every possibility." The club was mulling over numerous proposals but had no timetable for making a decision. "We need time to do this methodically and carefully," Lucchino emphasized. At the time, the owners were keeping their options open, hedging all bets.[182]

Just a few short months into the 2016 campaign, the PawSox closed its open-door policy. Bolstered by its refreshed friendship with the city, the team's leadership decided to grant Pawtucket a window of exclusivity. For the next year, the PawSox would only entertain proposals from their long-term hosts. In June, at a stately press conference arranged directly behind home plate, on the very spot where passed balls go to die, the team and the city announced that they would begin seeking proposals for a McCoy Stadium feasibility study, as promised in February's joint letter to the team's fans. It would be financed by three parties: the team, the city, and the state. Each was a major stakeholder. Pawtucket owned the stadium and leased it to the state, which subleased it to the PawSox. The parties would select the best company to conduct the analysis through an RFP process.[183]

The McCoy study would assess the possibility of extending the old ballpark's life either by patching up the current facility, renovating the existing structure to modern standards, or rebuilding a state-of the-art stadium on the current site. The analysis was expected to take months and include four major components: an evaluation of existing conditions at the

In June 2016, team executives, city leaders, and state officials announced a joint study to determine the feasibility of whether to improve, renovate, or rebuild McCoy Stadium. The PawSox also granted Pawtucket a one-year period exclusivity to get a deal done. *Photo by Ernest A. Brown, of the* Pawtucket Times.

stadium and its surrounding area, a survey of state-of-the-art and current trends in professional ballparks, a comprehensive list of necessary repairs and improvements, and a final report detailing the cost and preferred design of the improved ballpark. Lucchino said that the PawSox would deliver the tightly held 2015 study that estimated the stadium would need $50 million to $65 million in renovations. Grebien committed to contributing "every single study" the city had dating back to the 1999 McCoy renovation.[184]

Mayor Grebien was pleased with the cooperation. "This study of McCoy and the economic development opportunities within the ballpark district is going to help the city, the Pawtucket Red Sox, and the state determine the full potential at McCoy going forward through smart investments," he said. Grebien believed the prospects for retaining the team were growing more realistic by the day. He hoped the study would provide "a road map to ensure that the family-friendly, affordable brand of PawSox baseball can be enjoyed by the people of Pawtucket and Rhode Island for generations to come." The mayor could not avoid conjuring a baseball analogy cliché, calling the study the "next inning" of the team-city-state relationship.[185]

That hope was reinforced by the window of exclusivity the team provided to Pawtucket. The city's sole negotiating rights to consummate a stadium deal with the PawSox ran through the end of the state's legislative session the following June. The PawSox made their preferences known: the team would rather stay put…but it was making no promises.

FEASIBILITY

In late September 2016, Lucchino, Grebien, and Rhode Island Department of Administration director Michael DiBiase announced the selection of a Kansas City, Missouri architectural firm to conduct the feasibility study. The tri-party coalition selected Pendulum Studio II LLC from a list of four respondents to the RFP it published three months earlier. The study cost $105,000, a virtual bargain at $35,000 apiece.[186]

The Pendulum bid was anchored by cofounder Jonathan O'Neil Cole. His résumé included lead architect on more than twenty minor-league ballparks. Cole formerly worked for Populous Architects, PC, also of Kansas City. Populous had a long history of engagements with Lucchino. In 2004, Cole worked on the final punch list of Lucchino's San Diego Petco Field for Populous, although the two reportedly had not met then. Pendulum's proposal beat out Populous, along with Generator Studio LLC, yet another Kansas City firm, and Leshinsky Finance LLC, with offices in Boston, New York, and Providence.[187]

Lucchino was maintaining a wait-and-see posture on McCoy. He was not convinced that the stadium could be useful after the 2020 season, when the current lease ended. He claimed to be open-minded while pointing out the facility's leaky roofs and eroded kitchen pipes. McCoy needed lots of work to make it more appealing to today's fans "than it might have 75 years ago," Lucchino warned. Grebien remained optimistic for McCoy, pointing out that the parties would not have ponied up for the study without hope of finding a way to make McCoy viable. Cole stated the consultants did not have any preconceived ideas but also emphasized that baseball had changed in seventy-five years. The study would be completed before the end of January upcoming.[188]

As promised, the report—all 182 pages of it—was delivered to the stakeholders on January 26, 2017. It was thorough, detailed, scientific, artistic, and objective. Nevertheless, the preface foreshadowed the conclusion. "From the very early history of baseball through the mid-1990s," the lead paragraph states, "the concept of 'a day at the ballpark' has drastically changed." Somewhere along the way, the focus had shifted from what was happening on the field "to the entertainment that occurs during and in-between innings throughout the ballpark." A demand had evolved for "enhanced amenities that maximize the game-day experience for ballpark patrons."[189]

All hope must have vanished from McCoy supporters as they read on, "Unfortunately, most ballparks that were constructed prior to the mid-1990s

The PawSox held an annual event each winter that allowed fans and the media to interact with players. In 2017, the open house was called "A Touch of Spring" and featured former Pawtucket Red Sox star Dennis "Oil Can" Boyd. *Photo by Ernest A. Brown, from the* Pawtucket Times.

exhibit symptoms of aging in the form of limited infrastructure, structural deterioration, and outdated equipment." This was particularly true of "food service and premium amenities that present significant challenges" for tenant/operators "to maintain competitiveness in the entertainment marketplace."[190]

The gestalt of minor-league baseball in the new millennium dramatically altered the ballparks in which it was played. No longer did fans attend games for the enjoyment of the sport. Apparently, they were also there to be fed and entertained. Baseball was competing with all sorts of distractions, many of which were now a simple reach into the pocket and a few clicks away. It was going to be a heavy lift for McCoy to be transformed from your grandfather's baseball park into a modern entertainment complex.

The next chapter, "What We Love About McCoy Stadium," softened the blow. McCoy Stadium was nostalgic. According to the authors, baseball evokes the "emotional muscle memory"—that feeling fans get every time they pass through the gates—the recollection of good times. It is "why baseball purists are so passionate about preserving the look and feel of the old time ballpark. It's there to remind us of the good times we had with our fathers and our grandfathers just two generations back." McCoy Stadium, the consultants observed, does just that for most fans.[191]

The Pendulum authors waxed poetic. The history of the franchise was embossed along the ramp towers to the grandstands and corridors to the premium suites. The paintings recall the team's great players and special moments. McCoy Stadium was a place to see standout ballplayers from local communities play professionally. Like Providence College star and nearby Framingham, Massachusetts native Lou Merloni. Or like Seekonk High School standout Ken Ryan, who played four years for the PawSox in the town where he was born. McCoy was a throwback to a simpler era when spending time with family and "dreaming about what we can all strive to become if we just work hard at it" were esteemed virtues. But despite these emotions, the study team needed to make sure that the stakeholders "were not throwing good money after bad" to cure the stadium's deficiencies.[192]

The final report was divided into two major sections. Part 1 presented a "physical analysis of existing conditions through the eyes of Architectural and Engineering professionals with a proven track record in the sports facility design industry." It contained subsections on site conditions, structural systems and mechanical/electrical/plumbing/technology and concluded with an architectural assessment.[193]

The final pages of Section 1 summarized key findings. McCoy was steadily deteriorating due to a number of contributing factors. First among these was persistent water infiltration in major building systems. This was causing the stadium "to age much faster than what is typically deemed acceptable." Also, the ballpark was renovated in 1999, and some of the new additions appeared to be moving at different rates. The reasons for this shifting included poor soil conditions and deterioration below the footings caused by water infiltration. Finally, McCoy was plagued with major malfunctions resulting in operational inefficiencies caused by high humidity and moisture, lack of cohesive and modern building system controls, and the overall age of equipment. All those years above Hammond's Pond had taken a toll.[194]

The Pendulum Team believed that the life of McCoy could be extended for another twenty years by curing current deficiencies. The work would

The feasibility consultants acknowledged that McCoy Stadium was a throwback to a simpler era when hard work and spending time with family were esteemed values. *Courtesy of the Pawtucket Red Sox.*

cost $35.6 million. However, despite its historic charm, McCoy Stadium was "performing well behind competitive markets as it relates to the fan experience and revenue generation potential." This would jeopardize "the long-term feasibility of retaining an affiliated brand such as the PawSox in the City of Pawtucket." Based on this, the Pendulum Team found it "very difficult to make a convincing argument that the venue will continue to be competitive with comparable venues." It was also evident that McCoy's location was out of sync with the city's long-term strategy. Pawtucket's future development was going to be centered along the waterfront and downtown. McCoy Stadium was on the outskirts of the planned action and unlikely to serve as a catalyst for such development.[195]

Part 2 examined two more options: 1) renovating the existing McCoy Stadium into a state-of-the-art facility or 2) tearing down the existing structure and building a new facility on the excavated site. The authors began by analyzing five Triple-A ballparks: Victory Field in Indianapolis, Indiana; Coca Cola Park in Lehigh Valley, Pennsylvania; Huntington Park in Columbus, Ohio; Southwest University Park in El Paso, Texas; and BB&T Ballpark in Charlotte, North Carolina. The Pendulum Team also provided a brief mention of Louisville Slugger Field in Louisville,

Kentucky. Each ballpark's profile highlighted basic statistics and features, such as when they were opened, their seating capacities, their location in each city, how they contribute or benefit from their milieu, and what they cost to build in 2017 dollars. The authors also highlighted special features of each ballpark. If any new stadium in Pawtucket was to be successful in attracting and entertaining modern-day minor-league patrons, it must contain a combination of as many of these components as possible.[196]

The renovated McCoy Stadium called for structural improvements necessary to extend the life of the ballpark, along with a "building program to address pedestrian flow while dedicating appropriate spaces to service, hospitality, and storage." The renovation would relocate player clubhouses and batting tunnels. A premium club lounge with bar service would be added behind home plate at field level. The architects proposed bringing the first and third base seats closer to the field, thereby improving intimacy while reducing foul territory.[197]

The Pendulum Team's proposal also called for reclaiming three towers as symbolic entries. In left field, suites would be turned into rentable "party suites," and the mechanical pads in the corner would become a picnic deck. The designers recommended relocating the team administration, ticketing, and souvenir store to the right field main entrance. To improve traffic flow from the north, the renovations would add group areas at field level past the outfield fence, and an enclosed hospitality area would replace the tent in right field. A public park would be added along the right field line. New beer gardens would grace the concourse levels in left and right fields. The architects recommended expanding the press box and building twelve skyboxes adjacent to the press area. They also proposed demolishing the football field and track beyond right field to gain three hundred parking spaces.[198]

Renovating McCoy Stadium carried a price tag of $68.1 million. The benefits were impressive: preserving McCoy's historic charm, accommodating year-round events in new enclosed areas, increasing revenue potential for the tenant, improving the playing field, reducing game delays/cancelations related to improved drainage, accommodating other sports, expanding parking, growing naming rights, enhancing curb appeal, increasing intimacy of fan seating closer to the action, boosting energy within the stadium, elevating attendance, and completing construction within one or two off-seasons.[199]

Despite these advantages, a number of negatives outweighed the benefits: damage to McCoy Stadium might be much more extensive than anticipated; deficiencies may persist if they are not resolved permanently; the renovated ballpark would not be in the riverfront or downtown districts, which are the city's areas of future focus; a lack of visibility from Interstate 95; the distance from the new commuter rail station would require public transportation and visual links to McCoy; the McCoy "Stadium District" would need additional infrastructure; the renovation option did not cure McCoy's less-than-ideal field orientation; the surrounding residential neighborhoods presented significant redevelopment challenges; and the cost to repair, preserve, and enhance McCoy was close to that of building a new ballpark. In the end, Pendulum recommended exploring additional options that might "increase the potential to capitalize on opportunities for enhanced economic development."[200]

The opportunity the architects were thinking about was demolishing McCoy and building a new stadium in its place. This would allow correcting the ballpark's alignment. The architectural design team proposed running the third base line parallel with Division Street, which they believed provided opportunities to "strengthen a new Division Street corridor," something they declared "essential for creating a connection or link to the redevelopment focal point downtown." Home plate would be where the current left field foul pole sits. The new playing field would rotate ninety degrees from McCoy's existing orientation. A new entrance and primary façade would also run along Division Street, welcoming visitors from, and inviting development of, the north side of the stadium through "incredible curb appeal."[201]

The proposed replacement for McCoy would have all the features that ballpark advocates deem essential in state-of-the-art facilities. There would be new player clubhouses and batting tunnels, an open 360-degree ADA-accessible concourse, and an abundance of bars and sponsored destination areas. The architects designed a "Green Monster" scoreboard with seating in right field, not in left field like Fenway Park's famous feature. There would be views of and vistas into the new McCoy from the outfield. The plan would encourage future development of condos, office, retail, and parking decks. The proposed ballpark would incorporate banquet/club space overlooking the field from behind home plate, field-level premium seating and party decks, a Kids Fun Zone behind the "batter's eye," and, of course, grass berm seating.[202]

The price tag for the new stadium was pegged at $78.4 million. The difference between renovating McCoy and building a new stadium in its place was only $10.3 million. For that, the state, city, and team would have a spanking-new ballpark suitable for one of the prestigious teams in the entire minor-league system. It would last well beyond twenty years. However, tearing down McCoy Stadium would upset many Rhode Islanders, no doubt. The place had become a favorite of people throughout the state and region. Unfortunately, the new stadium would not remedy a number of McCoy's shortcomings—like its location not being part of the city's future development plans, the stadium being invisible from the highway and difficult to reach, or the housing stock issue (more than half of the houses in the McCoy Stadium area were rentals). The architects believed that success required more owner-occupied and mixed-use units.[203]

The Pendulum Group delivered what the team, state, and city asked. It examined three potential options and presented the pros and cons of each. For $35.6 million, the tri-parties could opt to make the necessary improvements to McCoy that might lengthen its life another twenty years. For $68.1 million, the stakeholders would receive a fully renovated McCoy Stadium, but spending that much money would not generate the full panoply of anticipated returns. Or, for $78.4 million, they could demolish the existing stadium and replace it with a modern facility. Of the three, the consultants favored the latter. Yet despite the fan-friendly new-age ballpark to host Triple-A baseball games and the additional economic prospects from the reorientation, the architects remained concerned that site limitations would hinder private investment and development.[204]

The company that performed the economic benefit analyses for the Pendulum Team, Brailsford & Dunlavey, believed there was scant opportunity "for ancillary economic development activity on the current site." The option would "likely generate minimal return on the public investment," the architects wrote, "other than the jobs and taxes generated by the construction and a modest level of increased recurring benefits generated by enhanced team operations."[205]

In the end, the real issue with spending any money on McCoy was the ballpark's location. It was not where the city wanted to grow, which was along the waterfront and downtown. Without that connection to Pawtucket's future, the city would be unable to maximize the potential community development aspect that planners ascribed to urban ballparks. On the other hand, if a catalyst like a Triple-A ballpark could be incorporated into the targeted riverfront or downtown geographies, it would accelerate desired development. The McCoy location would always be on its own peninsula, surrounded on two sides by firmly entrenched residential communities and a declining industrial area to its north.[206]

Pawtucket 20/20

The release of the Pendulum report signaled the end of the line for McCoy Stadium, even though the tri-party stakeholders said they needed time to digest the study. Seeing the glass as half-full, Grebien extracted value from the report. The study provided an "overall understanding of what the true needs are," he said. To Grebien, the study helped the city "build a very strong partnership with the PawSox." After the rocky start with the new owners, the mayor claimed, Pawtucket had "been able to build a value with them, they understand all the exciting things that are happening." Governor Raimondo spun the study as "the next step in the process of determining the best path forward for McCoy Stadium and the PawSox." She reiterated her oft-repeated preference that the team stay in Rhode Island, particularly Pawtucket. The PawSox were mum on the report, saying only that they would be examining it together with their partners, the State of Rhode Island, and the City of Pawtucket.[207]

Even before the study was released, though, Grebien began signaling that McCoy's goose might be cooked. In the middle of January 2017, Grebien was busy scouting alternative sites in Pawtucket for a new ballpark. Three options emerged. The most prominent was the underused Apex site on Main Street. The second was a tract of land on the Seekonk River near Taft Street. The third was at Morley Field on the city's west side near the Moshassuk River and the Providence line. Grebien honed in on the Apex property, calling it "a great location." Because Apex was so close to downtown, the mayor viewed it as a "very, very instrumental piece in the big puzzle," a catalyst to help boost the prospects of the reemerging center city. As winter turned to spring, the three parties that commissioned the McCoy study appeared to be pivoting away from the historic ballpark.[208]

By April, Pawtucket's leadership was riding a wave of optimism. There was growing consensus that the city was moving in the right direction. Grebien seized the moment to summon business leaders, public officials, residents, and investors to Slater Mill, where he introduced a collaborative forum dubbed "Pawtucket's 20/20 Downtown Development Vision." The director of the Pawtucket Foundation, Jan Brodie, cohosted the gathering. Interestingly, Brodie was the executive director of the I-195 Redevelopment District when the team tried to build a new ballpark there just two years earlier. Pawtucket was on the verge of a renaissance. It was at the "tipping point," Brodie said. Grebien predicted the "stars were aligning" for Pawtucket, and he wanted the city's business leaders to seize the moment.[209]

Grebien and Pawtucket Foundation director Jan Brodie kick off Pawtucket 20/20, a program to foster collaboration among the city's various economic development initiatives. *Photo by Erica Moser, from the* Pawtucket Times.

The day's event was to serve as a "pep rally for the city," Brodie said, and to connect the people working on the various projects that were spurring the evolution. That was the city's motto—"Join the Evolution." The major projects included the Pawtucket–Central Falls Commuter Rail Station, the Isle Brewers Guild, the Sandra Feinstein–Gamm Theatre, the Blackstone River Bikeway, the Blackstone Valley National Historical Park, Slater Mill itself, and, of course, the prospects of a new ballpark for the PawSox.[210]

Lucchino was among the speakers that day. He was reportedly the only one to receive a round of applause. That came when he declared, "Our very strong preference is to stay home. The PawSox belong in Pawtucket." The tone was set. Lucchino said the PawSox wanted to be part of Pawtucket's 20/20 plan. The team and a new ballpark would also be a beneficiary of the revitalization. General Manager Dan Rea found the forum "very inspiring," saying, "There's a lot of positive momentum going on in the city and it's exciting to hear that vision." The city leaders knew that growth and redevelopment were important to the PawSox. Private and public collaboration were no doubt important to the team. Later that day, the

Apex Companies, a Pawtucket institution since the 1930s, applauded the mayor's initiative. It also acknowledged having ongoing conversations with the PawSox about land for a new ballpark near downtown. The company looked forward to continuing those conversations.[211]

As April drew to a close, the PawSox surfaced the idea of a public park inside a ballpark located at the Apex site. The park would be open all year for people to use for exercise, like walking or jogging inside the stadium along the warning track. Once again, Rea confirmed that the team and Apex were in communication but remained mute on any details. The team followed that proposal with the results of an economic impact study it had co-commissioned with the city. Brailsford & Dunlavey was asked to assess the potential contribution of a stadium built on the Apex property compared to one at the Tidewater site. The consultants concluded that because the locations were so close to each other, they would provide similar "economic and fiscal" benefits to state. The Apex location would generate $129.8 million over thirty years compared to the Tidewater alternative of $95.8 million, a little more than $1 million per year. Nevertheless, the Apex property was continually gaining momentum as the favored site for a new Triple-A baseball stadium, which would soon culminate with a not-so-unexpected announcement.[212]

CHAPTER 5

The Ballpark at Slater Mill

A Good Deal

Drivers slow to a crawl when crossing into Pawtucket on I-95. If they don't, they find themselves in trouble as they attempt to navigate the city's notorious "S Curves." Legend has it that when I-95 was built through Rhode Island in the 1960s, the curves were designed to save a few of Pawtucket's historic buildings, particularly the once-exclusive To Kalon Club (TK Club) and Le Foyer, a French social club. Sitting on a one-acre parcel atop a rise that overlooks the winding thruway, the magnificent three-story Georgian brick TK Club was the meeting place for the city's movers and shakers. They gathered at the TK to dine, socialize, conduct business, play cards, and bowl in luxurious privacy. Le Foyer was a popular institution in a city where French was spoken on the streets and a Roman Catholic church celebrated masses in French. Roadbuilders had the good sense to let the structures be.

Not far away sits another notable edifice. At first glance, the building resembles a pyramid. Closer inspection reveals it to be a ziggurat—six rectangular white blocks stacked one on top of the other, each smaller than the one it sits on, stepping up to a peak. An upright trapezoid crowns the structure. Four bright-red letters proclaim this to be the Apex building, headquarters to the department store of the same name. An expansive asphalt parking lot surrounds the structure. The Blackstone River runs between the building and downtown.

The Apex building was built in 1969, the same year the state completed its most prominent structure, the iconic Newport Bridge. The building was conceived by noted architect, artist, and designer Andrew Geller while in the employ of Raymond Loewy, the father of American industrial design. Like most modernist structures, the building stokes advocates and detractors. Some want to bulldoze it as an eyesore. Others want to preserve is as a historic landmark. By 2017, city leaders were hoping the underused site might play a pivotal role in the city's happening renaissance, eager for it to become ground zero in the quest to keep the PawSox in Pawtucket.[213]

Grebien seemed pleased with Brailsford & Dunlavey's May 2017 conclusion that the Apex location outweighed the Tidewater option. "The numbers pretty starkly point to the Apex site being superior to Tidewater," Grebien said. "A ballpark at Slater Mill would be an impressive gateway into Rhode Island on 95 South, and would complement the new Blackstone River Valley National Historical Park," the mayor added. The Apex site offered a win-win opportunity. "We can preserve and enhance the affordable, family-friendly entertainment asset that is the Pawtucket Red Sox, while also driving economic revitalization and investment in our downtown." The PawSox were equally supportive of the economic consulting firm's findings. The team released a statement praising "the site as an extremely strong opportunity for real economic development for the City of Pawtucket."[214]

Following a weekend of cloudy and rainy mid-spring weather, with temperatures barely reaching a high of sixty degrees in Providence, Tuesday morning, May 16, 2017, broke sunny, jumping to eighty-one degrees by noon. It was a harbinger of warmer temperatures for the remainder of the week and foreshadowed the lazy days just a few months away. It was also a red-letter day for the PawSox, the City of Pawtucket, and the State of Rhode Island. The team enthusiastically announced that the three entities had agreed to build a new $83 million ballpark on the Apex property. The plan called for the PawSox to pony up $45 million. The State of Rhode Island would chip in $23 million, which would be derived from revenue generated by the ballpark. Pawtucket's share came to $15 million, two-thirds of which would pay for the Apex lot and the remaining one-third to improve surrounding infrastructure. The city was on the cusp of owning a modern stadium, and as a reward, the PawSox would agree to stay in Pawtucket for an additional thirty years, through 2050.[215]

A skeletal outline of the conceptual Ballpark at Slater Mill accompanied the announcement. The PawSox and city wanted the public to know what

The Apex building, targeted as the site for the Ballpark at Slater Mill. *Photo by James Ricci.*

they had cooked up. The team's new home would be located next to "historic Slater Mill." The nine-thousand-to-ten-thousand-capacity ballpark was intended to have "the same field playing dimensions as iconic Fenway Park." The new stadium would embrace the "Park in a Park" concept advocated by proponents just a few days earlier. It would be accessible to the public year-round and serve as an outdoor convention center hosting "a range of community events such as ice skating, college football, farmers' markets, and concerts." The team's $45 million "contribution" would become the "largest private investment in Pawtucket's history."[216]

Continuing its legacy of offering affordable family-friendly entertainment, the PawSox promised to freeze general admission ticket prices for children and senior citizens "for at least the first 5 years." More importantly, the team committed to pay for any stadium construction overruns, further protecting taxpayers from unexpected expenditures. And "like other minor league ballparks across the country," this one was going to "jump-start new economic initiatives and investments in the immediate downtown area," replete with "more jobs for Rhode Islanders."[217]

The announcement was well received by state leaders. Raimondo praised elements of the scheme by contrasting them with the doomed Providence

Larry Lucchino, Mike Tamburro, and Don Grebien were enthusiastic about the Ballpark at Slater Mill as a new home for the PawSox and a catalyst for economic development in the city. *Photo by Ernest A. Brown, from the* Pawtucket Times.

ballpark. She liked that the team and the city planned on paying most of the bill, rather than the state. The governor was satisfied with the team protecting taxpayers from escalating construction costs and ongoing maintenance expenses. Also, the new ballpark fit in with Pawtucket's economic and investment plans. Raimondo called it "radically much, much better," and she hoped that people would give the new ballpark a chance. Of course, she noted, legislation needed to be submitted to and considered by the state's General Assembly.[218]

One week following the announcement, state General Assembly leaders reined in the possibility of considering a stadium bill before the end of the current legislative session, which was scheduled to wrap up on June 30. Senate President Dominick Ruggerio said that he had not received any legislation from Governor Raimondo or Mayor Grebien. Without a bill to consider and only forty days left in the session, Ruggerio left no hope of expediting legislation through the Senate. "At this point," he clarified, "it is too late in the session for a thorough, public review of a proposal of this magnitude." If legislation were submitted, he said he "was not opposed to reconvening in the fall to consider it in a deliberative and public manner."[219]

House Speaker Nicholas Mattiello was less collegial. Earlier in the day, Mattiello's communication director, Larry Berman, said that bills needed to be submitted within the first forty days of the legislative session. That deadline passed twelve days earlier. In addition, Berman explained, all bills must receive permission from Speaker Mattiello, which was not going to happen unless Governor Raimondo backed the legislation. Berman said Mattiello was "not putting a deal before the House Finance Committee that was negotiated by the Governor…without her endorsement and her stamp of approval." Berman's remarks seemed odd given that Raimondo had already publicly backed the deal and that her Commerce Corporation played a major role in orchestrating the Ballpark at Slater Mill proposition.[220]

Later in the day, Mattiello stated bluntly that the Rhode Island House of Representatives was not going to consider a stadium financing bill. "It's not the appropriate time to even consider it," he said. Reemphasizing Ruggerio's point that nothing had been presented, Mattiello stated, "So we're not doing anything in the House." Adding to the confusion, Mattiello planted the idea that Raimondo was having second thoughts. "If the persons who have done all the work on it are equivocating," he declared, "it is absolutely the right thing" not to move forward. Mattiello hinted something might be "going on" in the governor's office, but he had "not been a part of that." In the Machiavellian mores of Rhode Island politics, excluding the Speaker of the House from backroom machinations was not the best way to expedite a piece of legislation, especially one with a short lead time.[221]

House Minority Leader Patricia Morgan opposed the stadium deal from the get-go. She objected to even considering legislation. "It's the people of this state who have put the brakes on this," Morgan said. She left no doubt how she viewed the proposal. The owners were millionaires. "They bought it to make money," the Republican leader pointed out. "Let them go pay for their own stadium."[222]

The governor, however, pinned the lack of legislation on Grebien. After crediting the mayor for "so passionately advocating for Pawtucket" and praising her own staff for guiding the team and the city "toward the framework for a deal that would protect Rhode Island's taxpayers," Raimondo said that final legislation from the city had yet to reach her desk. She agreed with Ruggerio that "consideration of a new ballpark" was "too important to rush [through] this legislative session." Mayor Grebien reserved comment while the bombshells dropped, keeping his powder dry for the following day.[223]

The next morning, Grebien appeared at the State House with copies of a bill he hoped would receive immediate attention. In actuality, he was taken aback by Ruggerio's announcement that the Rhode Island Senate would not consider ballpark legislation during the current session. The mayor had been working closely with Raimondo's Commerce wing and was under the assumption that the state agency was keeping the governor and legislators up to date. "We were finalizing all of this, so I don't know what happened yesterday," Grebien said. The bill could have been ready a month earlier but was delayed by the governor's request for the city to work with the Commerce Corporation to fine-tune the proposal. Grebien and Raimondo had met just days before Ruggerio's pronouncement, and the mayor believed everyone was on the same page.[224]

Grebien was troubled. One consequence of the delay was the upcoming expiration of the PawSox's promise to remain monogamous to Pawtucket. That agreement ended on July 1, 2017. The opportunity to deal with the team exclusively was slipping away. And this was a good deal, the mayor said. "The numbers in this agreement speak for themselves," Grebien harkened, "and are too good for Rhode Islanders and the City of Pawtucket to pass up." He pleaded that if "we can't put our political concerns aside; we risk losing the team and the nearly $2 million a year in existing state revenues they currently generate. That's $60 million of lost revenue over the next 30 years if the team leaves Rhode Island." "We have a choice," the mayor added. "Are we willing to invest $42 million—and that is with interest included—over the next 30 years to get $220 million aggregate state revenues? I think it's worth that investment."[225]

Grebien cautioned against letting the stigma of 38 Studios kill the ballpark deal. This opportunity had little in common with Schilling's gaming studio, the mayor said, enumerating the major differences. The ballpark proposal was publicly studied and vetted. The city and state were protected from cost overruns. The PawSox have been a successful business model with forty years of experience. "We cannot afford to be afraid of the politics of 38 Studios and let this great initiative pass us by," Grebien continued. "We can keep putting our heads in the sand and saying no or we can finally show true leadership and move our state and the city of Pawtucket forward."[226]

On the State House steps that morning, members of the Rhode Island Building Trades backed Grebien. Michael Sabitoni, the president of the organization, spoke in favor of the proposal. Besides the obvious benefit of the project bringing jobs to his constituency, Sabitoni pointed out that there were no other plans for the Apex parcel. The tradesman believed

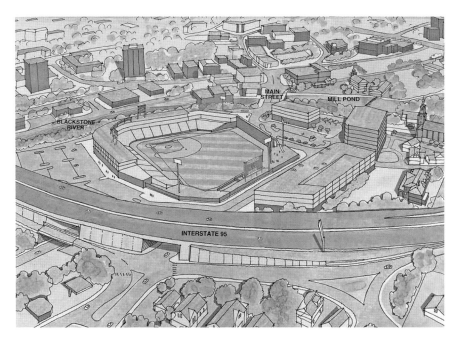

Schematic of the proposed Ballpark at Slater Mill, touted by proponents as a "gateway to Rhode Island." *Courtesy of the City of Pawtucket.*

that "if we don't do it in Pawtucket and on that site…nothing," adding the "Apex site may sit there for another couple decades." Sabitoni also noted the positive impact the stadium would have on Pawtucket, Central Falls, and the surrounding area. If this were popular owner Ben Mondor asking for money to renovate McCoy Stadium and keep the PawSox in Pawtucket, he would "already have the money," Sabitoni claimed. Recent proposals were complicated because the new PawSox owners were millionaires. But as the trade group head observed, incentives attract businesses.[227]

Raimondo continued to support Ruggerio's decision. The governor's press secretary released a statement reiterating her earlier buck-passing that Pawtucket was to blame. The governor's office claimed the city had "expressed concerns about its ability to make such a large financial commitment." Grebien and Lucchino were together the evening of Ruggerio's decree. Lucchino's disappointment was palpable in demeanor and conversation. The team was only committed to staying in Pawtucket through the 2020 season. Only six weeks remained on the city's exclusivity to reach a deal with the PawSox. Grebien did not want to lose them.[228]

S-0989

Finally, on June 26, just four days before the June 30 end of the regular legislative session, Senate Finance Chairman William J. Conley Jr. presented the ballpark bill. Upon passage, Rhode Island Senate Bill S-0989 would authorize the state to finance the construction of a new ballpark in Pawtucket and enter into lease arrangements with the Pawtucket Red Sox. The lease structure would be similar to the one in effect for McCoy Stadium, except that the city would be replaced by the Pawtucket Redevelopment Agency (PRA). The PRA would own the stadium and lease it to the state. The state, in turn, would sublease the ballpark to the PawSox.[229]

The bonds to pay for the new ballpark would be divided into three tranches: the team would be responsible for $33 million of Series A bonds, the state would be responsible for $23 million of Series B bonds, and the city would be responsible for $15 million of Series C bonds. Interest rates on tax-exempt bonds would be capped at 4 percent, with taxable bonds topped at 5 percent. The bonds were to be repaid within thirty years. A second bill, S-0990, would enable statewide redevelopment agencies to take properties by eminent domain even if they did not meet the definition of distressed or substandard. The sponsors of the bill did not believe that the targeted property qualified under existing law. Conley promised "vigorous public hearings" by his finance committee.[230]

Before Conley could schedule those hearings, other events swirled like cyclones around the state. The Rhode Island General Assembly failed to pass the state's fiscal budget before the June 30 conclusion of its regular session. Governor Raimondo finally signed the $9.2 billion budget on August 1, 2017. Pawtucket's Memorial Hospital, within a stone's throw of McCoy Stadium, was struggling to attract patients when its parent organization changed ambulatory policies and closed its maternity ward. Meanwhile, the PawSox's year of exclusivity with Pawtucket expired. Since then, the team had received inquiries from a number of Massachusetts cities, including Worcester, Springfield, Fall River, New Bedford, and Chicopee. The PawSox leadership confirmed that they had visited with Worcester officials and toured that city's up-and-coming Canal District.[231]

Toward the end of July, the PawSox also announced the hiring of Janet Marie Smith. She had been a valuable resource to Lucchino on ballparks and redevelopment in Baltimore and Boston. Since 2012, Smith had been vice-president of planning and development for the Los Angeles Dodgers. She had recently accepted a position at Yale University as the Edward

In the fall of 2017, Rhode Island state senator and Senate Finance Chairman William J. Conley Jr. spearheaded statewide public hearings on the proposed legislation for the Ballpark at Slater Mill. *Courtesy of the Rhode Island State Archives.*

P. Bass Distinguished Visiting Architecture Fellow for the fall semester. Consequently, Smith would be in the New England area and was ready and willing to help her former boss with another ballpark project.[232]

In August, Conley announced a schedule for the ballpark hearings. The sessions would stretch from mid-September through late October 2017. The opening and concluding hearings would take place at the State House, with five others sprinkled around the state. The committee comprised Senators Conley, Louis P. DiPalma, Walter S. Felag Jr., Ryan W. Pearson, Frank A. Ciccone III, Daniel Da Ponte, James E. Doyle II, Nicholas D. Kettle, James A. Seveney, and V. Susan Sosnowski. The Ballpark at Slater Mill and its associated legislation would be fully vetted.

24 POINTS

On September 13, 2017, the day before the first hearings, ballpark opponent Steven Frias published two dozen reasons to reject the ballpark deal. A Republican National committeeman, Frias had challenged and nearly defeated Mattiello for the Speaker's House seat in the 2016 election. He articulated his position in a detailed thirteen-page essay posted on the Republican Party of Rhode Island's website. While Frias may not have represented all of the various factions opposing the stadium, his twenty-four points undoubtedly covered most concerns. His analysis attempted to refute a number of claims presented by proponents as reasons to build the ballpark. He bolstered his case with 107 footnoted citations.[233]

First, Frias argued, a number of economists "have shown that public subsidies for new stadiums" do not make financial sense. After examining a number of subject matter experts—including economists Dennis Coates and Brad

Humphreys, who reviewed forty academic studies about public subsidies for professional sports teams—Frias questioned whether the financial benefits touted by proponents would come to fruition. "Proponents of a new PawSox stadium have never been able to refute these conclusions by economists or explain why a new PawSox stadium would be different," Frias wrote.[234]

Next, Frias declared, analyses produced by consultants like Brailsford & Dunlavey were unreliable. Some experts, Frias reported, proclaim that studies associated with stadium-building are no more than "bogus economic impact studies" produced to support claims by cities "that stadiums are good investments." Frias included the suggestion from one economist that these reports were not published in reputable journals because the authors manipulate them to say whatever the client desires. Frias relayed that other economists characterized the studies as "promotional literature" that suffer from "a long list" of problems. Frias warned the Brailsford & Dunlavey study on the Ballpark at Slater Mill was "comparable to the flawed economic impact studies typically used by promotors for tax subsidies of new stadiums."[235]

Frias also noted that Brailsford & Dunlavey used unrealistic tax revenue and attendance projections in its analysis. He highlighted discrepancies between Brailsford & Dunlavey's projections for the Providence plan and the Pawtucket plan. The consultants estimated the Providence proposal would generate between $2.1 million and $2.3 million, while the Pawtucket proposal would bring in between $3.2 million and $3.4 million. It did not make sense for the Pawtucket stadium to generate $1.1 million more than the Providence ballpark, Frias said. He deduced that the Brailsford & Dunlavey projections were not realistic; therefore, "the claim that a new stadium in Pawtucket will generate enough tax revenues to pay for itself was also not credible." Frias raised concerns about Brailsford & Dunlavey's attendance projections. He reported that comparisons with the Columbus, Ohio minor-league team were inconsistent. If its attendance projections were unreliable, he argued, it was reasonable to doubt the consultant's other forecasts.[236]

Frias then questioned revenue forecasts. He claimed the PawSox would not guarantee tax revenue projections because they knew the risks were material. If the PawSox were confident in the projections, he observed, they shouldn't have any issue guaranteeing the tax revenues. The team wanted a public subsidy "because they know stadiums are seldom financially attractive as private investments." He claimed the amount of tax revenues generated at McCoy had never been disclosed, presenting as evidence a comment made in 2015 by Antonio Pires, City of Pawtucket director of administration, that the city "was receiving no tax revenue from the team."[237]

Frias reasoned that general state tax revenues would be used to pay the bonds, not just taxes from the stadium. The proposed legislation did not prohibit the use of other taxes beyond those generated by the stadium to pay off the bonds. While some taxes are easy to associate with the stadium, others would not be so clear-cut. Frias also said the proposed legislation was ambiguous as to how the $33 million in bonds floated on the team's behalf would be covered. The bill called for the team to lease the stadium for $1 million for the first year, which escalated 2 percent each year, plus naming rights fees. That would not be enough to cover the debt repayment, which Frias calculated would reach $63.7 million over thirty years. "Although the PawSox have indicated they will pay the costs associated with this $33 million bond," Frias conceded, "the legislation is unclear about the responsibility of the PawSox to pay for these bonds."[238]

Frias also invoked 38 Studios and called for a statewide referendum on the PawSox stadium bonds. Because they would be moral obligation bonds, he wrote, the state would be in a similar position as it found itself following the failure of Schilling's computer venture. "Taking on public debt without voter approval for the benefit of a private company in the hopes of spurring economic development is quite comparable to 38 Studios," Frias warned. In addition, he stressed, moral obligation bonds are more expensive than bonds approved by a statewide referendum. Because the issue needed to be resolved quickly, Frias wanted the state to conduct a special election. It had done so many times. The cost, he proffered, would be less "than the difference in interest costs for a general obligation bond compared to a moral obligation bond."[239]

Furthermore, Rhode Islanders should have their say on the proposed legislation, Frias argued. The state constitution generally required such consideration prior to incurring public debt. Moral obligation bonds, he explained, started being used in Rhode Island as a way of getting around the requirement in the wake of voters rejecting bonds to fund low-income housing and economic development between 1969 and 1972. "Although the General Assembly legally can, it should not incur more debt to build a new PawSox stadium for which the taxpayers are responsible, without voter approval," Frias wrote. He said that proponents did not want a statewide referendum because they were afraid the proposition would be rejected. Frias also determined the legislation needed to pass both houses of the General Assembly by two-thirds plurality because the proposal fit a constitutional requirement when appropriating public funds for "local" or "private purpose."[240]

Frias observed it was "unclear how much it will cost taxpayers to acquire the land for the new stadium." Proponents estimated the Apex site would be in the $10 million range; however, its owners were supposedly asking twice as much. In addition, Frias said, there was a pending lawsuit concerning "environmental cleanup of the site," which, he pointed out, could result in the cost of the land to jump. And "because the Apex property had been contaminated by hazardous materials," both current and prior owners would be responsible for remediating the problem, raising the cost to Pawtucket taxpayers if the city acquired the land for the stadium.[241]

Eminent domain was problematic, Frias noted. First, the "proposed legislation significantly" expanded "the ability to use eminent domain" beyond property declared "blighted and substandard." And second, the use of "eminent domain in these circumstances could be unconstitutional." This included both the U.S. Constitution and the Rhode Island Constitution. After presenting precedents from both courts to bolster his point, Frias concluded there were major issues associated with taking land for private development.[242]

Frias proposed there were "better uses of taxpayer money than building a new PawSox Stadium." He explored the opportunity cost of taxes and agreed with economists who encouraged policymakers to "evaluate the best use of resources" by considering alternatives to which the money could be applied. Frias believed "the best use of taxpayer money is to allow taxpayers to keep their money so they can invest it or spend it as they best see fit." If, however, "policymakers decide that they know better than the taxpayers how to invest and spend their money, then there are other ways the government could spend $73.4 million over 30 years." For example, many of the state's schools needed attention. Frias cited one report that emphasized that "cities and towns need to spend about $1.7 billion to fully repair every school in the state." Fixing the schools, he proposed, would provide "temporary construction jobs" and "improve the learning environment" for the state's public school children. It would also be a "better use of taxpayer money."[243]

Frias also claimed the "new PawSox stadium is not necessary to assist the construction industry." He presented a conclusion from ballpark economists that declared construction unions are "a reason why new stadiums are built." But the state was already in a building boom, experiencing a 13.4 percent increase in construction jobs over the previous year. Frias claimed the increase was "driven by millions in taxpayer money being spent to repair roads and bridges and the millions in taxpayer subsidies for real estate development." He concluded, "Spending millions on a new PawSox stadium is unjustified because millions have been, and will be spent to benefit the construction industry."[244]

Frias suggested the new owners needed "a new stadium to increase the value of their investment." He said the "age of McCoy Stadium was not the primary reason" the PawSox wanted a new stadium. Because minor-league teams are not necessarily profitable, some new owners demand a new ballpark "to recoup and increase their investment." Because of this, new ballparks needed to produce much more revenue than their predecessors. Some economists, Frias declared, estimated that a new stadium could "double the value of a franchise." Taxpayers, Frias believed, "should not be required to subsidize the effort by PawSox owners to get a return on their costly investment."[245]

Frias was concerned that there was "no guarantee that PawSox tickets will remain affordable in the long-term." While the team repeatedly pledged that general admission ticket prices would remain the same for children and seniors for five years, nothing precluded the PawSox from raising those prices or reducing the number of favorably priced tickets over the remaining twenty-five years of the lease. The new breed of minor-league owners, Frias declared, needed to generate more revenue than in the past. The PawSox owners, he cautioned, without being legally bound, "will have the ability to increase the price of tickets or reduce the number of low-priced tickets in order to get a larger return on their multi-million-dollar investment."[246]

Frias asserted, "Massachusetts state taxpayers [would] not fund a new stadium." He based this claim on information reported in an August 13, 2017 *Worcester Telegram & Gazette* article. Massachusetts Senate Majority Leader Harriette Chandler, a Worcester Democrat, said her state's legislature had "an established precedent of not putting public money into sport stadiums." Massachusetts set the standard when it refused to finance a new stadium for the New England Patriots but rather agreed to pay for infrastructure improvements associated with the project. It was unclear, Frias stated, "why Rhode Island should not follow" the Bay State's example.

Frias also believed the PawSox were "in a weak bargaining position." In 2015, Frias said, the team "repeatedly indicated they may leave Rhode Island unless a new stadium was built in Providence." He said the PawSox were now saying the same thing about Pawtucket. Frias thought the team had "limited options," particularly with "the lease at McCoy Stadium ending after the 2020 season and the time needed for construction of a new stadium shrinking."[247]

Frias declared that the PawSox were a "poor investment even compared to other Commerce Corporation deals." Raimondo's economic development policy, with support from the General Assembly, relied on offering tax subsidies to specific businesses. The Rhode Island Commerce Corporation, Frias relayed, planned on granting $135 million in tax subsidies generating between 1,073 jobs to 2,287 jobs, as well as 2,141 temporary construction jobs. "For the PawSox deal," he reported, "state and local taxpayers" would be "spending $73.4 million…to build a new stadium" that "will directly produce only 162 permanent jobs, and 164 temporary construction jobs." In addition, Frias stated, Rhode Island would "not lose tax revenues if the PawSox leave." Rather, he said, consumers "would shift their recreation and entertainment expenditures to other recreation and entertainment venues."

Frias maintained that even if the team left Pawtucket, baseball could still be played at McCoy Stadium. He acknowledged it would not be another Triple-A team, but perhaps a Double-A, Single-A, or college team might fill the void. "McCoy Stadium may not generate enough profit for the new PawSox ownership," he reasoned, "but it may be sufficient for another team."[248]

Finally, Frias stated, a new ballpark would not be an economic catalyst for Pawtucket. He said that the city had spent millions since 1936 building and renovating McCoy "with little tangible economic benefits to show for it." Frias cited Pires's 2015 admission that "Pawtucket won't take a big economic development hit from the planned departure of the PawSox." He also referred to Rhode Island commerce secretary Stefan Pryor, who was the deputy mayor for economic development in Newark, New Jersey, when the Prudential Center was built in that city to house the New Jersey Devils NHL franchise and the Seton Hall University's men's basketball team. "No arena is a panacea," Pryor said.[249]

THE SENATE FINANCE COMMITTEE HEARINGS

On September 14, 2017, about a half hour before the first Ballpark at Slater Mill Senate Finance Committee hearing, trade workers jammed the State House rotunda to support the proposed legislation. Ironworkers donned orange shirts, while plumbers and pipe fitters sported yellow tops. Others wore red T-shirts with white "Pawtucket Is Home" in Red Sox MLB Tuscan font spelled across their chests. PawSox chairman Larry Lucchino and vice-chairman Mike Tamburro revved up the crowd. Tamburro led a call-and-response: "They say Rhode Island can't do great things anymore. Do you

Pawtucket mayor Don Grebien and PawSox executive Mike Tamburro lead a "Save Our Sox" rally in September 2017. *Photo by Ernest A Brown, from the* Pawtucket Times.

think that's true?" The crowd replied in unison, "No." "They say we can't build great things anymore. Is that true?" Tamburro asked. "No," the crowd responded. "Let's build the ballpark" Tamburro pleaded, "Let's do great things again." The crowd overwhelmingly agreed. The PawSox leaders headed to the hearing room serenaded by chants of "Save our Sox."[250]

Lucchino and Tamburro made it upstairs to room 313 in time for the presentations. An additional viewing room in the Senate Lounge handled the overflow crowd. The meeting started at 6:00 p.m. and ended seven hours and five minutes later. Conley kicked off the meeting by providing an overview of, and goals for, the hearings. The committee wanted to conduct a "transparent, accessible, and deliberative process." Senate Fiscal Advisor Stephen Whitney and Committee Legal Counsel Kelly McElroy outlined the two pieces of legislation, S-0989 and S-0990. This was followed by supportive testimony from a number of elected officers from around the state, mostly mayors. They represented Providence, Woonsocket, North Providence, Johnston, and Cumberland. Lieutenant Governor Daniel McKee also spoke in favor of the proposition.[251]

The following segment included presentations by the City of Pawtucket and the PawSox. Grebien and Lucchino outlined the reasons why the ballpark was a good idea. The major points were familiar. The stadium would complement and spur economic development in Pawtucket and the

Blackstone Valley. It would be self-sustaining, being paid for by tax revenue generated by the stadium. It would be a better option than renovating and preserving McCoy Stadium. The PawSox would contribute a larger share than most other Triple-A teams for their facilities. The team's contribution would be the largest amount a single private business ever invested in Pawtucket. And the proposed ballpark would not be a repeat of the failed 38 Studios deal.[252]

Grebien said it was Pawtucket's time to receive a piece of the pie. The state had invested significant sums in places like the Rhode Island Convention Center, Providence Place Mall, University of Rhode Island's Ryan Center, and Fort Adams in Newport. Once again, the mayor stressed, it "would be another crushing blow to the state of Rhode Island" if the PawSox left. Lucchino admitted that the new owners' attempt to move the team to Providence in 2015 was "a colossal mistake" and turned the public against the PawSox. Lucchino said the new proposal would not result in a "PawSox ballpark," but rather "a Pawtucket ballpark in which the PawSox [would] be a principal tenant." Rhode Island Commerce Corporation head Stefan Pryor praised the state's role in driving a hard bargain during negotiations. "Not every deal is a good deal for taxpayers," Pryor said, "but this one is."[253]

The Senate Finance Committee peppered the presenters with questions. At one point, committee member Senator Walter S. Felag Jr.—representing the East Bay towns of Warren, Bristol, and Tiverton—wanted to explore the risk to Pawtucket in relying on future real estate development to pay off the bonds. Grebien and Lucchino reaffirmed their commitment to develop the areas around the proposed stadium, although neither released details about such projects. Senator Donna M. Nesselbush, representing Pawtucket and North Providence, who co-sponsored the bill and participated in the hearings, inquired about plans for three buildings, including the TK Club and Apex Tire. Grebien confirmed that all three buildings were controlled by the same owner, who was also the proprietor of the proposed Apex site.[254]

After three hours of presentations, the citizenry finally had a chance to address the committee. More than seventy people signed up to speak. Of those, forty-eight favored the proposal, while sixteen objected. Only half of the folks who signed up got a chance to speak. Those in favor cited the economic development and job creation benefits associated with the proposal, along with other advantages of keeping the team in Rhode Island, including the charities to which the PawSox generously contributed. Opponents offered a litany of reasons why lawmakers should reject the proposal. These included giving public money to the team's wealthy owners for a profit-making business, borrowing funds that the state and city could not afford in the wake of a budget crisis, building a modern stadium in lieu of renovating McCoy, and questioning the proposed cost/benefit estimates laid out by the team and city.[255]

One opponent, Sam Bell, a leader in the Stop the Stadium Deal organization that surfaced during the 2015 Providence ballpark campaign, said his group assessed the Ballpark at Slater Mill and concluded that the team's contribution would be "negative $59 million," considering the lack of property taxes and other factors. And that was a conservative estimate. "We have analyzed this deal," Bell said, and concluded that it would be a "shockingly bad deal for Rhode Island and an especially bad deal for Pawtucket." He delivered the twelve-page report to Conley's committee. Another detractor was Frias, who submitted for consideration the previously discussed thirteen-page study detailing twenty-four reasons to reject the ballpark proposal.[256]

The opponents raised additional themes they wanted addressed. One of these concerned which party would be responsible for developing the adjacent waterfront properties. A Providence resident reiterated Frias's contention that funds would be better spent on the state's crumbling schools. One citizen feared that the ballpark could be named "something like Trump Stadium." The opponent said, "That doesn't sound very good," noting that there was nothing in the legislation that addressed such an eventuality. Apparently, she assumed that if such were offensive to her, it would be equally offensive to everyone else in the state.[257]

Conley caught flak from opponents because they did not get to speak until so late in the hearing. The chairman explained that participants who wanted to address the committee were called in the order they signed in before the meeting. Conley vowed to maintain that methodology at subsequent meetings. This led one dissatisfied opponent to respond, "So, the idea is to get here early. That's the trick. Thank you. I've got the trick." By the time Conley gaveled the meeting to a close at 1:05 a.m., the committee had much to chew on.[258]

Conley imposed tighter rules for the second hearing, which was held on September 26 at Pawtucket's Tolman High School, just a twenty-minute walk from McCoy Stadium. The chairman structured the second hearing to focus on the economic impact the stadium and ancillary development would have on Pawtucket. In an attempt to avoid another marathon meeting, Conley established it would start at 6:00 p.m. and conclude by 10:00 p.m. The stakeholders were limited to one hour, leaving three hours to hear from the public. Each speaker was limited to three minutes each. More than one hundred people signed up to talk. Of those, sixty-five favored the proposal, while twenty-five opposed. In the end, forty-eight addressed the committee.[259]

The first presenter was Pawtucket native son Attorney General Peter Kilmartin, who supported the deal. City of Pawtucket officers spoke next, led by Mayor Grebien, City Council president David Moran, Director of Administration Tony Pires, and City Commerce Director Jeanne Boyle. As with the first hearing, committee members pressed the advocates. Pawtucket director of administration Tony Pires debunked an initial parry from one senator who claimed the city was carrying a $5 million budget deficit. "That can't be further from the truth," Pires said. In 2011, when Grebien took office, the city had a $12 million deficit, a result of the Great Recession. However, that hole had since been plugged, and Pawtucket now enjoyed a $12 million surplus. "The city is on a strong financial footing," Pires declared. Felag probed deeper into the city's ability to pay its share of the costs and whether road repairs or new highway ramps would be required. Grebien said the city would not need either.[260]

Former Boston Red Sox pitcher and East Providence resident Dennis "Oil Can" Boyd, Colette Vacations CEO Dan Sullivan, and Providence Chamber of Commerce's Elizabeth Suever all spoke in favor of the ballpark legislation. They emphasized the PawSox's generous charitable contributions and the civic pride engendered by the team for the city and state. Opponents included former Pawtucket City Council president Henry Kinch Jr., who had lost the 2010 mayoral election to Grebien; Randall Rose from Operation Clean Government; and Libertarian Party chairman Pat Ford. Rose wondered if the International League would be capable of assuming the team's bond payments in the event the PawSox faltered financially. Ford pointed out two fictions being circulated concerning the proposal: that baseball teams attract additional development and that the city will lose the PawSox if the stadium is not built. Ford asserted the first was "pure fiction"; the second lacked "substantial proof."[261]

On October 3, the University Rhode Island hosted the third hearing at its main campus in Kingston. The meeting focused on questions that surfaced during previous sessions. Of particular interest was the financing plan for the new ballpark and the details of potential ancillary development from the stadium. Conley invited experts to address the issues. Brailsford & Dunlavey developed the economic analysis for the proposed Ballpark at Slater Mill in April 2017. The consulting firm discussed projected revenue streams for the state and city during ballpark construction, ongoing ballpark operations, and ancillary development. Ballpark attendance was a key variable in its assumptions.[262]

Conley invited Keenan Rice, founder and CEO of MuniCap, a municipal financial advising firm, to shed light on Tax Increment Financing (TIF), which was available for city redevelopment efforts in strategic locations. Rice informed the hearing about the ways Pawtucket could minimize its debt service during construction and initial years of operation before significant revenue could be generated.[263]

The committee also wanted to hear from minor-league baseball representatives. To that end, International League president Randy Mobley and Minor League Baseball president Scott Poley addressed the hearing. The two executives outlined the fiscal structure between the league and the teams. The committee asked the officers if the International League would assume the team's financial responsibilities if the PawSox were unable to meet its obligations. They said there are no guarantees, but a number of "safety nets" were in place to support the franchises. The executives also weighed in on the evolution of modern minor-league fans dating from when McCoy Stadium was built, buttressing the need for a new ballpark with modern amenities in a different location.[264]

Ernest Almonte, the former State of Rhode Island auditor general, supported the proposed stadium deal. He highlighted the $2 million the PawSox generated in annual taxes from McCoy Stadium. Almonte wanted to make sure that Conley's committee knew the economic impact if the team left Rhode Island and made it crystal clear to the hearing. "You're all aware that's $2 million that leaves." PawSox vice-chairman Mike Tamburro delivered a list of other benefits generated by the team. It included contributing $12 million up front for construction costs, hiring union workers to build the stadium, pledging to stay in Rhode Island for thirty years, continuing annual contributions to local charities, and budgeting $150,000 annually for capital expenses. As for ancillary development, Tamburro unveiled that "a select group of team owners" had agreed to develop at least fifty thousand square feet of real estate near the stadium.[265]

During the public comments, thirty-one people addressed the hearing: twenty in support, nine opposed, and two undecided. One opponent, Beth Richardson, owner of a small construction business in southern Rhode Island, spoke out against taxpayer subsidies. "I don't expect it, and I don't like paying for it," she said. Richardson wished the PawSox good luck with their new stadium. "I just don't want to pay for it." The meeting lasted three and a half hours, thirty minutes less than scheduled.[266]

Eight days later, the scene shifted from South County to Kent County, when the fourth committee meeting was held at the New England Institute of Technology. The goal of the meeting was for invited guests "to provide insight into the inner workings of the stadium deal." The state's general treasurer, Seth Magaziner, said his initial skepticism about the Ballpark at Slater Mill had dissipated. He now supported the deal. Magaziner declared the stadium was affordable and would contribute positively to Rhode Island. He recalled how in 2014 statewide voters favored by a large margin the $35 million bond bill to improve arts and cultural venues. Magaziner interpreted the result as a clear indication that the people of Rhode Island supported arts and entertainment facilities. "These are the things that make life worth living," Magaziner opined, "and they should be affordable to everyone."[267]

The general treasurer also declared the time had come to invest in Pawtucket. He painted a grim picture of the city's stagnant downtown, full of empty parking lots and a nearly vacant department store. Magaziner also described how the legislation could be improved. Better interest rates, he surmised, could be secured if the state's Commerce Corporation issued the bonds. The treasurer also suggested that although $71 million in bonds was needed to build the stadium, the state would most likely issue $84 million in bonds. The additional funds would be reserved for early interest and other costs that might arise before the ballpark generates sufficient revenue to cover the bonds. Magaziner reiterated his office would continue to help craft the best legislation possible to keep the PawSox in Rhode Island.[268]

Once again, Commerce Secretary Pryor addressed the hearing, this time sharing his "guiding principles of an exceptional deal." He favored the proposal as long as it cost less than renovating McCoy, paid for itself, and kept the PawSox in town for a long time. Pryor's guidelines also required the team to cover all cost overruns, commit to ancillary development, and donate a portion of its profits to charity for the first five years. Janet Lee, of the Public Resources Advisory Group, told the committee that the city and the state could both afford the deal. Finally, environmental experts determined that the proposed sites were compliant and produced letters from the Department of Environmental Management to that effect. Pawtucket resident Lynn Farinelli, speaking from the floor, wanted the people of Pawtucket to have the opportunity to vote on the legislation. Her comments reinforced Morgan's and Frias's calls for a statewide referendum on the proposal. Once again, the meeting wrapped up in three and a half hours.[269]

The following evening, October 12, Roger Williams University in Bristol hosted the fifth hearing. Conley invited two presenters, the Peregrine Group and the Pawtucket Redevelopment Agency. Peregrine's Colin P. Kane discussed the prospects for development in Pawtucket. The city had not seen any significant development in forty years, he said. Pawtucket needed a catalyst to encourage development and reverse the fortunes of what Kane claimed was a declining city. Without such a boost, Kane said, "nothing is going to happen" and the "death spiral" was going to continue. Kane, a former chairman of the I-195 Redevelopment District Commission, said that the riverfront properties in Providence and Pawtucket were both attractive, but Pawtucket had an advantage because its leadership was easier to deal with. Kane said that Providence's leadership had been "a significant barrier" to attracting investors from around the country.[270]

Roger Lemoie, chairman of the PRA, reaffirmed his organization's optimism about the city's future. He told the hearing that the PRA voted to support the legislation. The agency was the entity in line to issue the bonds. Lemoie mentioned that in the 1960s the PRA had acquired the land being targeted for the stadium and sold the property to Apex for $240,000. Jeanne Boyle, Pawtucket's commerce director, confirmed the city's intent to update its Redevelopment Plan to include a financing provision with mitigation strategies relating to the ballpark.[271]

When the committee opened the floor to the public, thirty people spoke—twenty-four supported the project and six did not. This meeting concluded in three hours, thirty minutes shy of the previous two hearings.[272]

The sixth hearing was held on October 19 at Bryant University in Smithfield. It focused on the economic impact study that Brailsford & Dunlavey presented to the committee during the second session. Paul Dion, chief revenue analyst for the Rhode Island Department of Revenue, began by cautioning the senators against his financial analysis providing "an unequivocal answer as to whether the state should go forward" with the deal. "One thing we know about estimates," Dion said, "is they're going to be wrong. Hindsight is 20/20." Dion said his department came to a different conclusion than the consultants. Their analysis used the same assumptions as Brailsford & Dunlavey but applied them to a different methodology, resulting in lower revenue estimates. Dion suggested part of the difference rested in how much income tax ballplayers contributed to the state. He believed the consultant's estimates "seemed rather rich." Brailsford and Dunlavey described its methodology and promised to return with additional information about its conclusions.[273]

As with the previous meetings, supporters outnumbered opponents during public testimony. One opponent, John Arcaro, looked Lucchino in the eye and told the PawSox leader he was brilliant and that he hoped Lucchino could find a way to keep the team in Rhode Island. Yet Arcaro opposed the current plan, he told the PawSox boss, because he did not condone the state diverting funds from people like his eighty-year-old handicapped mother. Arcaro did not want the team to leave. He wanted the PawSox to come up with a better plan. "But I can't let you burden my mother anymore," Arcaro said. "I'm very serious about that." Lucchino did not respond directly to Arcaro's plea. Lucchino later said he attended most of the hearings and collected numerous pages of handwritten notes. He wanted time to review his notes before he commented on them. The meeting lasted three hours and forty-five minutes.[274]

The Senate Finance Committee held its seventh and final hearing at the State House on Tuesday evening, October 24, 2017. The format allowed committee members to contemplate the legislation without offering time for public input. Invited guests included representatives from the state's Division of Capital Asset Management, which provided information about McCoy Stadium as an asset and how it was protected, and the Division of Municipal Finance, which delivered details of Pawtucket's finances. Paul Dion returned to the committee and fielded questions concerning tax exemptions and their role in generating tax revenues.[275]

Next, Pawtucket mayor Grebien, Chief of Staff Dylan Zelazo, and Commerce Director Jeanne Boyle fielded questions from the senators. Prior to the meeting, the city delivered a number of documents, including a list of frequently asked questions about the city with answers, along with a copy of its most recent audit. Senators asked the city representatives how Pawtucket would meet its financial obligations, particularly during the early years of the ballpark's life when the city was not projected to reap a significant amount of revenue. Boyle said the city could make payments from funds reserved in an account holding portions of the bond proceeds or even possibly assess a fee on property near the ballpark in advance of taxes that would be generated from additional development.[276]

Senator James J. Seveney suggested rewriting the legislation to allow the city to receive a surcharge on premium seats. Grebien said that would have to be renegotiated. Seveney emphasized that he was not worried about the state or the team's position. "I am worried about you guys," he said. All of a sudden, it seemed, many in state leadership were finally interested in Pawtucket's well-being.[277]

Concern about the city's financial commitment continued as the PawSox representatives assumed their seats at the hearing table. Team vice-chairman Tamburro said he believed the greatest risk inherent in the proposal was cost overruns, and the team had already settled that issue. As with Grebien, Lucchino was concerned about changes to the heavily negotiated deal, so when Senator Louis P. DiPalma asked if the PawSox would consider backstopping the city, the question was not well received. "To consider backstopping everyone's bonds," Lucchino said, "is perhaps unfair, considering what we're prepared to do to make this deal work." He reminded the committee that the team, state, and city had numerous conversations about risk. Nevertheless, he left the door ajar by saying the team would be willing to consider changes to the legislation and was willing to listen to the committee's suggestions.[278]

Conley wrapped up the hearings after three hours by acknowledging the committee would review all of the testimony and documents to determine if the proposed legislation would need revisions. Over a period of one and a half months, the Senate Finance Committee had held seven meetings in six municipalities throughout the state. The hearings consumed more than twenty-eight hours—twelve hours and forty-five minutes of which were dedicated to public testimony. The committee received 185 pages of written testimony and volumes of supporting documents from presenters representing twenty different organizations. While not all took the podium, 324 people signed in to address the committee, 234 said they supported the deal, 70 indicated they opposed it, while 21 claimed to be neither pro nor con.[279]

The committee also established a portal into which Rhode Islanders could deliver e-mails stating their opinions about the proposed legislation. Of the 138 citizens who delivered commentary, 62 percent "were at least generally supportive" of the proposal, 32 percent "were at least generally opposed," and 6 percent "provided suggestions and/or input without stating a position."[280]

Over the course of the hearings, two notable events occurred. On October 10, the House Finance Committee held a hearing on the proposed legislation in room 35 of the Rhode Island State House. The PawSox and the City of Pawtucket testified during that four-hour session. Lucchino told the committee that the PawSox had received interest from eighteen cities following the expiration of the team's self-imposed period of exclusivity. "We tried to get this done with the city of Pawtucket and the Commerce Department without exploring alternatives," Lucchino said. "Suffice it to say, we believe that the Triple-A franchise of the Boston Red Sox in a New England market that's crazy about baseball is a commodity that will be highly sought after."[281]

Then, on October 17, the Pawtucket City Council passed a resolution supporting the plan to build a new stadium for the PawSox. After hearing from city and team officials, twenty-seven citizens expressed their feelings to the city councilors: seventeen for, ten against. The resolution carried with a vote of six to two.[282]

If anyone took Lucchino's statement as an idle threat, they were not paying close enough attention. Public statements such as the ones he made during the closing hearing do not generally bode well for the home team. The pent-up frustration by the PawSox in dealing with Rhode Island leadership to get a deal done was beginning to spill over.

An Exhaustive Study

Two days following the last hearing, Conley declared that the Senate Finance Committee was not going to vote on the proposed legislation until the PawSox provided financial statements detailing its profits and losses. The committee had requested the information weeks previously, but the team was holding back the information. Instead, the PawSox provided a consolidated balance sheet, which team consultant Guy Dufault said was "a greater indicator of the team's financial stability" than yearly profit/loss comparisons. The balance sheet the PawSox submitted, along with a letter from the team's accounting firm, Providence-based Sansiveri, Kimball & Company, demonstrated the team possessed sufficient assets to continue "as a going concern for a reasonable period of time." Dufault indicated the PawSox were reconsidering the committee's request and would revert quickly.[283]

Meanwhile, Governor Raimondo, speaking on Gene Valicenti's popular morning radio show, encouraged the team to be fully transparent concerning their finances. After all, they were asking the state and city to contribute $38 million to build a ballpark. "If they want the state to be their partner, they can't hide anything from us," the governor said. "That's sort of part of the deal. And if they don't want to, then, fine. Finance it on your own." Conley asked Mike Tamburro to deliver the requested information to the Rhode Island auditor general under nondisclosure protection. That agency would review the information but not release confidential information to the public.[284]

By November 1, the PawSox relented and agreed to deliver additional financial statements to the state. Stressing the sensitive nature of the information, Senate President Ruggerio formally requested Auditor General Dennis Hoyle to analyze the data. Ruggerio understood that Hoyle's assessment would not be "a guarantee or predictor of any future Team financial operating results or financial measures." Hoyle's findings would, however, be shared with the Senate Finance Committee and the Speaker of the House and become part of the public record. Ruggerio told Hoyle that his findings could include a description of the materials but should not include any proprietary financial information. That same day, Hoyle met with PawSox owners Lucchino, Terry Murray, Tom Ryan, and Paul Salem, along with the team's attorney, Kim Miner. The committee waited for Hoyle's report.[285]

Five months following the expiration of the loyalty pledge from the PawSox to the City of Pawtucket, state leadership still lacked a sense of urgency to pass the Ballpark at Slater Mill legislation. It remained mired in the Senate Finance Committee, which was busy unpacking the information presented during its hearings. As the quagmire dragged on, students at Yale University's School of Architecture produced a ballpark design for Pawtucket under the direction of department faculty and visiting professor Janet Marie Smith. Lucchino said the PawSox would incorporate features of the Yale project into the new stadium. Interestingly, the students omitted a Green Monster replica in left field. More curiously, it turned out that the students designed ballparks for other cities, including Worcester. RISD professor Anne Tate spilled the beans, saying that the fledgling architects worked on designs for "two other unmentionable non–Rhode Island sites" for the PawSox.[286]

On December 1, 2017, Senate Secretary Greg Pare announced that the Senate would not vote on the proposed legislation until the new year. Pare laid out a schedule whereby the auditor general and the Commerce Corporation would deliver findings on the team's financial condition to the Senate Finance Committee within the upcoming days. In turn, the Senate Finance Committee would release a report on its investigation. Pare expected the committee to vote on the proposed legislation and refer the bill to the full Senate immediately following the opening of the General Assembly's session in January. Mattiello reiterated that the Senate was leading the ballpark legislation and that his House of Representatives would wait until it received proposed legislation from the Senate.[287]

Hoyle delivered his favorable report to Ruggerio and Conley on December 5, 2017. Ruggerio released the findings to the press: "The auditor general and the Commerce Corporation, in its separate review, determined that the team will be able to meet its debt service obligations under the proposal."

Hoyle confirmed the team's ability to generate sufficient revenue from increased attendance, along with executing plans to sell the team's naming rights. The Commerce Committee arrived at a similar conclusion. Jesse Saglio, managing director and head of investments for the Commerce Corporation, pointed to a 5 percent increase in league-wide attendance over the most recent ten years.[288]

On December 7, 2017, the Rhode Island Senate Finance Committee produced a final report of its hearings. Its sixty-seven pages contained a comprehensive analysis of the proposition. The Executive Summary highlighted the major issues the committee examined. These included eminent domain, the team's ability to meet its financial obligations, the city's wherewithal to uphold its end of the bargain, capital requirements to maintain the ballpark, the future economic impact of the stadium, public policy objectives of lease provisions, the accuracy of attendance projections, state backstops for the city, and environmental risks posed by the targeted Apex site. The committee's exhaustive study produced eleven amendments to the original legislation.[289]

Conley was pleased with his committee's work and the resulting improvements to the proposed legislation. He liked the deal. The Ballpark at Slater Mill will pay for itself, he declared. "Rhode Island should be proud to create great public spaces," Conley said. "This public space will be at the welcoming gateway to the Blackstone River Valley National Park." He proclaimed, "We should not turn our back on this opportunity to show ourselves off, not only to the rest of the state but the rest of our nation as well." The senator painted a compelling picture: "We can have our own baseball stadium with its lights shining above 95 as an iconic statement as to who we believe we are and what we believe the future of this state can be." Further, Conley exuded, "Our working families deserve a civic and cultural space that's affordable to them. They deserve to know that we're committed to that for them. We should not take this away from them, we should not lose this on our watch."[290]

The original legislation was no doubt improved by the hearings. It would be difficult to find any significant stone unturned. The proposition had been deconstructed from many angles. The committee particularly vetted the deal's financial benefits and associated risks to the State of Rhode Island and City of Pawtucket. Conley's committee presented the ledger in its sixty-seven-page report.

Now it was time for the Senate Finance Committee to vote whether to deliver the legislation to the full Senate or not. There were twenty-three days left in 2017. Earlier in the year, Ruggerio strongly hinted that he would convene a special session of the Senate to consider the bill. That meant before the end of the year. Curiously, Conley said that the committee was not going to address the bill until early in the next session, which would convene on January 2, 2018. House Speaker Mattiello had already declared the House would not consider the bill until 2018.

Yet time was of the essence. Worcester was gaining momentum. Just days earlier, Massachusetts governor Charlie Baker signaled that he backed the PawSox move to Worcester. The upcoming February would mark the third anniversary since the new ownership team acquired the PawSox. One thing was disconcerting: state leaders did not appear to be doing everything in their power to expedite keeping the team in Rhode Island.

DOOMSDAY

With the holidays approaching, Mayor Grebien continued to fret about losing the PawSox to Worcester. The threat was accelerating. On Monday, December 11, the PawSox released a statement hinting at their displeasure with the Senate Finance Committee's delay and its implication on ultimate General Assembly ratification. The press release doubted whether the stadium could be built by April 2020, "which was a stated, important, and collective objective." The PawSox were also concerned about some of the committee's proposed revisions to the deal. The team said they hoped "all partners and stakeholders" understood "the delicate balance achieved in the original agreement that followed months of negotiation in 2017 among the City of Pawtucket, the State of Rhode Island, and the Pawtucket Red Sox."[291]

The PawSox said they had lost a year but not hope—hope "that the House and Senate will exhibit the necessary leadership to allow the construction of a beautiful ballpark and a public 'park at the park' to revitalize our Riverfront and serve as a catalyst of a resurgent Downtown Pawtucket for the Gateway City of the Ocean State." The team emphasized what a good deal the proposed ballpark would be to the state and city. Tax revenues would exceed annual investment, and Pawtucket would end up owning "an innovative ballpark with year-round uses," along with a new city park sparking additional development and tax revenue for the city.[292]

The team reemphasized that it would be contributing the majority of the finances, committing to stay in town for the next thirty years, and assuming responsibility for any cost overruns "to ensure that this once-in-a-generation project comes to fruition for Rhode Island." The message from the PawSox to Rhode Island's leadership seemed to be "Enough is enough, let's get moving."[293]

As pressure continued to mount from central Massachusetts, Grebien's frustrations surfaced in a December 19 press conference at Pawtucket's city hall. As the legislature continued to sit on the proposed bill, the mayor urged the state's General Assembly to approve the deal. Grebien relayed rumors about the Worcester proposal supposedly being better for the PawSox. The team admitted that it had met with Worcester officials during the previous week. Reluctant to stand by and watch the Ballpark at Slater Mill become a victim of apathy or fear, Grebien served up Plan B.

If the legislature lacked the "courage" to act on the proposed Ballpark at Slater Mill, the mayor suggested that his city would assume the state's role in the deal. In return for absorbing the state's liabilities, Pawtucket would receive all of the existing revenue being generated by McCoy, between $1.9 million and $2.2 million in state income and sales tax each year. Pawtucket would use the incoming revenue stream to pay down the bonds. Grebien painted a grim picture. "What we nearly have reached is doomsday, when the team will be pushed out to another state, costing our residents one of the last few affordable, friendly entertainment options they have, and costing our state millions in revenue."[294]

Reaction from the Rhode Island Senate was reassuring. Conley had "complete confidence" in the Senate's plans, reiterating that his committee would consider the bill during the first week of January. Ruggerio said he wanted the Senate to vote on the bill as soon as possible, most likely by the second week of January. Vibrations were not so positive from the Rhode Island House of Representatives. Speaker Mattiello lauded Grebien's efforts. He said that if the bill passed the Senate, the House Finance Committee would hold a "thorough and transparent review." Mattiello then issued a note of caution. He said he was hearing from "a vast majority" of his House colleagues that their constituents did not want to spend taxpayer money on "this private venture." The Speaker suggested "the parties that put this deal together" should "renegotiate it in order to make it more acceptable to the citizens of the state." Unlike other issues that were so important state leaders needed to pull the public along, such as the controversial airport runway project, Mattiello believed that the PawSox deal was "not an impactful project." He cited the lack of development surrounding McCoy Stadium as evidence.[295]

Meanwhile, leaders in Worcester continued their workmen-like approach to snatching the team from its Rhode Island foothold. City Manager Edward

In December 2017, Mayor Grebien urged the legislature to approve the Ballpark at Slater Mill or allow the city to go it alone—what he called "Plan B." *Photo by Ernest A Brown, from the* Pawtucket Times.

M. Augustus Jr. issued a statement in response to Grebien's alternate approach. "We continue to have regular conversations with the PawSox," Augustus said, "and we did have another meeting with the team last week." Augustus left the impression that his city was making progress. "We look forward to continuing those conversations and seeing where they lead." He had no comment on pending legislation in Rhode Island.[296]

Grebien's Plan B did not receive much consideration from Rhode Island leaders, nor did his plea for immediate action by the General Assembly. Advocates for keeping the team in Rhode Island were left to enjoy the holidays and patiently look forward to the new year.

By mid-December, the legislation to build the Ballpark at Slater Mill had been deeply vetted. It would be grossly inaccurate for anyone to suggest otherwise. It appeared that a vast majority of Rhode Islanders wanted to keep the PawSox in Pawtucket, including high-ranking state officials. Many were in favor of the state and city providing financial support to make it a reality. Nevertheless, the prospect of losing the franchise seemed to be growing with each passing day.

CHAPTER 6

The Speaker's Gambit

A Brick-and-Mortar Project

Bitterly cold temperatures visited Rhode Island during the first few days of 2018. On New Year's Day, it was so cold that the traditional plunges into Narragansett Bay were either postponed or canceled. Biting single-digit temperatures greeted early morning risers. The high for the day peaked around fourteen degrees. Organizers of these events opted for safety over fortitude, and without doubt some of the hearty souls who planned to jump into the chilly forty-three-degree ocean were somewhat relieved when they heard they were off the hook.

In Pawtucket, the clock continued to tick on the city's prospects of retaining a visible source of civic pride, its Triple-A baseball team, the venerable PawSox. By then, it was well known that Worcester was making headway courting the team. In mid-December, Chairman Larry Lucchino visited the Massachusetts city and met with its leaders. Pawtucket mayor Don Grebien fully grasped the gravity of the situation. He pleaded with leadership in Rhode Island's General Assembly to act. Legislation enabling the state and city to issue bonds to help pay for a new ballpark near the birthplace of the American Industrial Revolution was pending approval by the Senate Financing Committee and, subsequently, the full Senate and House. The Senate president promised swift consideration. The House Speaker was less committed.

Before submitting the legislation to the Senate Finance Committee, William J. Conley Jr. made three additional changes to the legislation that he previously revised in December 2017. The amendments continued to strengthen revenues to the state, while re-conceding a few previously agreed-on provisions to the team. The PawSox publicly thanked the committee for progressing S-0989. The team had not yet reviewed the bill delivered on January 2 but were "glad to see it advance to the next step." The Senate Finance Committee scheduled a public hearing and vote on the bill for the following Tuesday.[297]

At long last, on January 9, the committee passed the Ballpark at Slater Mill legislation, but not before 38 Studios reared its disruptive head. Prior to the vote, Steven Frias, the avowed longtime opponent of publicly funded projects for private benefit, once again raised his concerns. Frias was also a vocal detractor of Mattiello. After losing to the Speaker in House District 15 by eighty-five votes in 2016, his shadow loomed over the upcoming 2018 election. Frias claimed the stadium deal did not pay for itself and declared that "putting debt on the taxpayers to support economic development sounds a lot like 38 Studios." He warned if that was what the Senate wanted to do, it "better bring it to the voters."[298]

Proponents, on the other hand, were all for taking risks to save the PawSox and revitalize Downtown Pawtucket. With eight union leaders in the room supporting the legislation, trades council president Michael Sabitoni voiced approval for the measure while debunking Frias's concerns. "This is not 38 Studios," the union leader said. "This is not a concept. This is a brick-and-mortar project, an investment, a classic public-private partnership." Senator Elizabeth Crowley, representing District 16, which includes sections of Pawtucket and Central Falls, concurred: the PawSox and 38 Studios were different at their very core. She believed that "most of the people in the state want to keep the Red Sox here." Crowley pleaded, "We already lost a hospital; we don't need to lose the Red Sox."[299]

Senator Donna Nesselbush, whose District 15 is home to both McCoy Stadium and the proposed Ballpark at Slater Mill, not to mention the about-to-be-shuttered Memorial Hospital, said there were few issues more important to her than the stadium legislation. The committee had spent hours combing through the details of the proposed deal, Nesselbush argued. "This particular proposal," she declared, "is good for the people." She added, "We carry on our shoulders the future of Rhode Island," Nesselbush said.[300]

The committee voted eight to one in favor of the legislation. The sole nay vote was from the only Republican on the finance panel, Nicholas D. Kettle, whose District 21 included Coventry, Foster, Scituate, and West Greenwich.

Kettle said most of his constituents opposed the deal. While they preferred to see the PawSox stay, Kettle said, "They don't want to pay for it." He characterized the ballpark as a "nice-to-have, not a need-to-have."[301]

Following the vote, Conley said he believed the full Senate would approve the bill. There was much uncertainty, though, surrounding Mattiello's intentions. He had previously promised to send the bill to the House Finance Committee upon the Senate's approval. Now, concern circulated as Mattiello stalled. Ruggerio wanted Raimondo to intervene, as the governor's Commerce Corporation helped negotiate the deal. Those close to Raimondo believed she would encourage Mattiello to push the bill forward. David Ortiz, the governor's spokesman, not to be confused with Big Papi, reminded folks that Raimondo had repeatedly advocated for legislative action. "She thinks it's a good deal," he said. "She thinks the Senate amendments are also good." Ortiz was certain the issue would "be on the short list of items the governor and the speaker discuss" at their next meeting.[302]

Mattiello's position on a publicly funded stadium to keep the PawSox in Rhode Island had shifted since the original 2015 Providence Ballpark Plan. Back then, he was all for it. He called the team "part of our social and cultural history." He believed the people of Rhode Island felt the same way. "There are folks out there that don't want to spend ten cents on any incentives," he elaborated. "That's a race to the bottom, and we're not going to do that." Three years later, the Speaker looked at the opportunity through a different lens. He said his change of heart wasn't because he barely escaped with his Senate seat in the 2016 election or because he feared the same capable Republican foe in the upcoming 2018 election. Rather, it was because he listened to his colleagues who claimed their constituents were overwhelmingly opposed to spending taxpayer money on a baseball stadium. He said they objected to projects lacking in "essential economic incentives."[303]

Projects such as the PawSox deal, Mattiello now believed, should be determined by voters through a referendum. He said that he would approve one for the upcoming November election if that was what the governor, the City of Pawtucket, and the PawSox wanted. November wasn't that far away, he said. He also stated that he would listen to survey results if one were properly conducted, asked the right question, and achieved a large enough sample size. He even proposed the question: "We have a proposal to build the stadium, to keep the PawSox in the state of Rhode Island. Do you want to put public money into this proposal or not?" He would change his opinion, he declared, if the result of such a survey favored the ballpark by 60 to 65 percent.[304]

On January 16, the full Senate passed the bill by a vote of twenty-six to nine. The next step was for the House Finance Committee to review the legislation. Speaker Mattiello had other plans. He said that he had no timetable for delivering the legislation to the House. What he did instead was call a closed-door caucus with House Democrats.[305]

Ball of Confusion

The November election that Mattiello suggested include a statewide ballot referendum on the Ballpark at Slater Mill was nine months away. Such a delay would have been far too long for the PawSox. The House of Representatives Democratic caucus recognized this. Representative Carlos E. Tobon characterized the delay as "an eviction notice." Representative Raymond H. Johnston Jr. observed, "If we wanted that, we should have done it in 2016." Mattiello got the message during the hour-long-plus meeting. The issue was going to be decided by the Rhode Island House of Representatives. It was that body's responsibility to vote on the deal. Rather than considering the Senate-approved legislation, though, House Democrats wanted to improve the current bill. To that end, four representatives from Pawtucket volunteered to work with their colleagues: Tobon, Johnston, Jean Phillippe Barros, and Mary Duffy Messier. Since the Democrats controlled the House by a wide margin, sixty-four to eleven, the full House would most likely support revised legislation crafted by the Pawtucket representatives.[306]

Immediately following the caucus, Governor Raimondo vented her frustration. The governor thought it was high time the House considered the legislation. "I think that it's time for them to take a vote," Raimondo declared. "This has been going on for months now. The Senate had excellent hearings; they passed the legislation. It's time for the House to do the same thing." The governor suspected that other cities and states would become attractive to the PawSox if the process dragged on much longer. The House, she concluded, needed to do its job.[307]

The remainder of January reinforced gonzo journalist Hunter Thompson's trenchant observation that "when the going gets weird, the weird turn pro." The PawSox took their campaign directly into the belly of the beast. On January 23, the team hosted an event called "Cranston Community Night." The venue was the Oaklawn Grange, a facility in Mattiello's voting district and of which the Speaker was a member. About one hundred people, including ballpark opponent Frias, showed up to hear what advocates had to say. They were treated to a presentation and slideshow by speakers from the City of Pawtucket and the PawSox.

Team consultant Guy Dufault said the team mailed 8,800 notices about the meeting and received only 48 responses. The team invited those respondents and local trade groups to the informational session. The PawSox claimed Mattiello was invited but did not respond. One resident, Paul Okolowitcz, refuted Mattiello's oft-repeated claim that he knocked on doors throughout his district and uncovered that his constituents did not want to contribute taxpayer funds for the proposed ballpark. Okolowitcz asked how many in the audience received a visit from Mattiello. Not one person raised their hand.[308]

Eight days later, at the well-attended Greater Providence Chamber of Commerce Legislative Luncheon at the Rhode Island Convention Center, Mattiello shared his thoughts on the PawSox Ballpark at Slater Mill with the 675 guests, including 4 from the PawSox's front office. In a conversation with reporters before his speech, Mattiello suggested that the PawSox needed to "learn what's important from the public." The Speaker meant having intimate open meetings, whether in school auditoriums or peoples' living rooms. "A lot of meetings, a lot of reach out. It takes a lot of work, but it needs to be done." He said that "real proposals" come from such "real conversations."[309]

Mattiello dismissed the Senate Finance Committee's twenty-eight hours of statewide public hearings on the topic. That was not what he was suggesting. "The average citizen does not go out to committee hearings," Mattiello said, "where you end up with a lot of interested parties on both sides of the equation. You don't get a flavor of what the public is thinking." Neither were meetings like the one at the Oaklawn Grange. That was by invitation only. Mattiello was talking about meetings that were open to the public. He said that the team needed "to reach out to folks, engage them, and have a real conversation." Ironically, Mattiello said he had not spoken to Lucchino since the previous fall. "If he were to call me up and said he had a different proposal," Mattiello explained, "of course I would have a conversation with him." The Speaker emphasized that "the PawSox can learn a lot from the public and vice versa."[310]

In his speech to the chamber, Mattiello suggested the PawSox should contribute more than $12 million to the project. "That would be a tremendous starting point." He also referenced a survey taken the previous fall that found two-thirds of the respondents opposed spending taxpayer money on a ballpark for the PawSox. The crowd chuckled when Mattiello said that he wasn't the one holding up the PawSox deal. "It's not up to me," he demurred. "Unfortunately, everybody likes to look at my district, but the House is going to reflect the view of the general public."[311]

Between February 5 and February 9, research firm Fleming & Associates contacted 425 registered Rhode Island voters to gauge their receptiveness to the proposal. Build RI, a Providence-based trade union, commissioned the survey. On February 26, it released the results. Seasoned pollster Joe Fleming delivered the findings. When survey participants were asked if they favored using tax revenue to fund a new stadium for the PawSox, 53 percent said no. However, after being told that the new stadium would pay for itself, that the PawSox were paying $45 million of the total $83 million, and that the team was covering all cost overruns, 56 percent said they would support the deal. The margin of error was pegged at 4.75 percent.[312]

James Carr, chairman of Build RI and CEO of H. Carr & Sons construction company, claimed the survey clearly indicated that "Rhode Islanders support this ballpark if the revenues it generates pays for its construction." Building & Construction Trades Council president Michael Sabitoni concurred, saying the survey results showed that "Rhode Islanders favor the current deal on the table to keep the PawSox in Rhode Island. At the very least, the General Assembly should give this Rhode Island institution the courtesy of a vote." So did Grebien. "This project has been discussed and vetted for over a year," the mayor said. It was clear, he pleaded, that "Rhode Island residents agree that this is the right investment and that we need to get this done now."[313]

Others read the results differently, including Mattiello. He was not surprised by the poll. "When given a neutral question," he observed, "only 40 percent of Rhode Islanders agree with the proposal." He continued, "Those numbers rise only when prompted with assumptions that are speculative at best and are presented in the most favorable light." On this point, Frias agreed with his long-term foe. "The truth is," Frias asserted, "that a new PawSox stadium will not pay for itself." Frias questioned the team's ability to generate projected sales and income tax revenues, doubted the jump in attendance attributed to the new ballpark, and mistrusted the amount Pawtucket would collect in tax revenues associated with the new stadium and ancillary development. Build RI did not disclose how much it paid Fleming for the survey, but it certainly did not seem to achieve its intended results—convincing doubters they should support the deal.[314]

Mr. Speaker

By late spring, the PawSox had good reason to be concerned. The insular world of Rhode Island election-year politics was heating up. The Ballpark at Slater Mill had become a hot potato between Senate President Ruggerio and House Speaker Mattiello. And Mattiello's every move on the stadium was being closely monitored by his campaign adversary and ballpark opponent. Now, a large gubernatorial field was choosing sides. Incumbent Gina Raimondo stood alone in favor of the legislation. Leading contenders for Raimondo's job had already opposed the stadium. These were Democrat Matt Brown, Republican Cranston mayor Allan Fung, House Minority Leader Patricia Morgan, and Independent Joe Trillo.

In addition, Mattiello was beset by several distractions. His narrow margin of victory over Frias in 2016 and the likelihood of a rematch in the fall seemed to drive his obsession with public opinion. Since that victory, controversies plagued Mattiello. One of his high-ranking staff members, Frank Montanaro, was found receiving $50,000 of free college tuition for two family members while on leave from his position at Rhode Island College. He would have been entitled to the benefit if he were still employed by the college. Mattiello also raised eyebrows by hiring the son of his political consultant Ed Cotugno. Finally, Rhode Island's board of elections ordered Mattiello to repay $72,000 to his Political Action Committee relating to campaign misspending. Nevertheless, Mattiello continued to exert firm control over the House of Representatives, including holding PawSox ballpark legislation in limbo.[315]

According to political science scholars, the balance of power in Rhode Island is heavily slanted toward the General Assembly and away from the governor—so much so that former governor Lincoln Chafee asserted that the state "constitutionally has a very strong legislature. That's a fact—the strongest in the country." He received corroboration from Peverill Squire, a professor at the University of Missouri specializing in state legislatures. Chafee's staff communicated with Squire while researching the 350th anniversary of the state's Colonial Charter of 1663. "We can always quibble about rankings," Squire said, "but every accounting puts the power of Rhode Island's governor at or near the bottom in terms of institutional powers."[316]

The reasons are not trivial. Power is generally granted to governors in some or all of the following ways: the bully pulpit, which requires strong communication skills and popularity from a receptive constituency; the ability to veto, particularly line items in a state budget; the right to select judges; the authority to appoint the state's attorney general; and the opportunity to appoint executive branch leadership, especially of regulatory agencies. Rhode Island falls short in a number of these areas. The state's governor lacks the ability to veto line items in a budget, being able to reject only entire budgets or appropriation legislation, which can, in turn, be overridden by the legislature. Because the state's General Assembly is so heavily controlled by one party, the legislature can easily muster the necessary votes to supersede a veto. Also, top general officers in Rhode Island are elected separately, not as part of a ticket. The governor, lieutenant governor, secretary of state, and attorney general are all elected independently. Because the governor and lieutenant governor do not run as a team, they are not always on the same page. Also, the governor's role in choosing judges is diminished, as the legislature recommends and approves such nominations.[317]

The governor of Rhode Island does make appointments to state agencies, boards, and commissions, which is critical to maintaining some semblance of balance. Because of their importance, such agencies have "metastasized." According to a 2003 study by Common Cause of Rhode Island, there were close to 430 such entities in the state around the turn of the twenty-first century, 73 of which were performing executive functions. The legislature found ways to wrest control of and assert influence over some of these administrative entities by channeling governing duties to boards of directors and granting those boards authority to appoint and remove the executive directors.[318]

In Rhode Island, power rests with the Speaker of the House. The Speaker controls the $12.7 billion state budget (fiscal year 2021), including who receives funding and who goes without. The Speaker decides which bills get presented to the full House and which are relegated to the back burner. The Speaker heads the Joint Committee on Legislative Services and its $45 million budget, meaning he can fill legislature staffing position with whomever he deems fit. Most of all, and perhaps the real source of the Speaker's power, is the ability to reward allies and punish opponents.[319]

The Speaker is elected by the full House. Before being selected, he— and it has always been a male—has generally served in a leadership role, typically either as House majority leader or House majority whip. When it is time for a new Speaker, the party's leadership puts forth its candidate. In Rhode Island, such transitions are usually preceded by the incumbent succumbing to some investigation or scandal. Since the mid-twentieth century, only a few of the twelve leaders have left office with their reputations relatively unscathed. For example, in 2003, Speaker John Harwood was forced to resign after purportedly paying off a female staffer who claimed that Harwood sexually harassed her. Harwood vigorously denied the allegation. Then, in 2014, Speaker Gordon Fox abdicated under a cloud of suspicion just days after the Federal Bureau of Investigation raided his home and State House office. Fox later pleaded guilty to accepting a bribe, wire fraud, and filing a false tax return.[320]

Nicholas Mattiello assumed the Speaker's position following Fox's fall from grace. He won the office by a majority of sixty-one to six, with six abstentions and two absentees. At age fifty, after serving as Fox's majority leader for four years, Mattiello said, "I'm taking over the leadership with a very heavy heart." He was referring to Fox's departure, with whom he "enacted some very important legislation." Before long, Mattiello began to mold the role to his own style.[321]

Mattiello was born and raised in Cranston, Rhode Island. During summers, he worked at his father's demolition company, Mattiello Drilling and Blasting, which was clearing the way for the new highways being laid down across New England in the 1960s and 1970s. His father, Anthony Mattiello, was born in Warwick, Rhode Island, in 1919, but his family returned to Italy when he was young. After serving in the Italian army during World War II, Anthony returned to Rhode Island and established his own business. Anthony stressed the value of hard work and education to his three children. He hoped that his eldest, Nicholas, would become a lawyer, which he did after graduating from LaSalle Academy in Providence, Boston College, and Suffolk University Law School. In 1985, one year out of law school, Mattiello married Mary Ann Montecalvo. They settled down in a white Colonial in the Hillside Farms neighborhood of Western Cranston, where they raised two sons.[322]

While Mattiello was completing law school, his uncle Ralph ran into lawyer Joseph Bevilacqua Jr. at a neighborhood filling station, told him about his nephew, and suggested that Bevilacqua hire him. Bevilacqua told Ralph to have Nicholas stop by and see him. Mattiello followed up on his uncle's lead and became a clerk for Bevilacqua Jr. Upon passing the bar, Mattiello rented office space from his mentor, who periodically sent him work. [323]

Within a year, then fledgling attorney William J. Murphy established an office in the same building. The two young lawyers became fast friends. In 1994, Mattiello was in Murphy's wedding party. "I started maybe a year before Bill," Mattiello recalled, "so I would show him the ropes, where the courts were, how to handle certain things." Within no time,

Mattiello had determined that Murphy was destined to "be a superstar in the law field….He quickly surpassed anything I could teach him," Mattiello said.[324]

Murphy entered politics in 1993, winning a House seat from West Warwick, and within a decade ascended to the most powerful position in the state. Murphy replaced the embattled Speaker Harwood. In 2006, Murphy urged Mattiello to run for office. The District 15 seat was opening up. The Republican incumbent was not seeking reelection, and Murphy wanted to fill it with a Democrat. Mattiello decided to run. His wife, Mary Ann, not enamored of politics, told him, "You can run for office, but you have to promise it will never change you."[325]

Rhode Island has seventy-five House of Representative districts. District 15 covers about a quarter of the land in Cranston, the state's second-largest city. Of the state's 1 million residents, 81,000 call Cranston home. District 15 has around 14,000 people, about 15 percent of the city's overall population. They reside in slightly more than 4,600 households. The median income of those households is close to $92,800, the fifth highest among the seventy-five districts. District 15's population is 85 percent white, almost 11 percentage points higher than the state as a whole. It has the third-highest concentration of Italian ancestry at 41 percent, while 21 percent claim Irish lineage. Of the district's residents twenty-five years of age or older, 91 percent possess a high school diploma or equivalent, while 39 percent have a bachelor's degree or higher. It is safe to say that District 15 is relatively wealthy, homogeneous, well educated, and suburban.[326]

Mattiello embarked on a grass-roots campaign. He rallied support from institutions with which he associated, including Immaculate Conception Church, where he was a lector, and the Cranston West Little League, where he was a coach. He eked out a win in the Democratic primary and then won by a landslide in the general election. In 2010, Murphy handed over the Speakership to Gordon Fox, who inserted Mattiello as majority leader. Fox praised Mattiello as a "very dedicated, intelligent and compassionate human being."[327]

Fox and Mattiello were unlike in many respects. Fox was a gay progressive who strongly advocated for same-sex marriage. The incoming Speaker was a self-described moderate Democrat, fifty years old, pro-business, pro-life, and Roman Catholic, with a passion for riding his Harley-Davidson Electra Glide. At first, Mattiello was against same-sex marriage but later voted for it after learning more about the civil rights impact of the legislation. He believed that the law's time had come. His pastor, however, was not so open-minded and furloughed Mattiello from the lectern. But most of all, Mattiello was interested in jobs, the economy, and changing the negative impression many Rhode Islanders had of their state. "That's got to change," Mattiello said. "This is the best state in the union."[328]

Mattiello hoped to bring a more collaborative approach to the Speaker's role. He stressed the importance of relationship building, discourse, and active listening. He also subscribed to the idea that leadership sometimes required dragging others along to a certain position for the greater good. To some observers, Mattiello was a micromanager who ruled the House of Representatives with an iron fist. If you crossed Nicholas Mattiello, you were no longer part of the team. Sometimes you lost a committee chairmanship, sometimes you were no longer consulted on important issues, sometimes you would get fired from your job, and sometimes he would actively campaign against you.[329]

The most powerful man in Rhode Island held the Ballpark at Slater Mill's fate in his hands. In 2017, he could have fast-tracked the bill at the end of the regular legislative session. Throughout the remainder of 2017, he could have worked with Senate President Ruggerio to convene a special session of the General Assembly to consider the proposed legislation. In January 2018, he could have followed up on the bill approved by the state Senate and moved it forward for a vote by the General Assembly. At any time, he could have advocated for a statewide referendum. Instead, he sat on it until the end of May 2018.

Pawtucket Agonistes

As the Speaker dawdled, a curious uprising of pro-stadium sentiment erupted from the editorial desk at 10 Dorrance Street, home of the state's major newspaper, the two-hundred-year-old *Providence Journal*. In a period of three months, the editors published five pieces about the Ballpark at Slater Mill. The number of editorials in such a short span was noteworthy. Granted, there was once a time in the state's history when the editorial opinion of the newspaper carried more weight than it did during the winter of 2017–18. In the new millennium, though, with newspapers fighting for readership against numerous internet-age options, editorial boards had lost much of their ability to shape public opinion. Nevertheless, the series presented cogent arguments in favor of keeping the PawSox in Rhode Island, a sentiment held by a large number of Rhode Islanders.

The first opinion appeared on December 17, 2017. The editors praised the work of the Senate Finance Committee, which, it said, "did not merely go through the motions" but "listened carefully to the public's concerns about the deal struck between the PawSox and the Raimondo administration." It lauded the revisions that Conley announced just a week earlier emanating from the finance committee's review. To the editors, the Ballpark at Slater Mill was "an excellent deal." The PawSox's willingness to cover more than 50 percent of the costs constituted "a far greater percentage of private money than other owners contributed to the 14 new Double-A and Triple-A ballparks built from 2006 to 2016." The paper noted, "The average for those stadiums was 21 percent."[330]

Governor Raimondo supported the deal, the editorial claimed, "because the state would lose more money in tax revenue if the PawSox were to depart." The state "would retain an asset that provides great enjoyment for families, boosts local pride, stimulates charity and advertises a vibrant place to the outside world." That was why other communities "kick in" so much for public stadiums. The editors understood that Mattiello remained "cool to the idea" and that many Rhode Islanders were "bitterly negative about public-private partnerships." While it would be a tough decision to vote for a baseball stadium in an election year, "strong leaders pushed through such measures as an airport expansion and a convention center, both of which have dramatically enhanced the vitality of Rhode Island, in the face of opposition." The opinion makers noted, "Courageous leadership is an essential ingredient of any thriving state." The piece concluded with a plea for the state's leaders to come together and "put the interests of the people of Rhode Island first."[331]

The editors struck again on Christmas Eve. This time they channeled the patron saint of perseverance and courage, Winston Churchill, who said, "The price of greatness is responsibility." The editorial board echoed the sentiment: "No political leader ever achieved great things for his or her city, state or country by avoiding the responsibility to lead." The state needed leaders to "step forward and solve problems, to dare great things, rather than surrender to the negativity that is endemic in Rhode Island's culture." The source of such negativity, the opinion makers suggested, had "been earned, in part, by the poor performance if not outright corruption of politicians in the past." Rhode Islanders should be cautious after the state's "bitter experience with such debacles as 38 Studios," the editors warned, but "not render us incapable of ever doing anything again."[332]

The senate, governor, and general treasurer all favored the stadium deal that would keep the PawSox in Rhode Island, along with its associated tax revenues, source of civic pride, entertainment value, tourist attraction, and charitable giving. "The sticking point," the editors wrote, was "House Speaker Nicholas Mattiello, who claimed most voters in his district did not favor the idea." No deal was going to get done without the Speaker's backing. "Since it would be folly for Rhode Island to turn its back on the project," the editorial urged that "the governor and other leaders will have to be determined and creative in making this proposal palatable to House members."[333]

In the February 19, 2018 edition, the editors piggy-backed on an opinion piece published in its newspaper eight days earlier by Johnson & Wales University professor Lee A. Esckilsen, an expert on venue and event management. Esckilsen observed that since 1992, the state had "used public financing to build, renovate and maintain public assembly venues at a cost of more than $300 million, benefiting Providence and the residents of Rhode Island." The projects included $16 million in 2014 to renovate Veterans Memorial Auditorium; $200 million in revenue bonds to build the Rhode Island Convention Center, which opened in 1993; and in 2005, $92.5 million in revenue bonds to acquire and renovate the Civic Center. That building, renamed the Dunkin' Donuts Center, hosts eighteen Providence College home basketball games and thirty-eight regular season Providence Bruins hockey contests. Providence College has an endowment of $200 million, and the P-Bruins are owned by a millionaire, the editorial noted. "Neither tenant contributed a cent to the acquisition or renovation of the building." Interestingly, "Almost no one said a word about it."[334]

The editors contrasted those projects to the proposed Ballpark at Slater Mill. The chief tenant in Pawtucket "would play 70 regular season games, more than the Friars and Bruins combined." But unlike the other teams, the PawSox would contribute 54 percent of the new stadium's cost. The editorial pointed out that the team's "remarkable pledge of $45 million would effectively permit the state to get a new public stadium, a significant economic generator, at better than no cost to the taxpayers—since tax revenues generated by the PawSox would more than cover the state's share." The opinion makers wondered aloud at "the hatred that some have stoked up against the owners for this extraordinary proposal," calling it "one of

During the winter of 2017–18, the *Providence Journal* published a series of editorials in favor of approving the proposed legislation and retaining the Pawtucket Red Sox. *Courtesy of the Pawtucket Red Sox.*

the wonders of Rhode Island politics, which can be irrationally negative at times." The editorial was counting on state leaders, including Mattiello, "to have the courage and sense to position Rhode Island for success." They concluded, "Spitting in the face of a plan for a new venue that would be a far better deal for taxpayers than any over the last three decades makes absolutely no sense."[335]

On March 16, the editors highlighted the proponents of the Rhode Island Convention Center as one example of "courage and imagination" in the face of "plenty of naysayers." And it paid off. It was the right decision, at least according to a study conducted by the Plano, Texas–based Conventions, Sports & Leisure International group. The analysis focused on the Convention Center, the Dunkin' Donuts Center, and the Veterans Memorial Auditorium. Between 2013 and 2017, the three venues generated $838 million in total economic impact. Such benefit far exceeded "the costs of running the facilities, including $23 million a year in state bonding costs." The venues drew an average of 1.4 million people to five hundred events each year, spending millions of dollars on tickets, concessions, and merchandise—not to mention the amount funneled "to the local economy through lodging, restaurants and bars, shopping and transportation." In addition, the three facilities supported 1,800 jobs that raised more than $12 million in state and local taxes.[336]

Beyond the positive economic impact, the editorial board highlighted a second but equally important contribution of the Rhode Island Convention Center: its impact on the "vitality of downtown Providence." "Let's face it," the editors implored, "the downtown would be something of a black hole without the remarkable energy the center generates." The Veterans Memorial Auditorium would be "shuttered," and "the Dunk would be a much inferior arena, left without the renovations it needed" if it weren't for the strong anchor provided by the convention center. The three venues "immensely improve the quality of people in and around Rhode Island." Now the Speaker was holding up the ballpark legislation, and the "naysayers, as in the past, are out in full force." As the Convention Center demonstrated, "Guts and vision make all the difference for a state." The opinion makers questioned: "Do Rhode Island's political and civic leaders still possess those qualities?"[337]

THE REVISED BILL

On March 5, the Speaker met with PawSox executives and city leaders at Pawtucket City Hall. Lucchino and Grebien and their top lieutenants attended the sit-down, as did the House representatives from Pawtucket. Mattiello wanted to speak with them privately to explain what was needed for a bill to get through the General Assembly during its regular session ending in June. Mattiello reaffirmed what he had been saying publicly: the risk had to be shifted from the taxpayers to the team. Of particular concern, the General Assembly would need to appropriate money in the state's annual budget to cover the projected costs associated with the bonds issued to build the new ballpark. Financial analysis provided to the Senate estimated that the amount would be between $3.5 million and $5.2 million each year. One participant in the meeting, Representative Tobon, said that he was confident Mattiello was "going to do what he has done historically, which is to put the brakes on things and improve [the deal] for the people of Rhode Island." Mattiello characterized the meeting as "cordial." Whether Grebien or the PawSox thought so remains doubtful.[338]

Little material information escaped from the negotiation table during the remainder of April. In early May, the PawSox public relations team broke the silence. On Saturday, May 5, the team held an open forum at the Pawtucket Public Library. Team president Charles Steinberg, General Manager Dan Rea, and Special Assistant to the Chairman Bart Harvey hosted a ninety-minute question-and-answer session. Attendance was sparse at only fifteen people, but they were fully prepared to engage in serious discourse with team brass about the ballpark proposal.[339]

The underlying theme was not uplifting. Steinberg confirmed that discussions between the team and Worcester were ongoing and that the two parties were getting close to a deal. Nevertheless, he repeated the PawSox's long-desired preference to keep the team in Pawtucket. Steinberg said that a "well-designed, well-located ballpark in the right part of downtown" could play a major role in revitalizing a city, like the ones he, Lucchino, and Janet Marie Smith brought to fruition in Baltimore and San Diego. The real question Steinberg wanted Pawtucket to consider was this: "How valuable is it to you for a family-oriented Triple-A baseball team to be in your town?" He painted a Dickensian future: "If the team goes away, you lose the profits, you lose the spirit, and you lose the place to take your children."[340]

Steinberg warned of further consequences. If the PawSox relocated to Worcester, Pawtucket would not be able to attract another franchise. Worcester's minor-league territorial radius would encircle Pawtucket, rendering it unable to host another professional baseball team. "If the club goes, you don't get a team back, you're in Worcester's territory, the door shuts," Steinberg said, making it clear that other towns would welcome the PawSox. "We'd like to keep it here, that's what we'd like."[341]

The PawSox officials clarified other points for the audience. Bart Harvey emphasized the importance of what seemed to have gotten lost about the project: the positive impact on Pawtucket and the state. Ballpark opponents have done a good job "mischaracterizing major components" of the proposal, he said. Upon entering Rhode Island on I-95, he noted, "We really think you could see this wow image, this gem of a ballpark as you're going by." As for the city, Harvey asserted, "The building stock and the bones are there, it's just waiting for the catalyst of development to come and we think the ballpark could be that catalyst."[342]

General Manager Rea provided insight into why renovating McCoy did not make sense, saying, "She's 76 years old." You can't drive a thirty-year-old car, he continued, and think it is a five-year-old vehicle. It would take $35 million to extend McCoy's life, but economic development would be constrained because it would still be in a neighborhood full of houses and schools. Also, while McCoy appears well maintained, "when you get downstairs, you're

In May 2018, PawSox president Charles Steinberg warned Pawtucket about a future without the PawSox and promoted the benefits of a "well-designed, well-located ballpark in the right part of downtown." *Courtesy of the City of Pawtucket.*

starting to see a fracturing in the cement causing a lot of drainage." Rea also blamed McCoy for the decline in attendance at PawSox games, citing McCoy's age and the "lack of establishments within walking distance, and limitations in amenities in and around the current stadium." Rea said the new stadium would raise attendance "to where it was in the heyday."[343]

Steinberg posed a series of pertinent questions: "You tell me where families are going to bring six-year-olds, eight-year-olds, consistently from spring 'til autumn?…Where is there a better opportunity for extremely affordable family outings?…How important is it for Pawtucket to have a half-million people come to a revitalized downtown Pawtucket?" They must have hoped that Speaker Mattiello would get the message.[344]

On May 16, the Northern Rhode Island Chamber of Commerce invited Mattiello to address its Eggs and Issues Breakfast at Kirkbrae Country Club. His keynote covered a range of topics, from the state budget to school construction, but many attendees were interested in the status of the ballpark legislation. "We are working on that," he said. "I said that it would have to be fair to the taxpayers and the taxpayers would have to understand and support the deal," the House Speaker elaborated. Mattiello knew that citizens get frustrated when politicians do not listen their constituencies but believed that the ballpark issue was moving in the right direction.[345]

Mattiello told the chamber of commerce that getting a public-private deal done was difficult when the public is against it. He cited a poll that said 60 percent of Rhode Islanders opposed the ballpark proposal until they were told the taxpayers' risk was eliminated from the equation. (Mattiello was most likely referring to the Fleming & Associates poll taken in February 2018.) He said that a "successful community economy" was difficult to achieve when people are "frustrated with their government." Mattiello expounded, "That means people like me had better make sure we listen to the public." Mattiello had a framework to serve the public's interest better. That included shifting the risk from the taxpayers to the team. He said that some people were willing to let the PawSox go to Massachusetts. He preferred they stay. He believed the PawSox were part of the fabric of the state.[346]

On May 31, more than four months after the Senate approved the legislation and passed it on to the House, Mattiello delivered his revised proposal to the House Finance Committee. The Speaker's revision called for eliminating the state guarantee. The Pawtucket Redevelopment Agency would own the ballpark. The PRA would issue the bonds. It would lease the ballpark to the team. The PRA would receive city and state tax revenue from an expanded Tax Increment Financing District (TIF). The addition of the state taxes to the previously identified city TIF would establish a so-called Super TIF. The PRA would pay back the bonds from revenues generated in the district. The agency would park excess revenue in an

In May 2018, Mattiello told the Northern Rhode Island Chamber of Commerce that the proposed ballpark legislation needed "to be fair to the taxpayers and the taxpayers would have to understand and support the deal." *Courtesy of the Rhode Island State Archives.*

account that would be used to pay for stadium improvements, along with infrastructural upgrades in and around the Downtown Pawtucket Redevelopment Project. The plan was intended to ensure that the project would "stand or fall on its own."[347]

The Speaker also introduced a companion bill re-addressing eminent domain, amending the definition of a blighted area to include lands, buildings, and improvements that together impact the entire area. The intent of the legislation was to make acquiring the Apex land easier and more reasonable. The new bill was drafted to clarify existing legislation that could require the city to pay owner Andrew Gates 150 percent of the assessed value for the five parcels of 12.41 acres being eyed for the project. The Speaker's revisions wanted to ensure that the city paid no more than 100 percent of the property's assessed value.[348]

Mattiello's proposal laid out the skeletal bones on which the House Finance Committee needed to add flesh. That job would be spearheaded by Representative Marvin Abney, from Newport, who chaired that committee. Nineteen people testified at the hearing, all but four in favor. Conley pronounced his gratitude to Mattiello for moving the bill forward. Republican Party chairman Brandon Bell issued a statement before the bill was presented objecting to Mattiello's plan. He said that even without backstopping the bonds, the state "will end up bailing out Pawtucket in the future when it lacks the funds to pay for these bonds." Mattiello rebutted the criticism. The revised bill would "allow the stadium to be built with no risk to Rhode Island or the Pawtucket taxpayers." The bonds would be special revenue bonds, "only payable through revenue. There is no other recourse against anyone." As for the PawSox, Steinberg said that the team would hold its comments for the time being. When asked if Worcester was a serious option for the team, Steinberg suggested that it would best to ask that city directly.[349]

At least one influential source praised Mattiello's revised bill. An editorial in the June 3 edition of the *Providence Journal* called it "encouraging news" that Mattiello "was working on keeping one of Rhode Island's superb amenities, Triple-A baseball, in Pawtucket." The opinion makers pointed out that for months the Speaker of the House "had been adamantly opposed to the project, in stark contrast to Governor Raimondo and the state Senate." While admitting that Mattiello's revised bill would make financing the stadium more expensive, the editors were encouraged by his engagement. The editorial called "the speaker's shift from stubborn opposition to fruitful involvement" a hopeful sign. "It suggests that he, like other leaders, wants to see Rhode Island become a more vibrant place to live and work, rather than a decaying shell of its former self."[350]

The editors acknowledged there was "unquestionably still significant opposition to the project from those who have grown, through bitter experience, to distrust the state's political leaders." They highlighted that some "have compared the project to 38 Studios, Rhode Island's notoriously rushed and poorly vetted investment in a highly risky video game venture." The opinion piece highlighted Mattiello's "knack for making good plans for the state better ones," holding up as example his contributions to the RhodeWorks legislation, Rhode Island's comprehensive approach to "finally repair its crumbling, worst-in-the-nation bridges and roads." It would become clear "in the coming days whether he is playing a similar role here." The editorial concluded that Mattiello's "dramatic shift has unquestionably boosted the chances Rhode Island will move forward with this exciting idea."[351]

On Tuesday, June 19, the House Finance Committee held a second hearing of Speaker Mattiello's revised Ballpark at Slater Mill legislation. A few details remained unanswered. For one, it was clear that the interest on the bonds would be more expensive without state backing. The exact amount was unknown, although some claimed it might be as much as $25 million. The legislation did specify that the bonds should be issued through a public offering, rather than by private placement. If the bonds had to rely on private placement, the legislation mandated that interest rates, prices, and yields should be at fair market value. The revised bill also did not set the boundaries for the Downtown Redevelopment District from which tax revenues would be generated to pay off the bonds. To accommodate the higher-priced bonds, some suggested the area would need to be larger than originally believed. Mattiello did not agree with expanding the district but acknowledged there were many details to be ironed out, which he was leaving "to the city and team."[352]

Several speakers addressed the committee assembled in room 35 of the State House. Once again, Pawtucket mayor Grebien carried the banner for his city. He virtually begged the committee to approve the bill. "Please pass this legislation," Grebien implored. "You will be shifting the risk and stopping the disaster of losing the Pawtucket Red Sox." The mayor said the PawSox were the third-largest tourist attraction in the state. He pictured the stadium and redeveloped downtown as an alluring gateway to Rhode Island. Opponent Jim O'Neil, a citizen testifying at the meeting, preferred the previously approved Senate version because state-issued bonds would receive more favorable credit ratings. "Interest rates are serious," O'Neil said, projecting an expense difference of tens of millions of dollars over the life of the bonds. The House Finance Committee delayed a vote until later in the week.[353]

Around 10:00 p.m. the following Thursday night, after an hour of deliberation, Abney's House Finance Committee passed the bill by a majority of fourteen to four. Committee members asked a number of questions that Fiscal Advisor Sharon Reynolds Ferland was unable to answer. Abney stepped in and reminded the committee that the bill was "just enabling legislation" and that "details would be worked out later." Mattiello moved the bill immediately to the full House for consideration but suspended discussion around 11:00 p.m. Some legislators asked for more time so they could read the twenty-one-page document. Others suggested it was too late to rush such an important bill. "It seemed as though trying to get it done was not the right idea," Mattiello conceded, "and hearing it tomorrow when everyone is fresh, after everyone has a chance to read it overnight is probably a good idea." The Speaker prepared House members that they were in for a long Friday and possibly Saturday.[354]

On Friday, June 22, 2018, with the end of the legislation session bearing down, the Rhode Island House of Representatives considered the revised bill. Despite lingering objections by some representatives, fifty-three members voted for the amended law versus thirteen opposed. Mattiello quickly marshalled the legislation to the Senate. The Rhode Island Senate—after months of analyzing, debating, revising, and approving legislation hammered out and agreed to by the governor, mayor of Pawtucket, and PawSox executives—now faced the unenviable task of approving or rejecting a bill it had never seen. It was a no-win situation. Voting for the revised bill would pass legislation that the team was unlikely to accept. Voting against the bill would further delay an agreement to keep the PawSox in Rhode Island.[355]

The Senate received Mattiello's bill early Friday evening. A financial analysis did not arrive until 11:00 p.m. Senate President Ruggerio called for

Above: Speaker Mattiello withheld ballpark legislation until the final hours of the 2018 regular legislative schedule. *Photo by Ernest A Brown, from the* Pawtucket Times.

Left: The Rhode Island House of Representatives passed Mattiello's revised ballpark legislation, 53-13. *Photo by Ernest A Brown, from the* Pawtucket Times.

a vote on one of the most influential bills in modern Rhode Island sports history in the waning hours on the last day of the legislative session. Senator Louis DiPalma of Middletown, who once opposed the stadium but came to favor it while sitting through the Senate Finance Committee hearing process, wondered why they were doing business this way. Senator Nesselbush of Pawtucket knew that passing the legislation was going to "kill the stadium." Conley himself knew the revised bill was problematic. He later recalled the frenzy of that evening to *Providence Journal* columnist Mark Patinkin. "We're screwed," he remembered thinking. "Now no one can afford it. The city, the ball club—it's dead."[356]

Nevertheless, the Senate approved the measure twenty-six to four. Despite his private beliefs, Senate Finance Committee chairman Conley publicly praised the result. "While the House version of the bill takes a slightly different approach, it still addresses and reconciles all the issues that were a concern to the Senate after studying and deliberating about the issue for so long," Conley said. It provided Pawtucket "the opportunity to pursue a ballpark partnership with the potential to anchor redevelopment in a downtown district at the northern gateway to our state." Representative Carlos Tobon concurred: "This will be the catalyst to make Pawtucket's downtown what it once was….This is no charitable giveaway to the PawSox. This is the city of Pawtucket asking…give us an opportunity."[357]

Others viewed it differently, citing the uncertainty of attendance ten to twenty years down the road and whether the redevelopment district would generate enough revenue to cover the cost of the bonds. Longtime ballpark opponent Patricia Morgan characterized the deal as "the very definition of risky." Also, the lack of communication from the PawSox disturbed Newport Representative Lauren Carson. "Their silence is just a little deafening," she said. "I'm concerned." Unanswered questions echoed in the summer air as the legislation was sent to Governor Gina Raimondo to be signed into law.[358]

Five months after the Rhode Island Senate approved a ballpark-funding bill in which the state would backstop the city if it was unable to pay down the bonds used to fund construction of the Ballpark at Slater Mill, the General Assembly ultimately approved legislation that shifted the risk to the investors of the bonds. Removing the state backstop escalated the expense of the bonds. According to a late-June analysis from Treasurer Magaziner's office, the city and state would have to pay about $3.2 million in principal and interest to bondholders each year, totaling $92 million over thirty years. The revised legislation would cost $900,000 more each year than the estimated cost of the bill the Senate passed in January. The treasurer estimated that revenue needed to be 1.6 times debt service. This meant the stadium and development district would need to generate between $5.1 and $5.2 million each year. The numbers could be reduced, Magaziner noted, depending on the PRA's "ability to use excess revenues to buy back the bonds—potentially saving millions in interest."[359]

Magaziner's memo noted that there remained "a high-degree of uncertainty regarding several key variables that would impact the market's appetite and, ultimately, the cost associated with these bonds." "The numbers presented in this analysis," he cautioned, "should be considered baseline projections with a wide margin for error." The treasurer's analysis determined that "the single most important factor to make this transaction successful and cost effective" would be the size of the Tax Increment Zone and noted that the legislation was "not specific in this respect." Nevertheless, the approved Ballpark at Slater Mill legislation was on its way to the governor for her signature.[360]

Late in the afternoon of Friday, June 29, just hours before the legislation would have become law without her signature, the governor signed the ballpark bill. Raimondo issued a statement announcing her approval, adding that as she had said all along, "The PawSox belong in Pawtucket." No one, she declared, "wants to see them end up in Worcester." With a nod toward the law being ambiguous about a number of details, Raimondo was pleased that the bill gave Mayor Grebien "an opportunity to work with the team over the coming months to keep them here, and it gives Pawtucket a shot at meaningful economic revitalization."[361]

In a project in which time was of the essence, the governor's allusion to months of work for the PawSox and city translated into further delays before a deal was sealed. It is unlikely the team relished the uncertainty. Furthermore, at this juncture, the team had remained mute on its feelings about Mattiello's revisions. They were no doubt unhappy with the absence of the state's backstop, which could double the cost to the team. Rumors of Worcester continued to swirl. That city had not released the details of any proposal it may or may not have made to the PawSox. Team spokesman Bill Wanless did release a statement saying that the team and city had been meeting during the week since the General Assembly passed the bill. "Analysis and talks will continue over the holiday week," Wanless said.[362]

In Rhode Island, the first two weeks of July are special. When the state was the capital of the jewelry industry from the 1950s to the early 1970s, most factories and ancillary businesses closed shop while numerous workers enjoyed an annual vacation. The state celebrated the Fourth of July with deep-seated traditions, foremost among them the longest continuous Independence Day festivities in the country. In 2018, Bristol's Fourth of July Parade marked its 233rd anniversary, in a country that was only 242 years old. Many also looked forward to the standout fireworks at McCoy Stadium, which had become a more recent ritual. Meanwhile, the PawSox were weighing their options. Rhode Islanders anxiously waited to learn the fate of their iconic baseball franchise.

CHAPTER 7

Bad News on the Doorstep

GOOD INTENTIONS

Rhode Island's deal was on the table. It was the product of a long and painful process, but there it sat…signed, sealed, and delivered by the Rhode Island Senate, House of Representatives, and governor. The original proposal for a Ballpark at Slater Mill was hammered out by the Pawtucket Red Sox, the State of Rhode Island, and the City of Pawtucket in May 2017. It was submitted to the Senate Finance Committee in June, vetted by more than twenty-eight hours of public hearings in September and October, revised as a result of those hearings in December, presented as a sixty-seven-page report, approved by the Senate Finance Committee in January 2018, and passed by the full Senate a week later. It lingered for five months until June, when it was revised by the Speaker of the House, delivered to the House Finance Committee, reviewed by that committee, approved by the full House, reapproved by the full Senate, and signed into law by the governor in late June. All of this to enable further negotiations between a team and the city to build an $83 million modern retro ballpark to continue hosting a Triple-A team in a New England mill city long abandoned by the industries that once served as a source of its prosperity.

As June evolved into July, the PawSox held their cards close to their vest. The 2018 campaign was in full swing. If the team was going to move, some observers speculated that it would be prudent to wait until the end of the season before making an announcement. Such a delay would postpone alienating the locals while minimizing any associated loss in attendance. It did not make sense from another perspective, though. The team needed to make a decision soon, as its lease in Pawtucket was up after 2020. From the very beginning, the PawSox said they wanted to be in a new ballpark for the start of 2021.[363]

The discrepancy in urgency between the state and the team was evident in comments made on June 28, the day Governor Raimondo signed the bill into law. The governor sounded like passing the legislation was the first step in the process. One reason for the lack of urgency on the part of some Rhode Island leaders may have been their belief that the PawSox were only using Worcester, or other cities for that matter, as a bargaining chip. The team was not going anywhere. After all, three years earlier, it had threatened to leave if it did not get a stadium in Providence. Hadn't the PawSox reiterated they did not want to leave Rhode Island and preferred to stay in Pawtucket?[364]

Also, some state officials believed that other cities, including Worcester, were not really serious about ponying up for the team. Some thought Worcester itself did not believe the PawSox were serious about moving and would put forth a halfhearted effort. By making a move for the PawSox, they reasoned, Worcester was demonstrating it would pursue legitimate economic development opportunities when they surfaced, even though its leaders felt it had little chance of landing this prize. Such miscalculations proved costly.[365]

Worcester was indeed very serious. The PawSox patience was undoubtedly wearing thin. The team was becoming leerier of what might happen in Rhode Island, especially considering its firsthand experience with the state between May 2017 and June 2018, from the Senate Finance Committee hearings to the General Assembly approval. The PawSox had been talking with Worcester for months. Worcester officials kept the dialogue going even after Lucchino rebuffed them in 2016, honoring the team's exclusivity pledge to Pawtucket. It was well known that Lucchino had been visiting with officials there since December 2017, if not earlier. When Mattiello's revision finally surfaced, removing state backstopping and shifting the risk to investors, the cost of the deal to the team escalated. In the spring of 2018, there was a noticeable flurry of activity between the Central Massachusetts city and the team.[366]

One critical meeting reportedly took place on May 14 when team executives met with Worcester business leaders. The PawSox wanted to get a feel for the corporate support they could expect in Worcester. That was a strength in Rhode Island, and the team valued such relationships. The Worcester meeting, organized by City Manager Augustus, was very successful. The

PawSox reportedly were "stunned" by the city's response, especially since it had just a short lead time to prepare. According to one reporter covering the Worcester scene, PawSox management spent "an enormous amount of time" in the city following the May 14 meeting, and the two sides were in the process of "talking particulars from lease details down to plans to have the main pedestrian access to a new ballpark come in from Greene Street."[367]

The PawSox fell silent for the month of July. Activity resumed and rumors began swirling in early August. First, a report circulated that Minor League Baseball applied for a trademark to protect the word *WooSox*. Next, Lucchino watchers tracked him traveling back and forth between Pawtucket and Worcester, as well as to Boston, where he reportedly met with economic development folks in the Bay State. The following Monday, he was back at McCoy meeting with Grebien, and then, that same day, off to Worcester for meetings with Steinberg and Rea. He returned to McCoy on Wednesday for the team's noontime game. By Thursday, a notice in the PawSox clubhouse announced a team meeting for Friday, August 17, which was the same day Worcester officials had scheduled a press conference to break their silence on proposed PawSox negotiations.[368]

Despite ominous speculation to the contrary, Grebien remained confident. That evening he released a statement saying, "The PawSox leadership is currently weighing their options and the City of Pawtucket is as committed today to our partnership as we have ever been throughout this franchise's storied 42-year history in Pawtucket." He remained steadfast "that the Ballpark at Slater Mill, in Pawtucket, Rhode Island, and the superior Greater Providence metro area" was the only home for the PawSox future. The mayor said that he "was excited to get to work building this world class destination with our partners, the Pawtucket Red Sox."[369]

A Bolt of Lightning

By then, though, the PawSox had already made their decision. It was divulged to the world during the Worcester press conference on Friday, August 17, at 2:00 p.m. in the Lincoln Levi Chamber, on the third floor of the Worcester City Hall. Massachusetts officials, city leaders, and PawSox executives announced the deal to an overflow crowd. The team had signed a letter of intent to move the franchise to Worcester. The city agreed to build a publicly owned, $86 million to $90 million, ten-thousand-seat ballpark in the Kelley Square neighborhood of its transforming Canal District, a former industrial area that was already well on the path to rejuvenation. The stadium would contribute to the district's progress rather than serve as an economic development catalyst, which was its expected role in Pawtucket.[370]

The City of Worcester would borrow $100.8 million by floating two bond issues to finance the ballpark. The city would pay off $70.1 million on one set of bonds through new tax revenue, fees, and parking income generated in a special eighteen-acre tax district established around the ballpark. The team would pluck down $6 million up front and repay $30.2 million in rent over the thirty-year term of the lease. The State of Massachusetts would contribute $35 million to improve infrastructure around the site, including housing incentives, a parking garage, and roadwork. The state would move up the schedule for improving the malfunctioning Kelley Square intersection. Madison Development Holdings LLC would provide the land for the project, a six-acre lot between Madison and Green Streets. Madison Development also planned to build 225 market-rate apartments, a 150-room hotel, another boutique hotel, and 65,000 feet of retail space and restaurants to the tune of around $90 million. A second phase would include 200,000 square feet of residential, office, and mixed-use development.[371]

The city would own the ballpark. At least 135 events would take place there each year. The city would have the advantage of running as many as 8 revenue-generating events at the venue, along with 10 community-focused days. The stadium would incorporate conference and meeting space for civic activities, and the ballpark would also serve as a polling location on election days. Every student in Worcester would receive a free ticket to a game each season. Some would have the opportunity to play baseball games at the stadium. Plus, the team pledged to donate $25,000 in 2019 and 2020 to help fund Recreation Worcester programs. The new ballpark would generate more than five hundred full-time and two thousand temporary jobs, including construction. If all went according to plan, construction would begin in July 2019. Triple-A baseball would begin play in April 2021. The team planned on staying in Pawtucket, where it would play out its remaining eight home games in 2018 and full schedules in 2019 and 2020.[372]

Worcester mayor Joseph M. Petty, City Manager Augustus, and City Councilor Candy Mero-Carlson shared the spotlight. They were joined by Massachusetts lieutenant governor Karyn Polito and Madison Properties president Denis Dowdle. The city leaders emphasized that Worcester's success was the result of collaboration. "It was a team effort all the way around," Petty said, while reserving special gratitude for Augustus, who he said "worked relentlessly while leading a process that contained few bumps or bruises, few delays or abrasions." While no one anticipated any future issues, the deal needed approvals from the Worcester City Council, the International League, and Minor League Baseball. The stadium would be called Polar Park, after a local bottling company, and it was later announced that the team would assume the WooSox moniker.[373]

Lucchino represented the PawSox. He said the team signed the letter of intent "with pride." He recalled the phone call he received from Petty during the team's exclusivity period with Pawtucket. "No, thank you," Lucchino said, "we are committed to Rhode Island." Worcester persisted, and negotiations picked up shortly after the monogamous window closed without a deal. "You go where you are wanted," the team's CEO said he learned from his mother, "not where there is controversy and opposition." The people of Massachusetts "are happy that we are here."[374]

Lucchino heaped praise on one Rhode Islander. "I thank the Mayor of Pawtucket, Don Grebien," who was "a wonderful partner, an honorable public servant, and an heroic champion of his city." The PawSox wished Grebien well, Lucchino said, adding that the team would "remain supportive of his efforts to improve his city." And he thanked PawSox fans, "who have loyally supported this ballclub for decades." Lucchino and Grebien had forged a special relationship. Steinberg would later say Lucchino "liked and even loved the mayor of Pawtucket."[375]

Lucchino felt certain that the deal would obtain the necessary approvals. The team and the city kept the city council and league offices appraised of the plans, so the parties were hopeful. "But in baseball," Lucchino said, "we don't count the no-hitters in the seventh inning. We wait until the ninth." It was difficult for the team to give up on Pawtucket, Lucchino admitted, despite "the political disagreements [it] faced in Rhode Island." The PawSox had "allowed time for a Hail Mary to keep the doors open for Rhode Island," he elaborated. "Fifteen months ago, if that deal had been approved by the General Assembly, we'd probably be building a ballpark right there now."[376]

It was a bittersweet moment for PawSox vice-chairman Mike Tamburro. He grew up in Worcester and graduated from the city's North High School. When Ben Mondor purchased the team in 1977, Tamburro was the first person he hired. He was a major cog in what the team became and what it meant to the city and state. The only person to be awarded the International League Executive of the Year five times, Tamburro had been elected and enshrined into the PawSox Hall of Fame just three months previously. He was already a member of the International League (2012) and Rhode Island Heritage Halls of Fame (2016). For the past six years, he had worked hard to

On August 17, 2018, the State of Massachusetts, the City of Worcester, and PawSox leaders announced the team's intentions to move to Worcester. *Courtesy of the Pawtucket Red Sox.*

keep the team in Rhode Island. "Sadness—absolutely," he said of the move. "I have great pride for what Ben and I accomplished in Rhode Island," Tamburro continued. "It was wonderful. We were blessed. It's a great fan base." Nevertheless, Tamburro was somewhat excited for his native city. "Worcester worked hard to make this happen," he added. "They wanted this club for a generation. They waited their turn, and they took advantage when the opportunity presented itself." But he was sad that the team was leaving Pawtucket because "that ballpark, that community, meant so much to us for so many years."[377]

The news hit Rhode Island like a shock wave. Reaction was immediate. Governor Raimondo expressed her disappointment. "It didn't have to be this way," she lamented. "My administration had negotiated a deal with the team over a year ago that paid for itself." The governor acknowledged that Worcester's deal was better than Pawtucket's. It was more than Rhode Island could afford. She did not regret doing more to promote the ballpark legislation.[378]

Cranston mayor Allan Fung, her challenger in previous and upcoming gubernatorial elections (2014 and 2018), capitalized on the opportunity to criticize Raimondo in a prepared statement. "Sad Sox fans can only reach one conclusion as they watch their team this year," Fung wrote. "We need a change." The candidate continued, "The dysfunctional relationship between the Governor, Speaker, and Senate President, prevented any deal from ever happening and now families and local businesses are paying the price." Fung did not mention that he had opposed the bill.[379]

Speaker Mattiello questioned the loyalty of the team's ownership. "It is very unfortunate and extremely disappointing that the PawSox have decided to leave Rhode Island," Mattiello said. "The state's proposal contained strong protections for the taxpayers and shifted the risk to the investors," he contended. "It is disheartening the PawSox did not show the same loyalty to the City of Pawtucket and the State of Rhode Island as the taxpayers and fans have shown to them for many decades." He failed to mention the major role he played in delaying House consideration of the bill or the impact his revised legislation had on the deal.[380]

Stadium opponent and Mattiello's antagonist Steven Frias also issued a statement. He argued that voters should have decided the issue. "Instead of giving the voters the final say through a bond referendum," Frias wrote, "Speaker Mattiello tried to fool people on both sides of the PawSox debate with his last-minute, junk-bond stadium plan." Frias claimed, "Because Mattiello's deal would have cost the taxpayers and the owners even more money, it ended up pleasing no one."[381]

Former Rhode Island secretary of state Matt Brown, also an opponent of spending public money for a ballpark, decried the loss of a "cherished institution that has been a big part of life for so many of us." Brown said it was "disappointing, but not surprising, that Governor Raimondo is trying to shift the blame. But the fact is: this is what happens when we have a governor who is more focused on out-of-state fundraising than being here at home, working for the people of Rhode Island."[382]

Mayor Grebien took the high road in a statement he released to his constituents. "The PawSox do not make Pawtucket. Pawtucket made the PawSox." He continued, "The city I am proud and honored to represent is made great by our resilient community and, no matter what challenge we face, Pawtucket will continue to move forward toward an even brighter future." Grebien said he knew that many of his neighbors "in Pawtucket and throughout Rhode Island are struggling today with the sudden news of this treasured piece of the fabric of our community being ripped out of its rightful home," but "no matter what" the city "will pursue other innovative ways to invest in our quality of life, as a community and with our fellow Rhode Islanders." Pawtucket had "a strong history of persevering," he crowed, "and, together, we will forge ahead to a brighter tomorrow."[383]

The phrase *sudden news* was well chosen. The announcement from Worcester was unexpected in general, but in particular to Grebien. "Up until Thursday night," he wrote, "and for the last three years, the City of Pawtucket and the State of Rhode Island had been working with the PawSox to keep this treasured institution, and the jobs associated with it, here in Pawtucket where they belong." After nurturing a strong working relationship with the PawSox, the mayor was miffed that he didn't at least get a heads up. "Sadly, we had to learn through media reports, like everyone else, that the ownership group had decided to take our team and move it to Worcester in light of substantial subsidies provided by Worcester and the State of Massachusetts." (In fairness, the PawSox hand-delivered a letter to the mayor's office, but it did not reach Grebien until later.) He had no details on the deal but promised he would "take the weekend to digest the limited information that was released this afternoon." He committed to holding a press conference "early next week to provide further comments and thoughts."[384]

The man who Larry Lucchino called "honorable" remained so in the wake of the disappointing news. No blaming Governor Raimondo. No blaming Mattiello. No blaming the opponents of the stadium. Grebien was a different type of political leader. He had established a special relationship with Lucchino. If anyone had the right to be disappointed, it was Don Grebien.

OUTWORKED

During the announcement in Worcester, Lucchino made a point of recognizing a man in the crowd. It was Gene Zabinski, president of the Canal District Alliance. Zabinski, and his wife, Donna, hatched the idea of sending postcards to the PawSox in an attempt to charm the team into moving to Worcester. Zabinski was reared in the Canal District and starred on the 1964 St. Mary's High basketball team that won the New England championship. His boyhood home was torn down during the 1960s to make room for Interstate 290. While he no longer lived in Worcester, he had a strong desire to see his old neighborhood come back to life.[385]

The origins of the successful crusade dated back to a November 2015 meeting of the Canal District Alliance. The area of Worcester took its name from the Blackstone Canal, which opened in October 1825, linking Providence and Worcester. The organization resolved to "move forward in making contact with the PawSox, and make every effort to encourage them to meet with us and discuss a possible project." Then President Mullen Sawyer said, "We'd like to invite them to the crossroads of New England."[386]

The postcard campaign was intended to encourage the team's new owners to consider the Canal District. Donna Zabinski suggested a letter-writing effort to whet the team's appetite. Gene came up with postcards, thinking that most people would not take the time or effort to write letters. He had 5,000 cards printed, bundled them into packages of 50, and delivered them to alliance members to distribute. "I'll be lucky if I get a couple of hundred cards," Zabinski thought. By January 2016, Rea acknowledged that the team had received around 1,100 cards. "I haven't counted them, so I don't know exactly how many, but we've kept them all and have them stored away." The postcards proved so successful that Zabinski had to order 5,000 more. In the end, the PawSox reportedly received about 10,000 direct pleas to consider Worcester.[387]

A color photo of the existing Madison Street Stadium graced the cover of the card. In iconic Red Sox font, the words "Worcester Red Sox" were printed boldly in red immediately under the picture. The organization's name and website address identified where they originated. The PawSox mailing address was preprinted on the back, directing the cards to the team's post office box. The message was also preprinted: "Dear Mr. Lucchino, a Triple-A stadium in the Canal District on the Wyman-Gordan site in Worcester, MA, has my vote! Please give serious consideration." There were lines for the signature and address of the sender. The Zabinskis later trekked to McCoy Stadium, where upon introducing themselves, they were directed to Rea. The general manager introduced Zabinski to Steinberg, saying, "This is the guy who sent the postcards."[388]

For his part, Zabinski later said, "The postcards were just the kindling that started the fire." He deflected credit for bringing the PawSox to Worcester. There were others who stoked the flame, like Worcester firefighter Steve Mita. Upon learning that there was a possibility the team might consider his city for its future home, Mita mapped out how a stadium could fit into the Canal District. Lucchino became aware of Mita's work.[389]

The Canal District Alliance's pursuit of the PawSox may have been embryonic, but it made a lasting impression. Thousands of postcards have a way of doing that. They carried some weight even if they were stored away in the team's archives. But this was early 2016, and the PawSox were on the verge of granting Pawtucket its period of exclusivity. Looking back on those early entreaties, Lucchino felt that the team would remain in Rhode Island. "I believed we were staying in Pawtucket, and I believed we should stay in Pawtucket," Lucchino said. He admitted that he was "not treating Worcester seriously" at that time—or any other city, for that matter, and there were

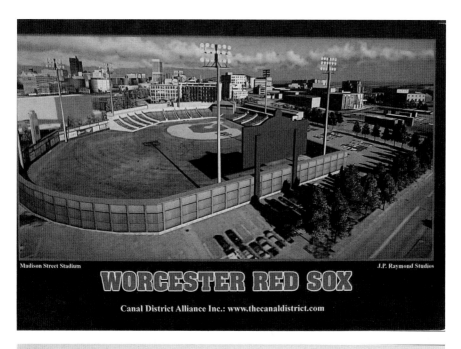

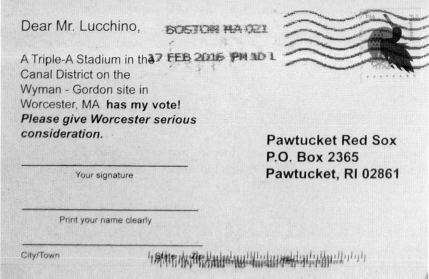

The PawSox received ten thousand postcards urging them to consider moving the team to Worcester's Canal District in a campaign devised by Gene and Donna Zabinski. *Courtesy of the Pawtucket Red Sox.*

indeed other suitors. In late 2016, Augustus dined with Lucchino and his wife at Toscano in Boston. Tim Murry, Worcester Regional Chamber of Commerce president; Robert Travaglini, a lobbyist; and Robert Bernard, Travaglini's former chief of staff, joined them. Travaglini was a former Massachusetts senator and president of the Massachusetts Senate. When the Worcester representatives expressed interest in the team, Lucchino rebuffed their offer. Lucchino was a man of his word, and he was sticking to his promise of exclusivity.[390]

Bringing the PawSox to Worcester was a grass-roots effort, Augustus observed. Lucchino said Worcester "outworked" Rhode Island. It was also an exercise in patience. In July 2017, immediately after the window of exclusivity closed on Pawtucket, Worcester was one of the first cities to let the PawSox know it was still interested. Over time, Lucchino began to consider Worcester as a possible challenger to Pawtucket, despite his inclinations to keep the team in its home of forty-five years. He would later say that his interest was a result of getting educated on Worcester and the redevelopment that was already happening in the Canal District.[391]

Both Lucchino and Augustus and their respective staffs deserve much credit for negotiating the deal that landed the team in Worcester. While ceding experience to the seasoned ballpark builder, Augustus, by all accounts, more than held his own. Mayor Petty urged the Worcester City Council to appoint Augustus city manager in January 2014. Augustus traveled a circuitous route to city hall. After graduating from St. John's High School and Suffolk University, the Worcester native was elected at age twenty-four to the city's School Committee. He subsequently became chief of staff for U.S. Congressman Jim McGovern before serving as a state senator for four years. He accepted the executive director position at the Children's Defense Fund of California, returning in 2010 to run McGovern's reelection bid. He then joined the College of Holy Cross as director of community relations. At first, the city manager post was only a nine-month arrangement, and Augustus fully expected to return to his job at the college. Instead, he signed on for three more years with the city.[392]

Recognizing that the city had gaps to fill, Augustus hired two consultants to help with the PawSox negotiations: Jeff Mullen, an attorney at the Foley Hoag law firm and a former Massachusetts secretary of transportation, and Andrew Zimbalist, the professor of economics and subject master expert Mattiello hired in 2015 to provide guidance during the Providence plan. Augustus did not want Worcester to be "extravagant" in its "enthusiasm for the project"—that might result in the city overreaching during the negotiations. He wanted the economist to temper the city's eagerness. "He knew baseball, which of course we didn't know."[393]

As negotiations dragged on, it became clear that Lucchino and Augustus shared a common vision. This long-term view helped keep the parties at the bargaining table. Augustus would later say that he and Lucchino "never had a harsh word" between them. Each could make strong points, the city manager explained, "but we always kept our relationship in a good place." Mayor Petty admired Augustus's perseverance. "He could have walked away several times and he didn't," Petty observed. "He knew this was important for Worcester and wanted to get it done." Zimbalist agreed with Petty's assessment that Augustus was effective in dealing with Lucchino. "If you're not on top of your game Larry will take advantage of you. Ed was at the top of his game." According to Jay Ash, the Massachusetts secretary of transportation and economic development, Augustus was "the single biggest reason why this thing happened for Worcester." He was most impressed with Augustus's ability "to keep Larry's interest in Worcester without giving away the store."[394]

A major reason Rhode Islanders were caught unaware by the August 17 announcement was because the Worcester dealings remained secretive. Augustus and his team went undercover. The city manager did not want the press seeing the negotiating teams at city hall or hearing they were there and "staking them out." Augustus wanted space to negotiate. He saw what had happened in Rhode Island "when there was no space, and [everyone] was reading into it or a leak would come out, it leaves you less room to figure things out." So, they moved around. They held meetings in Worcester at the American Antiquarian Society, Hanover Theater, Mechanics Hall, the Beechwood Hotel, and the chancellor of the UMass Medical Center's house. By doing so, Augustus reminisced, the Worcester team was able "to show off the depth and the contours of the city, the cultural assets, the cool, different neighborhoods of the city." The younger members of the negotiating teams would get together at night. They bonded at places in the Canal District along Green and Water Streets. They also held meetings in Pawtucket and overnight at Dan Rea's parents' home on Cape Cod.[395]

Toward the end, negotiations focused on costs. According to Augustus, Lucchino "wanted a budget big enough to build a great ballpark." A world-class Triple-A ballpark in a post-industrial city would be legacy achievements for both lead dealmakers. Augustus balanced the vision against what the city could afford. Lucchino wanted to be certain that the team received support from the Worcester business community. When Augustus organized the May 14 meeting to demonstrate that the community would back the team to the tune of $3 million in sponsorships, Lucchino could check off that box. Lucchino admitted that the team didn't get everything it wanted through the tense negotiations. "You have to give to get," he explained. "Both sides had to make some compromises."[396]

Disagreement persisted right up to the very end, including when to conclude negotiations and call it a deal. The city was ready to do so before the team. Lucchino said that deciding when to call it a deal was "one of the friction points." Augustus pushed Lucchino on the point. Augustus recognized that many constituencies needed to be satisfied: the team, the city, the state, a private developer and so on. All of the puzzle pieces had to fit. There was pressure to wrap things up. On Wednesday, August 15, Augustus ventured to Lucchino's Chestnut Hill home for dinner. He set the deadline for a decision. What followed, Lucchino said, was "a candid exchange of views…but we worked through it and we accepted the deadline the city was imposing." The PawSox went about scheduling a team meeting, while the city proceeded to schedule a press conference for the following day.[397]

At the Friday afternoon announcement in Worcester, lieutenant governor Karyn Polito summed it up. "Larry, you're a tough fish to catch, but we got you—and we're really happy about that." Months later, Augustus reflected on "what a big damn deal" it was for the city. He mused, "Long after I'm not in this role, long after I am not on this earth, probably, there's people that are going to go to that spot and have amazing memories with their families, amazing experiences, fall in love with the city, be proud of their city, and I had the opportunity to play a role in that."[398]

Augustus realized that everything was not always about economics. Community building also demanded enhancing the quality of life for its residents. Over time, an institution like the PawSox adds to the community's quality of life.

POLITICAL WILL

It takes political will to build a minor-league baseball park. Worcester civic leaders had a strong desire to bring the Triple-A team to their re-emerging Canal District. They believed that a brand-new, modern, urban ballpark would be a solid addition to their community. They nourished a consensus among state, municipal, and private proponents who became willing to stick their necks out and risk doing something worthwhile. Augustus was right when he said it was a big deal. Importantly, they were willing to pay for it.

The Worcester leaders reasoned that the new ballpark and its rebranded team complemented a broader vision, a renaissance that was already underway, with or without the PawSox. They were not just going to build a stadium in the middle of an urban frontier and hope it would spur additional development. This team was the top affiliate of the region's beloved Boston Red Sox—the same Boston club that sold out 820 straight home games at Fenway Park between May 2003 and April 2013. Worcester, like Pawtucket, was part of the heart and soul of Red Sox Nation. Worcester leaders waged an uphill battle to dislodge the team from its half-century home in Pawtucket, where it had endeared itself to several generations.

It was an upset of major proportions. Worcester's success rested on a foundation of cooperation. City leaders celebrated working together to achieve a common goal. The Canal District Alliance postcard campaign may have kicked it off, but it included the mayor, city manager, city council, city businesses leaders, and state leaders. Lucchino recognized the spirit and often highlighted it as a differentiator between the two contenders.

Rhode Island leaders did not want to lose their PawSox. That had been a common refrain for three and a half long years. They did, however, want to make sure the deal was a good one for the state's taxpayers. Economics became the dominant theme. Economics above all else. How much would the stadium cost? How much would each party contribute? How would the team, the state, or the city pay off its share of the bonds? What would happen if the team failed to draw enough fans? What would happen if the proposed development never panned out? What would happen if the project failed to generate sufficient taxes to support the stadium? How much would a new stadium contribute to urban redevelopment plans? Why should the state provide funds to wealthy team owners? What would happen, God forbid, if the state ended up with another 38 Studios on its hands? The focus was always on the liability side of the ledger.

There was little consideration from state leaders about the positive role institutions like the PawSox contribute to a community. Whenever non-economic benefits were raised, they were overwhelmed by potential financial risks. Institutions like the PawSox are assets. They provide affordable and alternative entertainment outlets. On seventy dates sprinkled throughout the spring and summer, cities with Triple-A franchises have one more option available to residents and visitors than cities that do not. They allow people to attend games featuring future stars on the way up to the major league or fading stars on the way down. Minor-league baseball teams are another small business in the community, providing income and work to neighbors and perhaps being the place where youngsters learn values and responsibilities on their first jobs.

Triple-A baseball provides the opportunity for shared experiences within families, among friends, and across generations. *Providence Journal* reporter Bill Koch summarized the sentiment at the conclusion of the lost 2020 season. "Government budgets and operating costs and tax breaks don't matter to a kid putting on a baseball glove for the first time. They're insignificant to someone with no backyard who casts a first glance on that spectacular green grass. A hot dog and some ice cream with your parents, your grandparents, your siblings, your friends—those moments are priceless."[399]

Local baseball teams can become a source of civic pride. Like the PawSox, teams can become tourist attractions in their own right. Triple-A teams frequently assume leadership roles in their communities—primarily because, by their very nature, they are highly visible institutions, but also because they become part of the fabric of the place. The good ones give back to their communities. The PawSox, for example, were highly regarded and recognized for their charitable contributions. Local professional ballplayers become role models, visiting schools to reinforce the importance of education, bringing encouragement to children in hospitals, holding instructional clinics to teach skills to aspiring youngsters, and more. All of which, of course, is very difficult—some would say impossible—to assign a value in a ledger book.

Political will requires vision, leadership, and advocacy. It demands actions as well as words. Don Grebien was a relentless promoter to keep the PawSox in Pawtucket. He worked tirelessly to strike a deal with the team for a Ballpark at Slater Mill and to encourage enabling legislation from the state. As did Senator William Conley Jr. But they needed help. And, unfortunately, Conley's hearings to vet a known entity like the PawSox delayed legislation between May 2017 and January 2018. Statewide office holders continually said they wanted to keep the team in Rhode Island but lacked the conviction and sense of urgency to step out front and lead the effort.

Case in point: In the early 1960s, Rhode Island Turnpike and Bridge Authority chairman Francis "Gerry" Dwyer and Governor John H. Chafee actively led the efforts to get the Newport Bridge approved despite persistent objections, particularly from the U.S. Navy and Jamestown town fathers, and built in the face of numerous obstacles. Governor Chafee was the proponent-in-chief. He was in favor of the bridge, always had been, and never wavered from his and Dwyer's vision. Rhode Island celebrated the fiftieth birthday of that iconic landmark on June 28, 2019. Just sixty-six days later, the Pawtucket Red Sox played their last home game at McCoy Stadium.

All that's Left to Linger On

Dirges in the Dark

From the moment the PawSox and Worcester announced they had signed a letter of agreement to move the team to Central Massachusetts, politicians, pundits, and interested citizens tried to make sense of the situation. Each storyteller seemed to have a different angle. As always, the truth was elusive. Fact and fiction intertwined. One thing was certain: by 2021, the beloved PawSox would join other long-lost bits of Rhode Island's cultural folklore on the dust heap of history, its memory invoked every now and then, particularly on special occasions—much like the Providence Reds hockey team, the Rhode Island Auditorium, Narragansett Park Race Track, the Outlet Company, Shepard's Department Store, Rocky Point Park, Crescent Park, Benny's, and so many others.

One of the more surreal events in Rhode Island took place just five days after the August 17 announcement when state and local leaders squeezed into an upstairs meeting room at historic Slater Mill to figure out what the future held for Pawtucket, as it was by then a foregone conclusion that the city would lose its Triple-A baseball team. Grebien, the optimistic mayor, could not disguise his dismay. "Let's be honest," he said, "we are still shocked and disappointed." Grebien acknowledged that many within the state were "struggling with the news of the loss of this treasured piece of our fabric that many of us took for granted. The city lost a rare opportunity." Grebien said that the city's only hope of retaining the team was during the period of exclusivity. "But," he observed, "the lingering of the cloud of 38 Studios threw a blanket over any attempt at a speedy resolution and that was why the process was so drawn out."[400]

The governor was somber but hopeful. "Friday was a sad day," Raimondo said. "Today we begin again." Raimondo made it seem as though Worcester simply outbid Pawtucket, sidestepping the actuality that Rhode Island fumbled away its opportunity. "The reality is that for whatever reason, Worcester has decided to offer an enormous subsidy to the team," she said. "It wouldn't have been responsible for us to try to compete with the offer that Worcester and Massachusetts have put in front of the team." Representative Carlos Tobon struck a third chord, saying that the House of Representatives should have acted with more urgency.[401]

Commerce Secretary Stefan Pryor looked to the future. The state was going to continue working with the city on two fronts: acquiring the Apex site and revisiting the McCoy feasibility studies. Raimondo was "confident" that "other excellent uses" would "give life to McCoy and provide affordable entertainment, sports and non-sports options." She added, "Let's make sure

Mayor Grebien and Governor Raimondo discuss the future of Pawtucket at Historic Slater Mill following the PawSox decision to move to Worcester. *Courtesy of Michael Salerno.*

the stadium is full." Neither Senate President Dominick Ruggerio nor House Speaker Nicholas Mattiello attended the event.[402]

Mattiello had a different bent. "A lot more people have been appreciative and thankful both within my district and outside of it and across Rhode Island that we listened to their will and did what they wanted us to do," he said at a ribbon cutting ceremony for a new casino in Tiverton. "Statewide," he added, "I think the tenor out there was that we love the PawSox and we'd love for them to stay but we do not want to guarantee that deal, so the outcome was to accomplish what the will of the people was at that time, and the outcome was what it was."[403]

Over the next few months, a series of events in Worcester triggered additional reflection in Rhode Island. One of those days was September 17, 2018, when the city officially welcomed the PawSox to what was now being heralded as the "Heart of the Commonwealth." It had all the hallmarks of a Lucchino/Steinberg production. During the day, blue bunting covered banners on city hall that seemed certain to be unveiled later that afternoon. The plaza of the Italianate landmark overlooking Common Park was an appropriate setting for speeches and celebration. Participants, wearing team jerseys emblazoned with "Worcester" across the front, made red-carpet entrances through a gauntlet of happy citizens.[404]

By the time the speeches began, Town Common was jammed. Banners were unfurled, the largest reading "Welcome to Worcester," with an image of the city's skyline in the background. In the month since the team and city announced their agreement, all of the pieces had come together. Every organization had subsequently approved the move, including Minor League Baseball, Major League Baseball, the International League, and the Worcester City Council, which voted 9-1 to approve financing for the ballpark. "It is now official," Lucchino declared. "You have chosen wisely," U.S. Representative Jim McGovern told team officials, adding, "Larry, you are family now." The largest cheers, however, were reserved for Augustus, who was becoming revered for luring the team.[405]

A number of former Red Sox legends and coaches attended the event. These included Sam Horn, Steve Lyons, Luis Tiant, Oil Can Boyd, Dwight Evans, Joe Morgan, Jerry Remy, Worcester native Rich Gedman, and Pedro Martinez. As usual, Pedro stole the show. He threw out a ceremonial first pitch to former catcher Gedman, who was stationed behind a home plate strategically placed on the red carpet. Martinez thanked Larry for choosing Worcester. "It is much closer to Boston," the special assistant to Lucchino and former ace said. "My trips are now a little shorter." In point of fact,

Pedro Martinez winds up to throw out a ceremonial first pitch during the "Welcome to Worcester" event at City Hall Plaza in September 2018. *Courtesy of the Pawtucket Red Sox.*

Worcester and Pawtucket are virtually equidistant from Boston. Lucchino was happy with the show, calling it a "great ceremony with a lot of spirit and energy." During his speech, Lucchino said that in his forty years in baseball, he had "never experienced as exciting, as warm, as sincere, as friendly a welcome as we have gotten from Worcester." Later that evening, the revelry continued in the Canal District as fireworks brightened the Central Massachusetts summer night.[406]

Another event occurred on July 11, 2019. That was the day the team and city broke ground for Polar Park. About one thousand people attended the ceremony at the corner of Washington and Plymouth Streets, the approximate location of the future left field foul pole. Mayor Joseph Petty called it "the day that our city once again will put its thumbprint on our nation's pastime." Augustus called the groundbreaking a milestone in the city's history: "Today is a special moment in Worcester's history—a line of demarcation separating Worcester before Polar Park and Worcester after Polar Park....Today we write the first words of a new chapter....This is the story of a new Worcester. Gone are the doubts, replaced by confidence."[407]

Lucchino, as always, reminded everyone how much work remained. "We have miles to go and dozens of problems to navigate, of course, but there is

Larry Lucchino and Lieutenant Governor Karyn Polito team up during the groundbreaking ceremony in July 2019. *Courtesy of the Pawtucket Red Sox.*

an experienced collaborating team working hard here," Lucchino said. "I hope you will see for yourself in the months ahead that such confidence in our experienced team is well-placed." He added, "We do not promise you a perfect ballpark, or a perfect overall project, or another eighth wonder of the world….What we do promise is a nice little ballpark, which we hope will be iconic, which will make you proud." After the speeches, each participant grabbed a red shovel and, in unison, tossed a spade-full of dirt over a mound of gravel.[408]

The groundbreaking ceremony had a different effect on Rhode Islanders. Columnist Mark Patinkin covered the event for the *Providence Journal*. "Were this a medieval tale of a great battle," he wrote, the gathering "would have marked more than the triumph of the kingdom of Worcester. It marked the disgraceful failure of our politicians to hold onto one of Rhode Island's crown jewels." The journalist "couldn't bear to stay for the actual shovel ceremony." He drove away "hearing waves of applause."[409]

A few days later, Armand Sabitoni, general secretary-treasurer of the Laborers' International Union of North America and New England regional manager, delivered an opinion piece to the *Providence Journal*. "The groundbreaking ceremony in Polar Park was another sad reminder of a commitment, loyalty, and history that once was but is no longer," the labor leader wrote. "It wasn't about you or me. It was about the history woven onto those PawSox jerseys." To Sabitoni, it was one more reminder that "while Massachusetts, and particularly Worcester, is open for business and swinging for the fences, Rhode Island once again remains waiting to suit up."[410]

Once again, Grebien took the high road. "The City of Pawtucket congratulates the Red Sox and the City of Worcester on their ceremonial groundbreaking," the mayor said. "The Red Sox were a great partner for Rhode Island for decades and their brand will be missed in this state."[411]

A Graceful Exit

Larry Lucchino told his executives that "people are often judged by their entrances and their exits." He wanted to leave Pawtucket with as much grace and appreciation as possible. The PawSox had grand plans for the final season at McCoy Stadium. Unfortunately, the coronavirus pandemic wiped out the team's final slate in Rhode Island. That did not stop the team from executing some of its plans without baseball games at McCoy Stadium, including special events for its fiftieth-anniversary celebration. The year 2020 marked the fiftieth year since the Double-A Red Sox affiliate moved to Pawtucket.[412]

Over time, the PawSox had become highly regarded as an organization for giving back to the community. In 1998, the team formalized its philanthropy by establishing the PawSox Foundation. Its major goal was "to use the power of PawSox Nation" to strengthen existing relationships, forge new community partnerships, and "improve the lives of children and adults across New England." The foundation focused on improving health, education, recreation, and social service programs in urban neighborhoods. It raised money through donations, special fundraising events, scoreboard messages, public address announcements, and 50/50 drawings. One of owner Ben Mondor's favorite traditions was providing members of the Boys and Girls Club of Pawtucket a chance to win trips to World Series games. Another longtime custom was scout sleepovers at McCoy. The team also donated baseball equipment to local organizations and awarded college scholarships to middle school students.[413]

In 2014, Minor League Baseball recognized the team's contributions by rewarding the franchise with the John Henry Moss Community Service Award. Beginning in 2013, Minor League Baseball began presenting the award to the club that "demonstrated an outstanding, ongoing commitment to charitable service and had exhibited support and leadership within its local community and the baseball industry throughout the season." The PawSox were the second organization to be so honored.[414]

At the time of the award, International League president Randy Mobley said, "The heart of the Pawtucket Red Sox is big enough to not only fill Rhode Island, but much of New England." He praised the organization for its "well-earned reputation for being a selfless regional treasure." Tamburro accepted the award at the Baseball Winter Meetings Banquet in San Diego. He elaborated on the team's philosophy: "The role of any successful franchise must be to help lift those in its community who are in need. The past four decades we have quietly tried to do our part." He added, "We take great pride in our ongoing efforts to enhance the quality of life within our community and for creating partnerships that have carried on for generations."[415]

As Rhode Islanders continued to grapple with the reality that only two seasons of Triple-A baseball remained at McCoy Stadium, PawSox executives planned the graceful exit Lucchino suggested. The team knew that its upcoming departure was going to have an adverse impact on its fans and wanted to ease their pain. The team wanted to express its "love and gratitude" for the support it had received over the past half century. Lucchino came up with a campaign called "50 Acts of Kindness," connecting the team's desire to celebrate fifty years in Pawtucket with its wish to say thank you to the people of Rhode Island.[416]

The PawSox had long understood that professional baseball clubs have the ability "to do a variety of small things that leave a big impression" on many people. "All good deeds, no matter how small, have the potential to affect more lives than one can imagine." Like hosting a bowling event in East Providence that provided a fun evening out for children and families while benefiting the Tomorrow Fund, an organization that helps children battling cancer. Or like players and staff pitching in to clean up a beach in Coventry. Or like serving guests at the Pawtucket Soup Kitchen, a stone's throw from McCoy Stadium.[417]

Many of the initiatives centered on education, which the PawSox long-valued as the vehicle for people to achieve their goals. For instance, in May 2019, the team spent time with the Family Literacy Center in Lincoln, and in June, it hosted the organization at McCoy. Also in May, the team partnered with the Rhode Island School for the Deaf in Providence, which led to a "Deaf Awareness Night" at McCoy where PawSox players wore jerseys that spelled out the team's name in sign language. Finally, the team pledged

$10,000 scholarships to eighth-grade students from Pawtucket, Central Falls, Providence, and Woonsocket. Plus, it granted $1,000 scholarships to two Smithfield High School seniors.[418]

Many of the Acts of Kindness supported youth baseball and softball. In 2019, team mascots Paws and Sox attended a number of Little League Opening Days. The PawSox Foundation provided scholarships to East Providence children so they could participate in Little League under the belief that "financial hardship should not hinder a child's ability to play ball." Later that summer, female PawSox front office members conducted a clinic for softball teams in Smithfield and encouraged them to consider careers in sports. The PawSox also visited senior centers in Lincoln and East Providence.[419]

The PawSox were "overwhelmed by the positive response" to the program. "From students, to families, to veterans, to first responders, the PawSox '50 Acts of Kindness' touched the lives of so many groups of people across Rhode Island." The team concluded it was so successful it continued the Acts in 2020.

THE LOST SEASON

One can only imagine what the final year at McCoy might have been like. Certainly, Lucchino, Steinberg, and Tamburro would have had a few special occasions up their sleeves. They understood pageantry, presentation, and publicity. But the worldwide coronavirus pandemic indefinitely delayed the season's opening. Then, on June 30, Minor League Baseball announced that it was canceling the entire 2020 season. Major League Baseball was not going to supply players, leaving teams to scratch out revenue the best they could. Some franchises had already implemented creative ways to survive. For example, the Pensacola Blue Wahoos and the Salem-Keizer Volcanos had turned their ballparks into bed-and-breakfast inns. Others had relied on farmers' markets, drive-in movie theaters, and anything else they could "dream up to get a few drops of revenue in an otherwise arid season."[420]

Minor League Baseball faced a number of challenges. The league shutdown made it easier for minor-league teams to plan events without worrying about game day scheduling for the remainder of the season. The unfortunate victims, however, were the players who were not on their team's player pool. Many hopefuls were not going to play baseball in 2020, interrupting their development, limiting their opportunities to showcase their skills, and curtailing their ability to earn a living beyond the $400 per week stipends many had been receiving since March. There was little doubt that 2020 would go down as the worst season for minor-league baseball since 1918, when the Spanish flu and World War I ravaged all but the International League's schedule.[421]

The announcement wiped out the PawSox's remaining thirty-one home dates at McCoy. While other minor-league baseball clubs could now focus on the 2021 season, the PawSox had two major concerns on their hands. The ballpark being built in Worcester was incurring coronavirus-related construction delays, and the farewell season in Pawtucket was now going to be game-less. Construction schedules could possibly be expedited, but a final season of a fifty-year-old state icon could never be replicated. The PawSox wanted to make 2020 a very special season at McCoy. Now they really needed to get creative. Steinberg was optimistic that the team would not disappoint. He acknowledged, "All of us recognize that the health, safety, and well-being of our players, fans, and entire community are paramount, but we will keep the faith." He added, "This may not be how the story ends."[422]

In late May, shortly after Governor Raimondo permitted outdoor gatherings of more than ten people, the PawSox brainstormed and came up with an event they called Dining on the Diamond. The team would offer on-field dining at McCoy Stadium on selected dates. For its first edition, the team planned to spread out twenty tables across the infield. The menu included typical ballpark food—hot dogs, hamburgers, French fries, and nachos—along with special meals of eggplant parmesan, barbecue platters, and "Grand Slam Hot Dogs" (bacon-wrapped hot dogs with pulled pork and mac 'n' cheese). The team publicized the concept on its website, along with the first two dates, June 5 and June 6. "Gentle ballpark music and photographs on the videoboard celebrating the 50th Anniversary of the PawSox will add to the pre-sunset ambiance," the announcement promised. The tables sold out in eighty-eight minutes. The team added a third outing for June 7, which also sold out in less than an hour and a half. During the first weekend, 162 people enjoyed a unique dining experience at the seventy-eight-year-old ballpark.[423]

Dining on the Diamond was an immediate success and received high praise. On June 9, with 800 families on a waiting list, the team announced it was expanding the program for the upcoming three weekends. They were also adding thirteen more tables for a total of thirty-three to honor the number of innings in the longest game. The new seating arrangement

In 2020, when the worldwide coronavirus wiped out the entire minor-league baseball schedule, the PawSox came up with Dining on the Diamond, the successful concept of using McCoy as an outdoor restaurant. *Courtesy of the Pawtucket Red Sox.*

extended across the outfield grass. The menu was broadened to include lobster rolls, chicken caprese, and steak tips. The team continued its creative table numbering scheme, christening each table with a name or event having special significance to the Red Sox. Table 9, for example, was adorned with a placard of Ted Williams. Table 8 honored Carl Yastrzemski, table 14 Jim Rice, table 26 Wade Boggs, and table 27 Carlton Fisk. Some of the tables recognized the importance of their specific location on the field, like "Table 2, Deep of First Base, where Dave Koza played in 'The Longest Game.'" Within twenty-four hours, fans reserved 400 tables. A waiting list for 1,000 more remained. By the end of August, the waiting list had ballooned to 3,700 groups.[424]

The event continued throughout the summer. McCoy Stadium had been selected for player training, but weekend evenings remained available for dinner. By the end of August, more than six thousand patrons had enjoyed a meal on McCoy Stadium's playing field. The program had become so successful it was being copied in ballparks across the land. The PawSox brought its special brand of the experience to another famous baseball park 1,175 miles away. Beginning the weekend of September 11–12, Dining on the Diamond debuted at the Field of Dreams in Dyersville, Iowa, made famous by the movie of the same name. It continued on subsequent weekends through October.[425]

The PawSox filled 2020 with other tributes to its fifty years in Pawtucket. The team created an audio documentary series of the team's ten most memorable games as determined by fan voting and counted them down on Sports Radio WEEI 103.7 FM. Beginning May 11, a new episode aired every Monday afternoon. The series, called *Solid Gold: Stories of the Best Games in PawSox History*, concluded with the number-one favorite, "The Longest Game."[426]

The final sendoff to the team began on Thursday, October 15, and ran through Sunday, October 18. The PawSox Foundation staged its first-ever Golf Classic at Pawtucket Country Club. The fundraiser sold out in advance. Dining on the Diamond returned to McCoy Stadium on Friday and Saturday evenings, with three seatings each night. On Saturday and Sunday, the team once again paid homage to the longest game in baseball history with "Grand Finale: A 33-Hour Marathon." The fun kicked off with a "Never Can Say Goodbye" tour where fans walked the warning track, received free PawSox gifts, chatted with mascots Paws and Sox, and reminisced about their times at McCoy. Saturday night was punctuated with a traditional "Scouts Sleepover," even though the temperatures dipped into the forties. Reveille sounded early Sunday morning when high school senior baseball and softball players, deprived of their final year of interscholastic baseball, showed up to take batting practice on a professional ballfield. Next, the Pawtucket Slaterettes, a forty-year-old girls' and women's organization that plays traditional hardball, took the field. A special Dining on the Diamond wrapped up the weekend, hosting Unity Fest, celebrating racial justice, equality, and the creation of the first African American charter school in New England.[427]

Despite some challenging weather, the team managed to hold its scheduled events that final weekend. "It was a chance to thank our fans, to have them come out to the ballpark one more time," said team spokesman Bill Wanless. "We are leaving, and we wanted to do it first class all the way with our heads held high, giving fans the best experience that we can." He continued, "That resonated through this season that never was, to do it right by everyone and not just mail it in." After a few last-minute chores—like holding a very successful virtual yard sale of jerseys, hats, and memorabilia—the team packed up the remainder of its belongings and memories and headed to Worcester. And with that, Rhode Island waved goodbye to a significant cultural artifact, leaving many in the state looking for an explanation.[428]

The Rhode Island Scene

Four days after the team selected Worcester over Pawtucket, an awkward *Providence Journal* editorial fingered the usual suspects for the villainy, including the PawSox owners, Governor Carcieri, Governor Raimondo, and Speaker Mattiello. The editorial ran under a picture taken at the Worcester press conference of Lucchino smiling and chatting with Polar Beverages president and CEO Paul D. Crowley Jr. From the very first phrase, it was clear that the editors were as disappointed as the team's most fervent fans. "It was a dark day for Rhode Island when the widow of legendary Pawtucket Red Sox owner Ben Mondor sold the franchise to a group of multimillionaire owners headed by Larry Lucchino." Despite the team's three-and-a-half-year effort to remain in the Ocean State, the editors portrayed the new owners as "abandoning the loyal fans who had made the PawSox one of the premier franchises of Triple-A baseball."[429]

The editorial board characterized the new owners as "stiff-arming Rhode Island," taking away "millions of dollars in tax revenues and charitable activities," and killing a plan "that would have helped revitalize Pawtucket, a city long down on its luck." The editors called it "a blow to the pride of Rhode Island" that "will do some damage to its quality of life," signaling, "once again, that the state is not up to snuff on economic development."[430]

The editorial writers summoned the ghosts of 38 Studios, calling it a "moronic decision by former Gov. Donald Carcieri and the legislature to back an incredibly risky investment." When it went bankrupt, the editors said, "the public soured on large-scale economic development projects, particularly anything associated with baseball." After the new owners "further poisoned the well" by initially demanding "taxpayers fund a new stadium in Providence" and "threatening to move the franchise elsewhere unless they got their way," the new PawSox owners and Raimondo's team crafted "an excellent deal for Rhode Island taxpayers, with the owners promising to put millions of dollars toward a new publicly owned stadium." But Raimondo failed to sell the plan to the state effectively."[431]

The editorial board claimed that the state's largest newspaper "spelled out, over and over, why the deal would benefit the public." After the "Senate passed a version of the plan, some negativity persisted," the editorial observed. "Speaker Mattiello refused to go along," the editors elaborated. "Burned by his initial support for the Providence idea, Mr. Mattiello feared defeat in this fall's election if he backed the Senate plan. Polling in his district showed strong opposition to a new ballpark." Instead, Mattiello "had the

House pass a plan to shift the risk from the state to private investors, which added millions of dollars to the cost of the project." But by that point, "the multimillionaires were fed up with Rhode Island. While the deal here kept getting worse, the deal in Worcester kept getting better."[432]

The editorial predicted that the "new stadium in Worcester will almost certainly be a smashing success for at least five to six years, and will doubtlessly generate significant economic activity for that city." Harboring deep parochial sentiments, the editorial board proclaimed, "Rhode Island is obviously a better baseball market—a separate state with a thriving capital city, a much stronger concentration of media, and a loyal fan base," which, the editors pointed out, "was painstakingly built up for decades by Mr. Mondor and his associate Mike Tamburro, good citizens in the community who treated customers like family." The editors pronounced, "The new owners have effectively destroyed their life's work." The piece concluded, "It is terribly sad that Rhode Island leaders could not get their act together to save this institution.[433]

In December 2020, the Pawtucket Red Sox relocated to Worcester. Polar Park was completed in time for Opening Day, May 11, 2021. The usual elements of a Steinberg Opening Day were front and center, including but not limited to banners unfurling, choreographed events with carefully selected musical accompaniments, a flyover, celebrity first pitchers, and a national anthem sung by James Taylor and his son Henry.

In Rhode Island, much has changed since August 17, 2018, the day the team announced its intentions to move to Worcester. In Providence, the acreage at P4 of the I-195 Redevelopment District remains a planned open-space park. That was where the Skeffington-led ownership team longed to build a stadium downtown, move the PawSox from Pawtucket, and rename the team the Rhode Island Red Sox. Whether the proposed ballpark would have been successful will forever remain unknown; however, it certainly would have changed the landscape of the city and potentially contributed to the revitalization of the former I-195 corridor.

In August 2019, the long-planned pedestrian bridge linking Providence's East Side to the Innovation District across the Providence River opened. It cost the state $21.9 million. The bridge has become an attraction in its own right. However, the price tag to the state for a 150-yard-long footbridge was roughly the same as the state would have floated in bonds to backstop an $83 million stadium for a fifty-year-old Rhode Island institution. And in contrast to the proposed Ballpark at Slater Mill, the bridge did not require twenty-eight hours of statewide public hearings.

Parcel P4 in Providence, where the new PawSox owners wanted to build a new baseball stadium, remains an open-space public park. *Photo by James Ricci.*

On December 2, 2019, Governor Raimondo and Mayor Grebien announced a $400 million Tidewater Landing project on one of the sites previously considered for a ballpark. As planned, the Fortuitus Partners–led Tidewater Landing Development would contain more than two hundred housing units and 100,000 square feet of retail, food and beverage, and other community space; an indoor sports event center; a 200-room hotel; and a 7,500-seat stadium that will house a USL Championship soccer team, expected to begin play in the 2022 season. The public financial commitment was announced to be 20 percent of the project, between $70 million and $90 million, with the state contributing $60 million to $80 million. The PawSox were seeking only $38 million in public funds.

The City of Pawtucket still does not own the Apex site, the targeted location for the Ballpark at Slater Mill. It was also included in Fortuitus Partner's plan for Tidewater Landing. The city continued to pursue avenues for obtaining the Apex site, including by eminent domain, but without it, the Tidewater Landing project was scaled back by about 25 percent in September 2020.

In November 2018, Governor Gina Raimondo won reelection over Republican opponent term-limited Cranston mayor Allan Fung, by a 12.6-point plurality. Independent candidate Joe Trillo, Donald J. Trump's

The new $22 million pedestrian bridge links South Water Street on the east side of the Providence River to Parcel P4 on the west, long designated as public open space. *Photo by James Ricci.*

state campaign director and former state representative from Warwick, added color to the contest but garnered a lowly 2.8 percent of the vote. During the campaign, Fung and Trillo faulted Raimondo for losing the PawSox. The incumbent claimed that she did her best to keep the team in Pawtucket and shifted the blame to the state's legislature for delaying for thirteen months the deal her administration had brokered. Other major campaign issues focused on the Raimondo administration's botched implementation of the $640 million public benefits computer system, causing long delays in processing food stamp benefits and Medicaid payments, and Fung's handling of a parking ticket scandal in the Cranston Police Department. In 2021, with two years remaining in her final term as governor, President Joe Biden selected Raimondo as U.S. secretary of commerce. On March 2, 2021, after a year of leading the state's effort to contain the coronavirus, she turned over the governor's office to Lieutenant Governor Dan McKee, before she could make good on her promise not to "rest until McCoy is filled."[434]

In 2018, Speaker of the House Nicholas Mattiello retained his District 15 seat by narrowly defeating persistent opponent Stephen Frias by 329 votes. The margin was more than the 85-vote victory Mattiello claimed over Frias in 2016, an election that turned on mail-in ballots and a recovered ballot box left behind at a precinct. Mattiello shouldered the blame for losing the PawSox, but Frias himself opposed any plan to use public funds to retain the team and advocated for putting the issue to a statewide referendum.

Democrat Mattiello was not so successful in his 2020 reelection bid. He was upended by Republican Barbara Ann Fenton-Fung, wife of Allan Fung, by a 17.6-point margin. It was the first time in more than one hundred years that a sitting Speaker failed to regain his seat. Mattiello campaigned on his ability as Speaker of the House to deliver for the city of Cranston, something a freshman representative could not. One of the many contributing factors to Mattiello's demise was a headline-producing, five-day bench trial days before the 2020 election. The proceedings shed light on alleged dirty tricks by the Speaker during his 2016 campaign. The defendant in that trial, Jeffrey Britt, maintained he was a fall guy for Mattiello and was exonerated six weeks after the November elections.[435]

Senator William Conley Jr. found himself on the wrong side of a controversial land acquisition and development project in his hometown of East Providence. The Senate Finance Committee chairman represented the company that purchased Metacomet Country Club from a group of owners led by professional golfer Brad Faxon. In April 2019, the private club, saddled with debt, confronted a declining membership. Faxon's ownership group, called the Metacomet Property Company, promised to continue operating Metacomet as a private golf course. In February 2020, ten months into their venture to restore the club to its previous glory, the new owners announced that they were selling Metacomet to Marshall Properties, whose intentions included turning the 105-acre club into a multi-use development.[436]

Metacomet Country Club is a Rhode Island institution in its own right. Nestled along a scenic Frederick Law Olmsted–designed parkway on the Providence River, Metacomet was designed by legendary golf course architect Donald Ross. It was home to some of the finest greens in the region and counted as members some of the state's more talented golfers. The proposed development ran into strong opposition from many fronts that coalesced into a powerful preservation group known as Keep Metacomet Green. Conley ended up representing an unpopular project against fierce, organized opposition from the people who once elected him. His opponent, Cynthia M. Mendes, was aligned with Keep Metacomet Green. In the September 2020 Democratic primary, Mendes buried Conley, winning 65 percent of the vote.

On July 29, 2020, former PawSox vice-president and general manager Lou Schwechheimer died from the coronavirus. He was sixty-two years old. Along with Ben Mondor and Mike Tamburro, Schwechheimer was the third leg of the Pawtucket Red Sox executive team that elevated the franchise from bankruptcy to state treasure during the late 1970s and early 1980s. He was a twenty-year-old college intern at the University of Massachusetts when he joined the PawSox in 1978, one year into the Mondor era. He remained a fixture with the team for thirty-seven years. Acting on a desire to own a team, Schwechheimer purchased controlling interest in the New Orleans Baby Cakes, a Triple-A franchise affiliated with the Florida Marlins. In 2020, the team was in the process of moving to a new ballpark in Wichita, Kansas, before the season was canceled.[437]

Schwechheimer won International League Executive of the Year in 1987 and 1992. He was selected to the International League Hall of Fame in 2019. Upon Schwechheimer's passing, Larry Lucchino said, "Minor League Baseball has lost a legend and a visionary." He added, "This deadly virus has robbed the baseball family of one of its most dedicated souls." To Tamburro, Schwechheimer's loss was "the saddest of news." "He was here morning, noon, and night, and there were nights when he even slept here," Tamburro marveled. "Every member of our business community, and tens of thousands of fans, knew him by name. He had remarkable interpersonal skills."[438]

In November 2018, Pawtucket citizens returned Mayor Don Grebien to his second-floor office at city hall for a fifth consecutive term. After Grebien ran unopposed in the previous three elections, David Norton stepped up to challenge the mayor. Norton, a Progressive Democrat, ran as an Independent with a "Hospitals Before Stadiums" campaign slogan. It was a clever way of reminding voters that Grebien had expended significant time and effort on economic issues at the expense of social issues. Norton claimed that Grebien "focused too much on trying to save a baseball team in an old mill city instead of preventing the local hospital from closing, at a cost of 1,200 jobs." Norton argued that Grebien lost an opportunity "to get in front of the TV cameras and fight for the hospital, which is more valuable socially and economically than a taxpayer-funded baseball stadium." He said the mayor had "no social objective policies."[439]

The down-to-earth incumbent defended his efforts to save the PawSox for the greater good. "I spent a lot of time on the PawSox because it was about revamping our downtown," Grebien explained. But that was not all he had been up to. Pawtucket city leaders worked "very aggressively" with state health officials to prevent Care New England from closing financially strapped Memorial Hospital. His team prevented the healthcare company from shuttering the building and was working to find another firm to run an emergency room and scaled-down hospital. He added, "I wish it was as easy as some people think it was."[440]

The mayor also touted other successes in his seven years at the helm, like turning the city around from the brink of economic collapse by reducing city staff, selling public buildings, and privatizing trash pickup. He was also proud of other city improvements, especially plans for a new MBTA rail stop and school renovations. "The quality of life here is improving," the mayor proclaimed. The voters of Pawtucket agreed. They reelected Grebien in a landslide, 70.7 percent to 28.6 percent.[441]

Two years later, Norton tried again, this time as a Democrat, by contesting Grebien in the September 2020 primary. The key issues in the campaign focused on what was going to happen to McCoy Stadium once the PawSox were gone, future plans for Memorial Hospital, the mixed-use Tidewater Landing development project, and the potential loss of toy manufacturer Hasbro Inc. Norton said he wanted to change the city's economic policies and economic strategies. The mayor stressed the importance of staying focused on Tidewater Landing, "the largest economic development project in our city's history," and the new Commuter Rail Station, as well as improving the city's schools. To Grebien, "Quality of life issues will always be a priority." Once again, Grebien easily defeated Norton, this time by 31 percentage points. He ran unopposed in the general election and secured the keys to his office for a sixth straight term. It is safe to say that the people of Pawtucket were satisfied with their mayor.[442]

Everything Solid Melts into Air

What once was is no longer. For the first time in fifty years, the city of Pawtucket lacks a professional baseball team. Without question, the remaining hole will be difficult, if not impossible, to fill. Whether by their own volition or not, most of the people involved in the PawSox departure had relinquished the spotlight well before Opening Day at Worcester's Polar Park. Leaders make decisions that affect the future of their state, city, or neighborhood and are long gone by the time the consequences of their actions begin to manifest. New leaders with new agendas have surfaced without ties to 38 Studios, the Providence Ballpark Plan, or the Ballpark at Slater Mill. They have other, more urgent issues to resolve.

Cars continue to snake their way on I-95 through Pawtucket. There is no shining new ballpark, no welcoming gateway—just the same Apex

Bill Wanless and Mike Tamburro on their final walk at McCoy Stadium, March 2021. *Courtesy of the Pawtucket Red Sox.*

building, standing sentinel over a long-ago once-vibrant New England mill town. Despite all the drama, McCoy Stadium remains empty, nestled in its neighborhood awaiting its fate.

This outcome might have been different. A number of ingredients were missing in Rhode Island that were evident in Worcester. Rhode

Island leaders lacked resolve. Many in the state believed that the PawSox were bluffing. State leaders were not on the same page. Cooperation was missing. Some reports claimed that the governor, Speaker, mayor, and team executives never sat down together to hammer out a deal. The governor professed she did not want the team to leave but expended little effort to sway public sentiment. Members of the Senate did not push for swift action. Members of the House of Representatives did not push the Speaker to act. When the House finally voted, it rubber-stamped a proposal submitted by the Speaker. The Senate, painted into a corner, voted to pass the Speaker's revised legislation knowing it was unpalatable to the PawSox owners.

Other issues clouded the proposed deal. Local developers did not step forward with concrete plans to breathe new life into Pawtucket. Rather, Rhode Island looked for the proposed stadium to spur redevelopment. There were no significant grass-roots uprisings to keep the PawSox in Rhode Island. Its citizens did not send ten thousand postcards to the team expressing their commitment, saying, "Please don't leave." They did not successfully pressure their governor or legislators to act more urgently. They did not fill McCoy's stands to convince the team that Pawtucket was a superior baseball town

Polar Park nears completion in time for the Worcester Red Sox home opener, May 11, 2021 *Courtesy of the Pawtucket Red Sox.*

the team couldn't afford to leave behind—or, perhaps, to demonstrate that maybe the stadium wasn't really the problem at all.

In the end, the departure of the PawSox can be viewed as the inability of proponents in the state to persuade detractors and fence sitters of the associated benefits of building a new stadium and retaining the team. What should have been a reasonably easy decision to support an institution with roots in the community dating back a half century became victim to the painful memory of an ill-advised deal to incentivize a Massachusetts-based computer game development company to relocate to Rhode Island; to the missteps of an overly aggressive new ownership group to move the team from one city to another; and to the insistence—at the last minute—of the state's most powerful elected official to alter the terms of a deeply vetted deal. Aside from Pawtucket mayor Grebien, the state lacked proponents with sufficient political capital, savvy, and wherewithal to marshal the proposal to a successful conclusion.

The Pawtucket Red Sox have gone to Worcester, leaving generations of Rhode Islanders with treasure chests of memories and the reaffirmation that not all stories have happy endings.

Photo by James Ricci.

Notes

*T*he actions detailed in this book were covered extensively by a number of dedicated journalists from local media outlets. Foremost among them were Kate Bramson, Paul Grimaldi, Katherine Gregg, Patrick Anderson, Bill Koch, and Mark Patinkin of the *Providence Journal*; Brendan McGair and Jonathan Bissonnette of the *Pawtucket Times*; and Mary MacDonald of the *Providence Business News*. You will find their names copiously sprinkled throughout the endnotes. In the earlier articles, the date included for each entry is the day the story ran in the printed newspaper. At some point along the way, as digital media gained popularity, the dates in the notes shift to the day the article was filed. In many instances, the headlines of the digital stories differ from the print versions. To preserve space, I have omitted the digital link and access date. Each newspaper is accessible by its web address (for example, www.providencejournal.com or www.pawtuckettimes.com). Endnotes are included at the end of paragraphs pointing to the source(s) that informed each paragraph and/or from which quotations derive. I have used a semicolon to separate multiple entries in a note.

Prologue

1. "PawSox 5, Iron Pigs 4, 10 Innings: Sturgeon's Three Homers Give Pawtucket Season-Ending Win," *Providence Journal*, September 2, 2019.
2. See David Borges, *The Pawtucket Red Sox* (Charleston, SC: Arcadia Publishing, 2002); Minor League Baseball, "Pawtucket Red Sox," milb.com/pawtucket.

3. Borges, *Pawtucket Red Sox*.

4. Ibid.

5. Ibid.

6. Dan Barry, "A City Braces for Its Ballpark to Go the Way of Its Mills," *New York Times*, February 24, 2015; Larry Kessler, "Tireless Tamburro Inducted into PawSox Hall of Fame," Minor League Baseball, May 29, 2018, milb.com.

7. Peter Abraham, "Ben Mondor, 85; Owner Revitalized R.I.'s Red Sox," *Boston Globe*, Obituaries, October 5, 2010.

8. "Talking PawSox," Kimball Crossley interview with Ben Mondor and Mike Tamburro, YouTube, https://www.youtube.com/watch?v=Pvx75VvCe9w.

9. Ibid.

10. Ibid.

11. "Pawtucket Red Sox Owner Ben Mondor Looks Back at His Career," WPRI, October 4, 2010, YouTube, https://www.youtube.com/watch?v=jEY6nSrrzHw.

12. *Solid Gold: Stories of the Best Games in PawSox History*, "Game #1—April 18, 1981; The Longest Game (Part 1)," presented by Cox Communications and WEEI 103.7 FM, 2020. Note: For a comprehensive account of baseball's longest game, see Dan Barry, *Bottom of the 33rd: Hope, Redemption, and Baseball's Longest Game* (New York: Harper Perennial, 2012).

13. J.M. Murphy, "The Longest Game in Baseball History, Pawtucket vs. Rochester, April 18 & 19, and June 23, 1981," unpublished, 1991; Art Martone, "Morgan, Boggs, and Others Commemorate Baseball's Longest Game," *Providence Journal*, June 23, 2006.

14. Brendan McGair, "Wonderful Memories: Looking Back at the PawSox Era at McCoy Stadium," *Pawtucket Times*, September 20, 2020; Benjamin Hill, "Revisiting Baseball's Longest Game," Minor League Baseball, June 24, 2011, milb.com.

15. *Solid Gold: Stories of the Best Games in PawSox History*, "Game #3—July 1, 1982; Fidrych and Righetti Duel at McCoy."

16. Ibid. Note: This was only the second time a rookie pitcher started the All-Star Game. The first was in 1961, when Westerly, Rhode Island's Dave Stenhouse started for the American League.

17. Ibid.

18. Ibid.

19. *Solid Gold: Stories of the Best Games in PawSox History*, "Game #4—September 13, 1984; Pawtucket Captures Governor's Cup Title."

20. See year-by-year statistics for the Pawtucket Red Sox on Stats Crew, https://www.statscrew.com/minorbaseball/roster/t-ps13687; McGair, "Wonderful Memories."

21. *Solid Gold: Stories of the Best Games in PawSox History*, "Game #10—April 14, 1999; Opening of Remodeled McCoy."

22. Ibid.

23. McGair, "Wonderful Memories."

24. Ibid.

25. Ibid.

26. "Ben Mondor, Longtime Owner of Pawtucket Red Sox, Dies," *Providence Journal*, October 5, 2010; Jim Donaldson, "Mondor's Help Reached Beyond McCoy," *Providence Journal*, October 21, 2010.

Chapter 1

27. Leigh Montville, *The Big Bam: The Life and Times of Babe Ruth* (Boston, MA: Random House, 2006), 161–64; Dan Shaughnessy, *The Curse of the Bambino* (New York: Dutton, 1990), 7–8.

28. Dan Shaughnessy, "Pedro Martinez Invokes Babe Ruth After Beating Yankees," *Boston Globe*, May 31, 2001.

29. For an excellent account of the Boston Red Sox, including the 2003 and 2004 seasons, see Seth Mnookin, *Feeding the Monster: How Money, Smarts, and Nerves Took a Team to the Top* (New York: Simon & Schuster, 2006). One of the best ways to understand the intensity, excitement, and drama of the 2003 and 2004 American League Championship Series between the Boston Red Sox and the New York Yankees is to watch the games or game highlights. They are available via YouTube and can be accessed by Googling "2003 ALCS" or "2004 ALCS." The 2004 World Series can be found in the same manner.

30. Game 5 started at 5:11 p.m. and lasted five hours and forty-nine minutes.

31. Ryan Fagan, "The Eight Best Pitchers Who Didn't Win a Cy Young Award," Sporting News, November 18, 2015, www.sportingnews.com.

Chapter 2

32. E-mail from Tim Gray, Tim Gray Media Inc., to Kattie Leighton, Leighton Communications Inc., December 18, 2009; Ted Nesi, "E-mail, Schilling Invited RI Leaders to Infamous Fundraiser," WPRI, October

2015, https://www.wpri.com/news/email-schilling-invited-ri-leaders-to-infamous-fundraiser.

33. Rhode Island Department of Labor and Training, "Media Advisory," March 19, 2010. Also see Leonard Lardaro, "Rhode Island Unemployment," *Communities and Banking (Federal Reserve Bank of Boston)*, Fall 2010, https://www.bostonfed.org/home/publications/communities-and-banking/2010/fall-2010.aspx.

34. See Ballotpedia, "Donald Carcieri," https://ballotpedia.org/Donald_Carcieri; Donald Carcieri for Governor website, www.carcieirforgovernor.com.

35. Donald Carcieri for Governor; Thomas S. Mulligan, "Governor Praised for His Handling of Crises," *Los Angeles Times*, February 24, 2003, https://www.latimes.com/archives/la-xpm-2003-feb-24-na-carcieri24-story.html.

36. Donald Carcieri for Governor.

37. Mulligan, "Governor Praised for His Handling of Crises."

38. Donald L. Carcieri, State of the State Address, January 26, 2010, State of Rhode Island and Providence Plantations, *Journal of the Senate* 137, no. 9, Ninth Legislative Day (January 26 and January 27, 2010).

39. Ibid.

40. See Matt Bai, "Thrown for a Curve in Rhode Island," *New York Times*, April 20, 2013.

41. State of Rhode Island General Assembly, "Document 04 2014-07-24 Corso Exhibit D-131," http://www.rilin.state.ri.us/Special/House%20Oversight/Forms/AllItems.aspx. Note: All subsequent "documents" from this source will omit the repetitive website address.

42. Ibid.

43. State of Rhode Island General Assembly, "Document 07 2013-11-05 Stolzman Depo Exh 034"; State of Rhode Island General Assembly, "Document 05 2014-07-24 Corso Exhibit D-135."

44. State of Rhode Island General Assembly, "Document 07 2013-11-05 Stolzman Depo Exh 034."

45. Paul Grimaldi, "38 Studios Documents—Loan Deal Had Secret Start," *Providence Journal*, September 25, 2015.

46. Bai, "Thrown for a Curve in Rhode Island"; Grimaldi, "Loan Deal Had Secret Start"; Andrew Stewart, "38 Studios Document Release: Murphy's Deposition," Rhode Island Future, September 25, 2015, www.rifuture.org.

47. Bai, "Thrown for a Curve in Rhode Island"; Tom Mooney and Katherine Gregg, "How an Extra $75M Made Its Way into 2010 Jobs Bill," *Providence Journal*, September 25, 2015; Grimaldi, "Loan Deal Had Secret Start."

48. Grimaldi, "Loan Deal Had Secret Start"; State of Rhode Island General Assembly, "Document 13 2014-07-22 Costantino Exhibit 625"; State of Rhode Island General Assembly, "Document 14 2013-11-05 Stolzman Depo Exh 046."

49. Rhode Island Economic Development Corporation, Meeting of Directors, Public Session, Meeting Minutes, June 14, 2010.

50. Strategy Analytics in Association with Perimeter Partners, "Evaluating a Video Game Cluster in Rhode Island," PowerPoint Presentation to RIEDC Board, June 14, 2010.

51. Ibid. Note: In 2012, the Providence/Fall River/New Bedford Statistical Metropolitan Region ranked 91 out of 100 in *American City Business Journal*'s ranking of best cities in which to start a new business. The same year, *Forbes* magazine ranked the area 178 out of 200 among "Best Places for Business and Careers." In its 2012 "Top States for Doing Business," Rhode Island finished on the bottom of overall business climate. And *Chief Executive Magazine* concurred, ranking Rhode Island 39th of "Best/Worst States for Business" that same year. Also, in late 2008, Carcieri had selected Al Verrecchia, CEO of Hasbro Inc., to lead a review of the EDC. The report, released in 2009, pointed out significant deficiencies in Rhode Island's economic-development efforts, with the EDC calling the agency "fragmented, disjointed and without focus." See Kate Bramson, "Verrecchia Said He Relied Entirely on EDC Staff to Report on 38 Studios Finances," *Providence Journal*, September 25, 2015.

52. Wells Fargo Securities, "38 Studios: Rhode Island Economic Development Corp. ("RIEDC") Discussion Materials—Interactive Entertainment Industry Overview," June 14, 2020.

53. Ibid.

54. Rhode Island Economic Development Corporation, Meeting of Directors, Public Session, Meeting Minutes, June 14, 2010.

55. Ibid.

56. Ibid.

57. Ibid.; see also State of Rhode Island, Superior Court, *Rhode Island Economic Development Corporation v. Wells Fargo Securities, LLC; Barclays Capital, PLC; First Southwest Company; Starr Indemnity and Liability Company; Curt Schilling; Thomas Zaccagnino; Richard Webster; Jennifer MacLean; Robert I. Stolzman; Adler Pollack & Sheehan P.C.; Moses Alfonso Ryan Ltd.; Antonio Alfonso, Jr.; Keith Stokes; and J. Michael Saul*, Max Wistow, Esq., Wistow & Barylick Inc., Providence, Rhode Island, November 1, 2012.

58. Ibid.

59. Ibid.
60. State of Rhode Island General Assembly, "Document 29 2014-06-12 Della Rocca Exhibit 367."
61. Ibid.
62. Ibid.
63. State of Rhode Island General Assembly, "Document 30 Esten D 117 and Della Rocca Depo."
64. State of Rhode Island General Assembly, "Document 43 2014-05-23 Gallogly Exhibit D-12."
65. Edward Fitzpatrick, "Some Tried to Stop the 38 Studios Train Before It Derailed," *Providence Journal*, September 27, 2015.
66. State of Rhode Island General Assembly, "Document 45 2013-12-04 Stolzman Exhibit 103,"
67. Ibid.; Michael W. Chippendale, "38 Studios: The Deal that Could Have Saved Rhode Island…Twice," PowerPoint presentation, 2014.
68. State of Rhode Island General Assembly, "Document 38 2014-06-18 Zaccagnino Exhibit 376."
69. State of Rhode Island General Assembly, "Document 36 2013-11-19 Alfonso Depo Exh 061."
70. Ibid.
71. Ibid.
72. Rhode Island Economic Development Corporation, "Executive Session Briefing: Video Game Industry & 38 Studios Opportunity," PowerPoint presentation, RIEDC Board Meeting, July 15, 2010.
73. Ibid.; *Rhode Island Economic Development Corporation v. Wells Fargo Securities et al.*
74. Rhode Island Economic Development Corporation, "Executive Session Briefing."
75. Ibid.; *Rhode Island Economic Development Corporation v. Wells Fargo Securities et al.*
76. Rhode Island Economic Development Corporation, Executive Session Briefing.
77. Bai, "Thrown for a Curve in Rhode Island."
78. Chippendale, "38 Studios."
79. Molly Ball, "Why Did Lincoln Chafee Even Run?" *The Atlantic* (October 23, 2015), https://www.theatlantic.com/politics/archive/2015/10/lincoln-chafee-2016/412141.
80. Ibid.
81. Ibid.
82. GoLocalProv, "Gov. Lincoln Chafee's 38 Studios Deposition and Exhibits," September 24, 2015, https://www.golocalprov.com/news/gov.-lincoln-chafees-38-studios-deposition-and-exhibits.

83. Ibid.

84. Ibid.

85. Bai, "Thrown for a Curve in Rhode Island."

86. Ibid.

87. Ibid.

88. GoLocalProv, "Gov. Lincoln Chafee's 38 Studios Deposition and Exhibits."

89. Bai, "Thrown for a Curve in Rhode Island."

90. Ibid.

91. Ibid.; Jason Schwartz, "End Game: Curt Schilling and the Destruction of 38 Studios," *Boston*, July 23, 2012.

92. Chippendale, "38 Studios"; "Timeline of Events Preceding, After 38 Studios Deal," *Providence Journal*, September 24, 2015, updated July 30, 2016.

93. Ibid.

94. Curt Schilling, "Inept Chafee Helped Doom 38 Studios (opinion)," *Providence Journal*, October 16, 2016.

95. Ibid.

96. *Rhode Island Economic Development Corporation v. Wells Fargo Securities et al.*, 2.

97. GoLocalProv, "Top Attorney Wistow Urged Criminal Charges Be Levied on 38 Studios, but AG and RISP Did Not Pursue," June 8, 2017, https://www.golocalprov.com/news/top-attorney-wistow-urged-criminal-charges-be-levied-on-38-studios; Kate Bramson, "38 Studios: The Cost to R.I. Taxpayers," *Providence Journal*, September 26, 2016; GoLocalProv News Team and Kate Nagle, "Last Defendant in 38 Studios Settles—After Legal Fees, RI Secures $49M," February 2, 2017, https://www.golocalprov.com/news/new-last-defendant-in-38-studios-settles-after-legal-fees-ri-secures-49m.

Chapter 3

98. Samuel A. Coren, "Interface:Providence and the Populist Roots of a Downtown Revival," *Journal of Planning History* 16, no. 1 (2017): 6.

99. Vincent "Buddy" Cianci Jr., with David Fisher, *Pasta and Politics: How I Prosecuted Mobsters, Rebuilt a Dying City, Dined with Sinatra, Spent Five Years in a Federally Funded Gated Community, and Lived to Tell the Tale* (New York: Thomas Dunne Books, 2001), 2.

100. Coren, "Interface:Providence," 3–23.

101. Jay Farbstein, Emily Axelrod, Robert Shibley, and Richard Wener, Chapter 4, "Providence River Relocation, Providence, Rhode Island," in *Creative*

Community Building: 2003 Rudy Bruner Award for Urban Excellence (Cambridge, MA: Bruner Foundation, 2004), https://www.rudybruneraward.org/wpcontent/uploads/2016/08/06_providence.pdf.

102. Ibid.

103. Boston Roads, "East Providence Expressway: Historic Overview," http://www.bostonroads.com/roads/I-195_RI.

104. Kip Fry, "$450M Relocation of I-195 Revs Up in Providence, RI," *Construction Equipment News*, Northeast Edition, November 5, 2002; Elizabeth Abbott, "Removing a Barrier," *New York Times*, November 10, 2010.

105. Stephen Beale, "Is Rhode Island Squandering Its Opportunity to Redevelop I-195," GoLocalProv, January 16, 2014, https://www.golocalprov.com/news/is-rhide-island-squandering-its-opportunity-to-redevelop-i-195.

106. CKS Architecture and Urban Design, "Rhode Island Interstate 195 Surplus Land: Redevelopment and Marketing Analysis," RI Economic Development Council, September 2009.

107. Ibid.

108. Alex Speier, "Pawtucket Red Sox Sold; Group Eyes Providence," *Boston Globe*, February 23. 2015.

109. Ibid.

110. Ibid.

111. Barry, "City Braces for Its Ballpark."

112. Speier, "Pawtucket Red Sox Sold; Group Eyes Providence"; Richard Sandomi, "Rhode Island City May Lose Its Red Sox and, Mayor Says, Its Heart," *New York Times*, February 23, 2015.

113. Matthew J. Smith, "The Real McCoy in the Bloodless Revolution of 1935," *Rhode Island History* 32, no. 3 (Summer 1983): 67–86.

114. Ibid.; Barry, "City Braces for Its Ballpark"; Barry, *Bottom of the 33rd*.

115. Barry, *Bottom of the 33rd*.

116. Barry, "City Braces for Its Ballpark."

117. Kate Bramson, "Owners Seek State Payments, Tax Relief," *Providence Journal*, April 16, 2015; Kevin Reichard, "New Providence Ballpark Renderings Unveiled," *Minor-League Baseball News*, April 15, 2015.

118. Bramson, "Owners Seek State Payments."

119. Kate Bramson, "PawSox Owners Want State Lease, 30 Years of Property Tax Abatements for Providence Stadium," April 15, 2015; Amy Anthony, "New PawSox Owners Seek Stadium in Downtown Providence," *Morning Call* (Lehigh Valley, PA), April 16, 2015; John Kostrzewa, "PawSox

Stadium Pitch Looks Good, but It Doesn't Go Deep," *Providence Journal*, April 20, 2015.

120. Kostrzewa, "PawSox Stadium Pitch Looks Good."

121. Ibid.

122. Kevin Reichard, "Lawmaker: Voters Should Decide on New Providence Stadium," *Minor League Baseball News*, March 26, 2015; Cassius Shuman, "Filippi Questions Tax Deal for PawSox Owners," *Block Island Times*, April 24, 2015; GoLocalProv, "Bill to Require Voter Approval for PawSox Stadium in House Finance," June 6, 2015.

123. Kate Bramson, "Pawtucket Red Sox—New Owner Outlines Field of Dreams," *Providence Journal*, April 3, 2015.

124. GoLocalProv, "PawSox Owners Combined World Rank as 10th Richest Owner in Sports," June 29, 2017.

125. Paul Grimaldi, "Pawtucket Red Sox—Ballpark Proposal Could Hit Roadblock at Federal Level—Federal Land Plan May Present Roadblock to PawSox Ballpark Proposal," *Providence Journal*, March 3, 2015; Paul Grimaldi, "I-195 Commission Looks for Alternative to Park Restrictions," *Providence Journal*, August 28, 2015; Paul Grimaldi and Kate Bramson, "Federal Agency Insists on Reimbursement if Park Land Used for PawSox Stadium," *Providence Journal*, August 28, 2015; Associated Press, "Feds: Land Eyed for R.I. Stadium Must Be Sold for Market Value," *Lowell Sun*, August 30, 2015; David Brusart, "Dr. Downtown: The Red Sox and the PawSox," GoLocalProv, March 2, 2015.

126. Neil DeMuse and Joanna Cagan, *Field of Schemes: How the Great Stadium Swindle Turns Public Money into Private Profit* (Lincoln, NE: University of Lincoln Press, 2008).

127. Paul Grimaldi, "Proposed PawSox Stadium's Value Can Be Difficult to Measure," *Providence Journal*, April 16, 2015: Kostrzewa, "PawSox Stadium Pitch Looks Good, but It Doesn't Go Deep."

128. Ibid.

129. Grimaldi, "Proposed Paw Sox Stadium's Value Can Be Difficult to Measure."

130. Ibid.

131. Katherine Gregg, "R.I. House Hires Consultant to Analyze PawSox Stadium Plan," *Providence Journal*, May 5, 2015; Kevin Reichard, "RI Brings in Zimbalist to Consult on Ballpark Funding," *Ballpark Digest*, May 5, 2015.

132. Kevin Reichard, "RI Gov: Providence Ballpark Deal Alive," *Ballpark Digest*, May 6, 2015.

133. Katherine Gregg, "Consultant Tells Mattiello PawSox Stadium Request 'Not Outlandish,' Offers Options," *Providence Journal*, May 9, 2015.

134. Above section from "Obituary of James J. Skeffington, Sr.," J F Skeffington Funeral Home, May 17, 2015, https://skeffingtonfuneralhome.com/obituaries/obit_view.php?id=90; "PawSox Owner James Skeffington Dies," *Providence Journal*, May 19, 2015.

135. Barton Gellman and Dale Russakoff, "The Life of Bill Bradley: At Princeton, Bradley Met Impossible Demands," *Washington Post*, December 13, 1999; Ron Donaho, "Lucchino!" *San Diego Magazine* (June 1999); Major League Baseball, "Larry Lucchino, President/CEO Emeritus," *Boston Red Sox: Front Office Directory*, https://www.mlb.com/redsox/team/front-office/larry-lucchino; Anuj Basil, "From Jadwin to Fenway Bluegrass," *Daily Princetonian*, January 7, 2005.

136. Ibid.

137. Ibid.

138. Bill Nowlin, "Fenway Park (Boston)," SABR, https://sabr.org/bioproj/park/fenway-park-boston; National Park Service, "National Register of Historic Places Program: Fenway Park, Boston, Suffolk County, Massachusetts," https://www.nps.gov/nr/feature/highlight/fenwaypark/fenwaypark.htm.

139. Larry Lucchino, "Downtown Park Will Be a Gem (opinion)," *Providence Journal*, May 27, 2015. Note: Lucchino's reference to the Providence Grays evokes the legendary 1884 local nine that won the first "World Series" between the American Association and National League, behind the mythical performance of Hall of Famer Charles "Old Hoss" Radbourn, who pitched the last twenty-seven games of the season and wound up with a 60-12 record.

140. GoLocalProv, "Pawtucket Fights to Keep PawSox: Mayor Grebien's Letter to Larry Lucchino," May 22, 2015, https://www.golocalprov.com/news/Pawtucket-Fights-to-Keep-PawSox-Mayor-Grebiens-Letter-to-Larry-Lucchino.

141. Kevin Reichard, "Options Abound for Pawtucket Red Sox," *Ballpark Digest*, May 17, 2015.

142. Kate Bramson, "Lucchino Seeks to Keep 'Jim's Dream' Alive," *Providence Journal*, May 28, 2015.

143. Paul Grimaldi, "Baseball CEO Pitches Benefits of Proposal," *Providence Journal*, June 4, 2015.

144. Paul Grimaldi, "PawSox—Team Owners Call for 'Fresh Start' Over Stadium Bid," *Providence Journal*, June 10, 2015; Joseph Kahn, "Charles Steinberg Is the Maestro of Red Sox Magic," *Boston Globe*, June 5, 2012.

145. Kate Bramson, "195 Land—Bridge Too Far: River Walkway Delayed" *Providence Journal*, July 19, 2015.

146. Ibid.

147. Kate Bramson, "Owners to Take Plan on the Road," *Providence Journal*, July 3, 2015.

148. Kate Bramson, "'Listening Tour' Gets an Earful in Smithfield," *Providence Journal*, July 8, 2015.

149. Ibid.

150. Paul Grimaldi, "Opponents of Ballpark Stage Protest," *Providence Journal*, July 14, 2015.

151. Tracee M. Herbaugh and John Hill, "Route 195 Tax-Break Proposal Advances," *Providence Journal*, July 10, 2015; John Hill, "Tax Breaks OK'd for 195 Developer," *Providence Journal*, July 24, 2015.

152. Donita Naylor, "In Barrington, 'Listening Tour' Heads in a New Direction," *Providence Journal*, July 28, 2015.

153. Ibid.

154. Steve Ahlquist, "Public Opposition to Downtown Stadium Builds," Rhode Island Future, July 28, 2015, http://www.rifuture.org/public-opposition-to-downtown-stadium-builds.

155. Kate Bramson, "PawSox Intensify Pitch for Stadium," *Providence Journal*, July 29, 2015; Kate Bramson, "Stadium-Opponent Steele Says She Was Invited to N.C. by PawSox Owners," *Providence Journal*, July 30, 2015.

156. Kate Bramson, "Durham Stadium Grew from Different Ballgame," *Providence Journal*, August 9, 2015.

157. Minor League Baseball, "Durham Bulls History," milb.com; Bramson, "Durham Stadium Grew from Different Ballgame"; Kate Bramson, "In Durham, PawSox Pitch the Benefits of a Downtown Ballpark," *Providence Journal*, August 6, 2015.

158. Bramson, "In Durham, PawSox Pitch the Benefits of a Downtown Ballpark."

159. Ibid.; Kate Bramson, "Mattiello Says State, Team 'Very Close' to New Proposal," *Providence Journal*, August 7, 2015.

160. Katherine Gregg, "Assembly Unlikely to Deal with Stadium This Year," *Providence Journal*, August 20, 2015.

161. Kate Bramson, "Letters, E-mails Indicate Opposition Remains High," *Providence Journal*, August 22, 2015.

162. Kate Bramson, "Opposition Mounts to PawSox Stadium Downtown," *Providence Journal*, August 26, 2015.

163. Ibid.

164. Paul Grimaldi and Patrick Anderson, "PawSox Owner Scouts Victory Place Site," *Providence Journal*, August 27, 2015.

165. Kate Bramson, "Mattiello Stresses Obstacles to Deal," *Providence Journal*, September 4, 2015.

166. Ibid.

167. Ibid.

168. Ibid.

169. Kate Bramson, "PawSox Riverfront Proposal Is Off; No Word about Alternate Providence Site," *Providence Journal*, September 20, 2015.

170. Ibid.

171. Ibid.

Chapter 4

172. Larry Lucchino and Donald R. Grebien, "PawSox Will Focus on McCoy Experience," *Providence Journal*, February 5, 2016.

173. Ibid.

174. Ibid.

175. Kate Bramson, "Team, City, State Weigh Upgrade Plan," *Providence Journal*, February 10, 2016.

176. Ibid.

177. Ibid.

178. Above section from Brendan McGair, "Hats Off to Mayor for Current State of the PawSox," *Pawtucket Times*, April 9, 2016.

179. Jonathan Bissonnette, "PawSox Brain Trust Have a Lineup of Ideas for Transforming Fan Experience," *Pawtucket Times*, February 19, 2016.

180. "PawSox Enjoy Win-Win Weekend at McCoy Stadium," *Pawtucket Times*, January 18, 2016.

181. Ibid.

182. Kevin Reichard, "Lucchino: All Options for Future PawSox Ballpark on Table," *Ballpark Digest*, November 10, 2015, https://ballparkdigest.com/2015/11/10/lucchino-all-options-for-future-pawsox-ballpark-on-table.

183. Brenden McGair, "What's Next for Our Ballpark," *Pawtucket Times*, June 7, 2016; "Officials Announce Request for Proposals on McCoy Stadium Study," *Valley Breeze*, June 6, 2016.

184. Ibid.

185. Ibid.

186. Kate Bramson, "Kansas City Architect to Study Fate of McCoy Stadium," *Providence Journal*, September 27, 2016.

187. Ibid.

188. Ibid.; Brendan McGair, "Sliding Away: Long Search for New Ballpark Took PawSox from Providence to Pawtucket to Worcester," *Pawtucket Times*, August 21, 2018.

189. Pendulum Studio II LLC Team, "McCoy Stadium Study—Final Report," January 26, 2017, 1.

190. Ibid.

191. Ibid., 20.

192. Ibid.

193. Ibid., 1.

194. Ibid., 63.

195. Ibid.

196. Ibid., 67–85.

197. Ibid., 137.

198. Ibid.

199. Ibid., 145.

200. Ibid., 146.

201. Ibid., 147.

202. Ibid.

203. Ibid., 152–54.

204. Ibid.

205. Ibid.

206. Ibid.

207. Ibid.

208. McGair, "Sliding Away"; Jonathan Bissonnette, "Downtown Site Best for New Ballpark?" *Pawtucket Times*, February 18, 2017.

209. Erica Moser, "A 2020 Vision: Grebien & Co. Tout Pawtucket's Future at Forum," *Pawtucket Times*, April 4, 2017.

210. Ibid.

211. Brendan McGair, "PawSox Want to Be Part of City's Evolution," *Pawtucket Times*, April 4, 2017.

212. McGair, "Sliding Away."

Chapter 5

213. "Apex Department Store," ArtInRuins: Documenting Change Since 2002, http://artinruins.com/arch/ ?id=stillinuse&pr=apex#top1.

214. Jonathan Bissonnette, "Stadium Study Details Economic Benefits," *Pawtucket Times*, May 11, 2017.

215. Kate Bramson, "PawSox Stadium Plan Gets Official Support, Faces Opposition from Tax Groups + Poll," *Providence Journal*, May 16, 2017; Jonathan Bissonnette, "PawSox Announce Cost Figures for Proposed Downtown Pawtucket Ballpark," *Pawtucket Times*, May 16, 2017.

216. Bissonnette, "PawSox Announce Cost Figures for Proposed Downtown Pawtucket Ballpark"; City of Pawtucket and the Pawtucket Red Sox Baseball Club, "9 Things to Know About the Proposed Ballpark at Slater Mill," *The Ballpark at Slater Mill: Overview*, http://www.pawtucketri.com/sites/default/files/uploads/images/PressReleases/The%20Ballpark%20at%20Slater%20Mill-%20Overview.pdf.

217. Ibid.

218. Joseph Nadeau, "Gov. Raimondo On Board with New Stadium Plan," *Pawtucket Times*, May 17, 2017.

219. Jonathan Bissonnette, "Legislative Leaders Say They Won't Consider Proposal for New PawSox Stadium," *Pawtucket Times*, May 23, 2017.

220. Ibid.

221. Ibid.

222. Ibid.

223. Ibid.

224. Jonathan Bissonnette, "Park Plea: Grebien, at Statehouse, Goes to Bat Again for New Stadium," *Pawtucket Times*, May 25, 2017.

225. Ibid.

226. Ibid.

227. McGair, "Workers: Striking Out on Deal a Big Blow to City," *Pawtucket Times*, May 25, 2017.

228. Bissonnette, "Park Plea."

229. Steph Machado, "PawSox Stadium Legislations Introduced, Will Be Vetted This Fall," WPRI, June 27, 2017.

230. Ibid.

231. Jonathan Bissonnette, "Senate Sets Hearing on Stadium Bill," *Pawtucket Times*, August 5, 2017.

232. Brendan McGair, "Lucchino Tabs Familiar Face Janet Marie Smith for New PawSox Ballpark Input," *Pawtucket Times*, July 31, 2017.

233. Steven Frias, "Why Rhode Island Should Reject the New PawSox Deal," Republican Party of Rhode Island, September 13, 2017, www.ri.gop.

234. Ibid.

235. Ibid.

236. Ibid.

237. Ibid.
238. Ibid.
239. Ibid.
240. Ibid.
241. Ibid.
242. Ibid.
243. Ibid.
244. Ibid.
245. Ibid.
246. Ibid.
247. Ibid.
248. Ibid.
249. Ibid.
250. Kate Bramson and Katherine Gregg, "Senate Panel Opens Hearings on Proposal," *Providence Journal*, September 15, 2017; Katherine Gregg, "Cheering 'Save Our Sox,' Pro-PawSox Construction Workers Rally at RI State House," *Providence Journal*, September 15, 2017.
251. Senate Fiscal Office, "Ballpark at Slater Mill Senate Finance Hearings, S-0990 & S-0898, Final Report," December 7, 2017, State House Room 117, Providence, Rhode Island, www.rilin.state.ri.us/senatefinance.
252. Ted Nesi, "PawSox Stadium Backers, Critics Air Views at First Hearing on $83M Plan," WPRI, https://www.wpri.com/news/pawsox-stadium-backers-critics-air-views-at-first-hearing-on-83m-plan/1044332759.
253. Ibid.; Bramson and Gregg, "Senate Panel Opens Hearings on PawSox Stadium Proposal."
254. Bramson and Gregg, "Senate Panel Opens Hearings on PawSox Stadium Proposal."
255. Senate Fiscal Office, "Ballpark at Slater Mill Senate Finance Hearings"; Nesi, "PawSox Stadium Backers."
256. Nesi, "PawSox Stadium Backers."
257. Ibid.
258. Kate Bramson, "Pawtucket Red Sox Stadium Hearing Stretches Over 7 Hours," *Providence Journal*, September 16, 2017.
259. Senate Fiscal Office, "Ballpark at Slater Mill Senate Finance Hearings."
260. Kate Bramson, "Pawtucket Officials Grilled at Senate's PawSox Hearing + Videos," *Providence Journal*, September 26, 2017.
261. Ibid.
262. Senate Fiscal Office, "Ballpark at Slater Mill Senate Finance Hearings."
263. Ibid.

264. Ibid.

265. Ibid.

266. Kate Bramson, "Financing Focus of PawSox Hearing in South Kingstown," *Providence Journal*, October 3, 2017.

267. Senate Fiscal Office, "Ballpark at Slater Mill Senate Finance Hearings"; Kate Bramson, "Magaziner Calls PawSox Stadium Proposal an 'Affordable' and Appropriate Investment," *Providence Journal*, October 12, 2017.

268. Bramson, "Magaziner Calls PawSox Stadium Proposal an 'Affordable' and Appropriate Investment."

269. Ibid.

270. Kate Bramson, "Pawtucket Open to Financing Options for PawSox Deal," *Providence Journal*, October 13, 2017.

271. Senate Fiscal Office, "Ballpark at Slater Mill Senate Finance Hearings"; and Bramson, "Magaziner Calls PawSox Stadium Proposal."

272. Senate Fiscal Office, "Ballpark at Slater Mill Senate Finance Hearings."

273. Ibid.; Kate Bramson, "Plenty of Support, but Also Calls for Voters to Decide on PawSox Stadium Support," *Providence Journal*, October 19, 2017.

274. Bramson, "Plenty of Support."

275. Senate Fiscal Office, "Ballpark at Slater Mill Senate Finance Hearings."

276. Kate Bramson, "Senate Panel Weighs Helping Pawtucket Cover Its Costs for New PawSox Stadium," *Providence Journal*, October 24, 2017.

277. Ibid.

278. Ibid.

279. Senate Fiscal Office, "Ballpark at Slater Mill Senate Finance Hearings."

280. Ibid.

281. McGair, "Slipping Away."

282. Ibid.

283. Kate Bramson, "Senate Finance Chairman: No Vote on PawSox Stadium Without Info on Owners' Finances," *Providence Journal*, October 27, 2017.

284. Ibid.

285. Donita Naylor and Kate Bramson, "PawSox Owners Agree to Share Profit and Loss Statement with RI Auditor General," *Providence Journal*, November 2, 2017; Jonathon Bissonnette, "PawSox Owners Share Financial Info," *Pawtucket Times*, November 2, 2017.

286. Kate Bramson, "Yale Students Unveil Their Vision for PawSox Ballpark," *Providence Journal*, November 17, 2017.

287. Jonathan Bissonnette, "No Vote on PawSox Stadium until Next Year, *Pawtucket Times*, December 2, 2017.

288. Ethan Shorey, "Finance Committee Will Report on Stadium Thursday, but No Vote Yet," *Valley Breeze*, December 5, 2017.

289. Senate Fiscal Office, Ballpark at Slater Mill Senate Finance Hearings; Kate Bramson, "New PawSox Legislation Would Split Stadium-Naming Rights, Increase Amount of Bonds | Documents," *Providence Journal*, December 7, 2017.

290. Jason Bissonnette, "Revised Ballpark Bill Released," *Pawtucket Times*, December 8, 2017.

291. Ted Nesi, "PawSox Express 'Concern' About New Stadium Bill; 2020 Opening Off the Table," WPRI, December 12, 2017.

292. Ibid.

293. Ibid.

294. Kate Bramson, "Pawtucket Mayor Has a 'Plan B' if Legislature Won't Approve Ballpark Proposal," *Providence Journal*, December 19, 2017.

295. Ibid.; Katherine Gregg and Patrick Anderson, "R.I. House Speaker Raises Doubts about Support for New PawSox Stadium," *Providence Journal*, December 18, 2017.

296. Gregg and Anderson, "R.I. House Speaker Raises Doubts about Support for New PawSox Stadium."

Chapter 6

297. Kate Bramson, "PawSox Stadium Legislation Tweaked Ahead of General Assembly Session," *Providence Journal*, January 2, 2018; Kate Bramson, "PawSox Still Evaluating Revised Stadium-Financing Bill," *Providence Journal*, January 3, 2018.

298. Kate Bramson, "R.I. Senate Finance Panel OKs PawSox Proposal," *Providence Journal*, January 9, 2018.

299. Ibid.; Jonathan Bissonnette, "Ballpark Bill Gets Committee Approval," *Pawtucket Times*, January 10, 2018.

300. Bissonnette, "Ballpark Bill Gets Committee Approval."

301. Bramson, "R.I. Senate Finance Panel OKs PawSox Proposal"; Bissonnette, "Ballpark Bill Gets Committee Approval."

302. Bissonnette, "Ballpark Bill Gets Committee Approval."

303. Kate Bramson, "Listen: Mattiello Explains Switch on PawSox Referendum" (interview audio embedded), *Providence Journal*, January 11, 2018.

304. Ibid.

305. Patrick Anderson, "Mattiello Calls Closed-Door Caucus to Discuss PawSox Stadium," *Providence Journal*, January 17, 2018.

306. John Hill, "Mattiello: PawSox Stadium Proposal Not Likely to Go to Referendum," *Providence Journal*, January 18, 2018.

307. Jonathan Bissonnette, "Raimondo: Time for House to Vote on PawSox Bill," *Pawtucket Times*, January 20, 2018.

308. Brendan McGair, "Cranston Forum Lends Support to PawSox, New Ballpark Plan," *Pawtucket Times*, January 23, 2018.

309. Brendan McGair, "Speaker: Hold More Meetings on Ballpark," *Pawtucket Times*, January 31, 2018.

310. Ibid.

311. Ibid.

312. Kate Bramson, "Construction Group Tries to Woo Mattiello with PawSox Stadium Poll," *Providence Journal*, February 26, 2018; Chris Bergenheim, "Poll: Rhode Islanders Support PawSox Stadium If Deal Pays for Itself," *Providence Business News*, February 26, 2018; GoLocalProv, "Union Poll on PawSox Fails to Change the Game in RI," February 27, 2018.

313. GoLocalProv, "Union Poll on PawSox Fails to Change the Game in RI."

314. Bramson, "Construction Group Tries to Woo"; Katherine Gregg, "GOP's Frias Disputes Poll's Findings on PawSox Stadium Costs," *Providence Journal*, February 26, 2018.

315. GoLocalProv, "RI House Approves Record $9.6B Budget, PawSox Bill Posted for Tuesday Hearing, Frias Awaits," June 16, 2018.

316. Kate Mulvaney, "Gov. Lincoln Chafee Says R.I. Legislature Is Strongest in U.S.," Politifact, November 30, 2014.

317. Carl T. Bogus, "The Battle for Separation of Powers in Rhode Island," 56 Admin. L. Rev. 77, 134 (2004), Digital Commons.

318. Ibid.

319. Ibid.

320. For a more comprehensive look at corruption in Rhode Island in the late twentieth century, see H. Philip West Jr., *Secrets & Scandals: Reforming Rhode Island, 1986–2006* (Riverside: Rhode Island Publications Society, 2014).

321. *Turn to 10 WJAR*, "Mattiello Elected RI House Speaker," March 25, 2014, turnto10.com.

322. Tom Mooney, "R.I. House Speaker Mattiello's Path from Blue-Collar Roots to Pinnacle of Power," *Providence Journal*, May 3, 2004; Mike Stanton, "Who Is Rhode Island House Speaker Nick Mattiello?," *Rhode Island Monthly*, September 29, 2014.

323. Stanton, "Who Is Rhode Island House Speaker Nick Mattiello?"; "Joseph A. Bevilacqua Dies at 70; RI Judge Linked to Mob," *New York Times*, June 22, 1989.

324. Mooney, "R.I. House Speaker Mattiello's Path"; Stanton, "Who Is Rhode Island House Speaker Nick Mattiello?"

325. Stanton, "Who Is Rhode Island House Speaker Nick Mattiello?"

326. Demographic Statistical Atlas of the United States, https://statisticalatlas.com/United-States/Overview.

327. Mooney, "R.I. House Speaker Mattiello's Path"; Stanton, "Who Is Rhode Island House Speaker Nick Mattiello."

328. Stanton, "Who Is Rhode Island House Speaker Nick Mattiello?"

329. Ibid.

330. "Editorial: Refining the Stadium Deal," *Providence Journal*, December, 16, 2017.

331. Ibid.

332. "Editorial: A Test of R.I. Leadership," *Providence Journal*, December 23, 2017.

333. Ibid.

334. "Editorial: The Venues of Rhode Island," *Providence Journal*, February, 18, 2018.

335. Ibid.

336. "Editorial: The Virtue of Guts and Vision," *Providence Journal*, March15, 2018.

337. Ibid.

338. Katherine Gregg, "R.I. House Speaker Meets with PawSox Executives to Discuss Pawtucket Stadium Deal," *Providence Journal*, March 9, 2018.

339. Jonathan Bissonnette, "Steinberg: PawSox would 'Like to Keep It Here,'" *Pawtucket Times*, May 6, 2018.

340. Ibid.

341. Ibid.

342. Ibid.

343. Ibid.

344. Ibid.

345. Jonathan Bissonnette, "Stadium Deal the Hot Topic at 'Eggs and Issues,'" *Pawtucket Times*, May 17, 2018.

346. Ibid. Note: A June 2018 poll sponsored by GoLocalProv and conducted by John Della Volpe, director of polling at Harvard Kennedy School's Institute of Politics, returned similar results, with 59 percent either strongly or somewhat opposed to using public funds to finance a stadium for the PawSox.

347. "Mattiello: Revised PawSox Ballpark Plan Would Remove Taxpayer Risk," *Pawtucket Times*, May 29, 2018; Patrick Anderson, "New Financing Plan for PawSox Stadium Would Use State, Pawtucket Taxes," *Providence Journal*, May 30, 2018; Brendan McGair, "Speaker, Statehouse Leaders

Support New Ballpark Plan; and Steinberg Says Team Needs to Study Details," *Pawtucket Times*, June 1, 2018.

348. McGair, "Speaker, Statehouse Leaders Support New Ballpark Plan."

349. Ibid.; Anderson, "New Financing Plan for PawSox Stadium."

350. "Editorial: Momentum for a New Stadium," *Providence Journal*, June 2, 2018.

351. Ibid.

352. Jonathan Bissonnette, "With Legislative Session Near Close, House Finance Committee Re-Visits PawSox Ballpark Legislation," *Pawtucket Times*, June 18, 2029; Patrick Anderson, "PawSox 'Interested' in Mattiello's Proposed Financing Legislation," *Providence Journal*, June 20, 2018.

353. Mary MacDonald, "House Committee Reviews PawSox Ballpark, No Vote Taken," *Providence Business News*, June 19, 2018; Rachel Nunes, "End of Session PawSox Battle Continues in House Finance Hearing Tuesday Night," GoLocalProv, June 20, 2018.

354. "PawSox Pitch: House Finance Committee Approves Revised Bill," NBC 10 News (WJAR), June 21, 2018; GoLocalProv, "Big Controversies Hit State House as General Assembly Tries to Adjourn," June 22, 2018.

355. Mark Patinkin, "How Rhode Island Lost the PawSox," *Providence Journal*, September 7, 2018.

356. Ibid.

357. Mary MacDonald, "GA Approves Pawtucket Red Sox Ballpark Financing Plan," *Providence Business News*, June 23, 2018.

358. Patrick Anderson, "Raimondo Signs PawSox Stadium Bill; Team Still Mum about Future," *Providence Journal*, June 29, 2018.

359. Ibid.; Patrick Anderson, "Magaziner Revises Estimate of PawSox Stadium Plan Cost," *Providence Journal*, June 26, 2018.

360. Ibid.

361. Ibid.

362. Ibid.

Chapter 7

363. Anderson, "Raimondo Signs PawSox Stadium Bill."

364. Ibid.; Bill Ballou, "Worcester or Pawtucket? Time for PawSox to Step to the Plate," *Providence Journal*, July 1, 2018.

365. Ballou, "Worcester or Pawtucket? Time for PawSox to Step to the Plate."

366. Bill Ballou, "Two Moves Define Early Success of Red Sox Manager Alex Cora," *Worcester Telegram*, May 26, 2018.

367. Ibid.

368. McGair, "Sliding Away."

369. Brendan McGair, "Worcester Scheduled to Unveil PawSox Ballpark Proposal; Front Office Scheduled to Meet with Team on Friday," *Pawtucket Times*, August 16, 2018; Patrick Anderson, "PawSox Plan Move to Worcester, Team Says R.I. House to Blame," *Providence Journal*, August 17, 2018; Barry M. Bloom, "Red Sox Affiliate, a Minor League Gold Mine, Is Leaving Pawtucket for Worcester," *Forbes*, August 21, 2018.

370. Patrick Anderson, "PawSox' Lucchino Says Team Is Going 'Where You Are Wanted,'" *Providence Journal*, August 17, 2018.

371. Ibid.; Walter Bird Jr., "Person of the Year: The Dealmakers," *Worcester Magazine* (December 27, 2018).

372. Bird, "Person of the Year."

373. Ibid.

374. Ibid.

375. Brendan McGair, "PawSox Announce Plans to Leave Pawtucket, Move to Worcester, Mass," *Pawtucket Times*, August 17, 2018.

376. Bill Ballou, "Worcester's Approach to PawSox Shift Made all the Difference," *Worcester Telegram*, August 17, 2018.

377. Ibid.

378. Anderson, "PawSox' Lucchino Says Team Is Going 'Where You Are Wanted.'"

379. Ibid.

380. Ibid.

381. Ibid.

382. Ibid.

383. "Statement from Mayor Grebien on PawSox," City of Pawtucket, Office of the Mayor, August 17, 2018.

384. Ibid.

385. Bill Ballou, "PawSox Move to Worcester Started with Gene Zabinski's Postcard Campaign," *Worcester Telegram & Gazette*, August 18, 2018.

386. Ibid.

387. Ibid.; Bill Ballou, "Worcester Group's Postcard Campaign to Attract PawSox in Full Effect," *Worcester Telegram & Gazette*, January 15, 2016; Ballou, "PawSox Move to Worcester Started with Gene Zabinski."

388. Ballou, "PawSox Move to Worcester Started with Gene Zabinski."

389. Ibid.

390. Bird, "Person of the Year: The Dealmakers."

391. Ibid.

392. Ibid.

393. Ibid.

394. Ibid.

395. Ibid.

396. Ibid.

397. Ibid.

398. Ibid.

399. Bill Koch, "A Final Farewell: PawSox End Decades-Long Love Affair with Rhode Island," *Providence Journal*, September 25, 2020.

Epilogue

400. Patrick Anderson, "PawSox Leaving: Raimondo, Grebien Look Ahead After RI Strikes Out with PawSox," *Providence Journal*, August 22, 2018.

401. Ibid.

402. Ibid.

403. Brendan McGair, "PawSox Departure Was People's Will," *Pawtucket Time*, August 30, 2018.

404. Brendan McGair, "Worcester Case Scenario: Mass City Celebrates as PawSox Receive Final Approval for Move," September 17, 2018.

405. Ibid.

406. Ibid.

407. Cyrus Moulton, "Groundbreaking Held for Worcester's Polar Park," *Worcester Telegram*, July 11, 2019.

408. Ibid.

409. Mark Patinkin, "In Worcester, Groundbreaking for a New PawSox Stadium a Stark Contrast of Political Leadership," *Providence Journal*, July 11, 2019.

410. Armand Sabitoni. "We Lost So Much More than Money (opinion)," *Providence Journal*, July 17, 2019.

411. Edward Fitzpatrick, "PawSox Fans Bitter as Worcester Breaks Ground on a New Stadium," *Boston Globe*, July 11, 2019.

412. Benjamin Hill, "33 In the Books: PawSox Say Goodbye to McCoy," Minor League Baseball, News, https://www.milb.com/news/pawtucket-red-sox-stage-33-hour-grand-finale-at-historic-mccoy-stadium.

413. Minor League Baseball, "The Pawtucket Red Sox," https://www.milb.com/pawtucket/community/about-pawsox-foundation.

414. Minor League Baseball, "John H. Moss Community Service Award," https://www.milb.com/pawtucket/community/about/awards; Bruce Weber, "John Henry Moss, Head of Minor League for 50 Years, Is Dead at 90," *New York Times*, July 13, 2009.

415. Minor League Baseball, "PawSox Win Moss Community Service Award," milb.com.

416. "PawSox Community Involvement Is AOK (as in 50 Acts of Kindness)." This is a write-up that was intended to be included in the PawSox 2020 Program, which was never printed.

417. Ibid.

418. Ibid.

419. Ibid.

420. J.J. Cooper and Josh Norris, "The 2020 Minor League Season Is Cancelled. So What Happens Next?" *BA Newsletter*, June 30, 2020, https://www.baseballamerica.com/stories/the-2020-minor-league-season-is-canceled-so-what-happens-next.

421. Ibid.

422. Brendan McGair, "Cancellation of 2020 Minor League Baseball Season Means the PawSox May Have Already Played their Final Game at McCoy Stadium," *Pawtucket Times*, June 30, 2020.

423. Gary Santaniello, "When a Farewell Season Was Wiped Out, the Outfield Became a Diner," *New York Times*, July 3, 2020; Minor League Baseball, "PawSox Introduce 'Dining on the Diamond' at McCoy Stadium," May 27, 2020, https://www.milb.com/pawtucket/news/diamond-dining-at-mccoy.

424. Minor League Baseball, "Dining on the Diamond, Seats 162 Families This Past Weekend; Dates Added Next Three Weekends, Including Father's Day," June 9, 2020, https://www.milb.com/pawtucket/news/diamond-dining-at-mccoy; Minor League Baseball, "PawSox Fans 'Bat 400' as They Reserve 400 Tables in 24 Hours for 'Dining on the Diamond,'" June 12, 2020, https://www.milb.com/pawtucket/news/diamond-dining-at-mccoy.

425. Minor League Baseball, "Pawtucket Red Sox to Expand Dining on the Diamond Program to Iconic 'Field of Dreams' Movie Site," June 12, 2020, https://www.milb.com/pawtucket/news/diamond-dining-at-mccoy.

426. Minor League Baseball, "PawSox to Relive Greatest Games in Team History," May 8, 2020, https://www.milb.com/pawtucket/news/diamond-dining-at-mccoy.

427. Brendan McGair, "PawSox Announce Plans for 'Final Weekend Celebration' at McCoy Stadium," *Pawtucket Times*, October 8, 2020; Hill, "33 In the Books."

428. Hill, "33 In the Books."

429. "PawSox Snub Their Loyal Fans," Editorial, *Providence Journal*, August 20, 2018. Note: The original group was headed by Jim Skeffington, not Lucchino.

430. Ibid.

431. Ibid.

432. Ibid.

433. Ibid.

434. Jack Brock, "Gubernatorial Candidates Face Off in Debate," *Brown (University) Daily Herald*, September 28, 2018.

435. Katherine Gregg and Patrick Anderson, "Mattiello's Loss Leaves a Power Vacuum in the RI House. Here's Who Could Step Up and Take Rhode Island's Most Powerful Position," *Providence Journal*, November 3, 2010; Karen Mulvaney, "Jeffrey Britt Cleared of All Charges Linked to Mattiello's 2016 Campaign," *Providence Journal*, December 16, 2020.

436. Joel Beall, "Brad Faxon Saved His Childhood Club. Members Are Now Suing Him for Fraud. The Curious Case of Metacomet Golf Club," *Golf Digest*, September 20, 2020, https://www.golfdigest.com/story/brad-faxon-saved-his-childhood-club-members-are-now-suing-him-for-fraud-the-curious-case-of-metacomet-golf-club.

437. Bill Koch, "Passages: Long-Time PawSox General Manager Lou Schwechheimer, 62," *Providence Journal*, June 29, 2020.

438. Ibid.

439. Tom Mooney, "Pawtucket Mayor's Race: Incumbent's 'Hard Financial Approach' vs. Challenger's Call for Focus on Social Issues," *Providence Journal*, November 1, 2018.

440. Ibid.

441. Ibid.

442. Paul Edward Parker, "Norton Again Challenges Pawtucket Mayor Grebien," *Providence Journal*, August 31, 2020; Jonathan Bissonnette, "Grebien Bids for 6th Term as Mayor," *Pawtucket Times*, June 25, 2020.

About the Author

*J*ames M. Ricci is a native Rhode Islander. He holds a doctorate degree from Salve Regina University in Newport, where he explored the city's efforts to reinvent itself from a sailor town to a tourist center following World War II. This led to a particular interest in the quarter-century struggle to build the Newport Bridge, which resulted in *The Newport Bridge*, published by The History Press in 2018. A lifelong baseball fan, he became curious about the details surrounding the departure of the Pawtucket Red Sox from Rhode Island to Worcester, Massachusetts. Jim has spent more than three decades in financial services and holds Master of Arts and Bachelor of Arts degrees in American studies from the University of South Florida. He has published articles on bungalow architecture and the Florida Land Boom of the 1920s. Jim is an avid golfer and serves on the board of directors of the Narrows Center for the Arts in Fall River, Massachusetts. He and his wife, Cheryl, live in Bristol, Rhode Island.

Visit us at
www.historypress.com